HOPKINS IN IRELAND

→ Hopkins in 1888 ←

HOPKINS IN IRELAND

⇥⟩⟨⇤

Norman White

UNIVERSITY COLLEGE DUBLIN PRESS

PREAS CHOLÁISTE OLLSCOILE
BHAILE ÁTHA CLIATH

First published 2002
by University College Dublin Press
Newman House, 86 St Stephen's Green,
Dublin 2, Ireland. *www.ucdpress.ie*

ISBN 1 900621 71 1 hardback
ISBN 1 900621 72 X paperback

British Library Cataloguing in Publication Data
A catalogue record for this title is available
from the British Library

Typeset in Ireland in Caslon and Walbaum
by Elaine Shiels, Bantry, Co. Cork

Text design by Lyn Davies

Printed on acid-free paper

Printed in England by MPG Books Ltd,
Bodmin, Cornwall

for Jess and Pippa

Contents

Preface

Gerard Hopkins is buried in Ireland. His grave is emblematic of his isolation, alienation, and sense of lonely duty during the last five years of his life which he spent in Ireland.

In the Prospect Cemetery, Glasnevin, in north Dublin, a 160-foot thin round tower, the O'Connell memorial, towers over everything, on an island surrounded by gravestones, including, most prominently, those of other patriots. A white stone with the legend 'Roger Casement/ 1864–1916/ R.I.P.' is uneasily propped against a larger black one, flat in the ground, which translates it into Irish and angular Celtic minuscule, 'ruari mac easmainn'. Parnell has a stone of Wicklow granite in an impressive, honoured position; his surname only, written in large letters, and with a bright green ribboned wreath. By the cemetery entrance are the two most pompous individual tombs, looking appropriate for Italian princes of five hundred years ago: Cardinal McCabe, Archbishop of Dublin and Primate of Ireland, with a richly ornamented stone canopy over him, supported by thirty-six grey marble pillars in carefully unequal clusters, and an elaborately tessellated mosaic around the catafalque. McCabe died in 1885 and was replaced as Archbishop and Primate by the Most Reverend William J. Walsh, D.D., who now rests a few feet from him, both in body and in princely robed effigy. His white marble tomb has a grey stone canopy, and on his catafalque an inlaid pavement of variously coloured marble, with pink predominating, and then yellow-grey. The two most powerful figures in the Irish Church in Hopkins's time, and they both voted against Hopkins's appointment to University College Dublin, and resigned from the Royal University Senate in protest when their wishes were ignored.

In contrast to the packed avenues in the main body of the cemetery, the Jesuit plot is alone, separate in a forlorn corner by the wall, with the noise of unseen motor traffic on the other side. About forty feet square, strictly delimited by white double rows of spear-topped railings, chest-high, set in a low wall; surrounded not by graves but by stretches of waving grass and tall, mournful evergreen trees. The plot is bare gravel except for, at the far end, a large ornamented memorial cross, whose carved names have overflowed onto subsidiary stones. 'Orate pro Defunctis/ Patribus et Fratribus/ Societatis Jesu'.

Four types of Celtic interwoven ornament in panels beneath the figure of the crucified Christ on the main memorial, with its few hundred names.

There are forty-nine names on the front of the base, dating from 1878 to 1917, including 'P. Gerardus Hopkins obiit Jun. 8 1889 aetat. an. 44', with Irish names above his – O'Reilly, Farrell, O'Neill, O'Callaghan, Moloney, Callan – and Irish names below – Tuite, Scully, Lynch, Gaffney, Murphy. Odd names among the 'Sacerdotes' stand out, of priests who played a part in Hopkins's Dublin life: 'P. Gulielmus Delany' (William Delany, the courageous first Jesuit President of the new but already ailing University College); 'P. Matthaeus Russell' (Mat Russell, editor of *The Irish Monthly*, and one of the rare handful to publish Hopkins during his lifetime, albeit translations of Shakespeare into Latin); 'P. Thomas Wheeler' (who was with Hopkins during his final illness). Each of these outlived Hopkins by more than twenty years, but on another side of the base, under 'Scholastici', Hopkins's companion in life, in eccentricity, in delicate health, and in a premature death, 'F. Robertus Curtis obiit Sep. 29 1893 aetat. an. 41' (of whom Hopkins wrote: 'he is my comfort beyond what I can say and a kind of godsend I never expected to have').

In his Dublin life Hopkins was frequently misnamed 'Gerald' (in the annual list of priests in *The Irish Ecclesiastical Record*, for instance), and in death his name was latinised. When I first saw the grave in the 1960s his carved name was also obscured by moss, fungi, dirt, and weathering.

* * *

This book is not a conventional biography; it does not aim to be an account of Hopkins's doings in Ireland. The important things that happened to him in Ireland were mental; and so *Hopkins in Ireland* is an account, an exploration of the poems he wrote in Ireland largely as a form of psychological biography, working outwards from his most intimate creations. We have often been told that we should not read poems as biography, but we usually do, and I am not sure it is wrong when the poems draw so deeply on the life and mental states of the author as do Hopkins's.

If the outer details of Hopkins's life are needed, the reader is invited to consult my *Hopkins: A Literary Biography* (Oxford, 1992). But in the present study, the poems are the biography. The events of the life (the world without) are used as context to this world within.

I have placed a simple chronology, indicating events and poems, with their dates of composition, immediately after this Preface to emphasise that chronological narrative is not the point of the rest of the book; I hope that this skeletal picture of the outside facts will free the body of the book to explore the inner life, the ways in which the poems draw on a huge background of thought, and the fascinating webs of connection.

An examination of the composition and complexities of 'Spelt from Sibyl's Leaves' forms the first and most detailed study, demonstrating the book's general aim that exploring the intricacies of the poem is to explore the intimacies of the mind of its author; to see the various elements, religious, linguistic, psychological, social, personal, and literary that make up the poem is to get nearer an understanding of Hopkins's mind and life in the Dublin years.

* * *

I am most grateful to Clare Hall, Cambridge, and to the University of Birmingham for Fellowships and pleasant study facilities; my work was also aided by a President's award from University College Dublin. Barbara Hardy read an early version of this book and gave sound advice; Nest Price's generosity enabled me to live and work in Hopkins country in North Wales, and Diana Golledge played a similar role in his favourite part of Devon; R. K. R. Thornton's help has been invaluable, as friend, Hopkins expert, and critical reader; J. C. C. Mays has offered sympathetic encouragement over a long period; Richard and Catherine O'Rourke and their family have kept up Monasterevin's reputation for warm and relaxing hospitality when Dublin was unbearable; Elaine and Liam Murphy, also of County Kildare, have been helpful to me and this book; Catherine Phillips's friendship has been very welcome; I am indebted to Ann Stephens in more ways than I can say; I am most grateful to the late Fergal McGrath SJ (whose father had been a colleague of Hopkins's), for his helpfulness and generosity at Lr Leeson St; Joseph J. Feeney SJ has remained a good friend, in spite of my continuing incomprehension of his religion. And finally, Barbara Mennell has been the most considerate and yet the most efficient of publishers

Norman White
Dun Laoghaire
March 2002

List of Illustrations

✦

Frontispiece: Hopkins in 1888

Between pages 78 and 79:
Revd William Delany SJ

Archbishop William Walsh

Thomas Arnold (Jr), Professor of English at University College Dublin

A. W. M. Baillie

St Stephen's Green (West)

Phoenix Park, the Wellington Memorial

Katharine Tynan, by John B. Yeats
Courtesy National Gallery of Ireland

Monasterevin

The Cassidy house, Monasterevin

Stonyhurst, the boys' bathing place (the Epithalamion)

Hopkins's last known sketch

Glasnevin cemetery, late 1960s

Monasterevin, statues of Miss Cassidy and Hopkins

Abbreviations

+>-<+

HALB Norman White, *Hopkins: A Literary Biography* (Oxford, 1992).

HQ   *The Hopkins Quarterly*

HRB   *The Hopkins Research Bulletin*

J.   *The Journals and Papers of Gerard Manley Hopkins*, ed. Humphry House and Graham Storey (1959).

L1   *The Letters of Gerard Manley Hopkins to Robert Bridges*, ed. C. C. Abbott (1935, 1955).

L2   *The Correspondence of Gerard Manley Hopkins and R. W. Dixon*, ed. C. C. Abbott (1935, 1955).

L3   *The Further Letters of Gerard Manley Hopkins*, ed. C.C. Abbott, 2nd edn. (1956).

P.   *Gerard Manley Hopkins* (The Oxford Authors), ed. Catherine Phillips (Oxford, 1986). (This is the edition of poems I have generally used, but I have sometimes preferred my own manuscript readings.)

S.   *The Sermons and Devotional Writings of Gerard Manley Hopkins*, ed. C. Devlin (1959).

Chronological Tables

→>→←←

1884   February, Hopkins appointed Professor of Greek at University College, Dublin, and Fellow in Classics of the Royal University of Ireland. His appointment opposed by Cardinal McCabe and Dr William Walsh. For the remainder of the academic year H. has examining but no teaching duties.

     By April, Hopkins in bad depression, exacerbated by frequent and heavy exam-marking. Friendship with Robert Curtis. Renews his interest in music. In charge of a greenhouse at no. 86. Although invited to stay with his family at Hampstead, he spends Christmas in Dublin.

1885   Cardinal McCabe dies, and Dr Walsh appointed Archbishop of Dublin. H. upset by political unrest in Ireland. By end of March severely depressed; melancholia lasts throughout Spring and Summer. End of July visits his family and Coventry Patmore in England, returning to Ireland 19 August. 21 August, retreat at Clongowes Wood College. Christmas 1885 again spent in Dublin, in spite of family's invitation to Hampstead.

1886   April–May, H. on holiday in England, partly at Oxford and with Bridges at Yattendon, but mainly with his family in London. June–September, much examining. Then holiday with Curtis in Scotland, returning to more examining. Meets Katharine Tynan and the Yeats family. Christmas at Monasterevan, where he starts 'On the Portrait . . .', then on retreat at Tullamore.

1887   H. starts his Epithalamion, but cannot complete it in time for his brother Everard's wedding in April. Starts collecting 'Irish dialect' words for the *English Dialect Dictionary*. Complains about his health, the weather, examining, and Irish politics: Gladstone is particularly blamed. Increasingly patriotic on behalf of England. Growing sense of failure at his academic writing projects. September, retreat at Dromore.

1888   Valuable friendships with the McCabes of Donnybrook, the O'Hagans at Howth, and the Cassidys at Monasterevan, where he spends Christmas.

1889 January, H. in retreat at Tullamore. *The Times* v. Parnell: Pigott confesses his forgery. H. dies of typhoid, 8 June.

1918 (December) Hopkins's *Poems* published, edited by Bridges.

Chronological Table 2: Poems

1884 (most of) 'Spelt from Sibyl's Leaves' (finished in 1886). Perhaps 'The times are nightfall', and 'Hope holds to Christ'.

1885 Spring/Summer: the 'Sonnets of Desolation', viz.: 'To seem the stranger', 'I wake and feel', 'No worst', 'My own heart', 'Patience, hard thing'. August: 'Not, I'll not, carrion comfort', 'To what serves Mortal Beauty?', '(The Soldier)'. Also, probably, 'To his Watch', 'Not of all my eyes see', 'Thee, God, I come from', 'Strike, churl', 'The sea took pity'.

1886 'On the Portrait of Two Beautiful Young People'.

1887 'Harry Ploughman', 'Tom's Garland'.

1888 The Epithalamion (January), 'That Nature is a Heraclitean Fire', 'St Alphonsus Rodriguez', 'What shall I do for the land that bred me?'

1889 'Thou art indeed just', 'The shepherd's brow', 'To R.B.'.

Chapter One

HOPKINS IN ENGLAND, WALES AND SCOTLAND

→>–<←

Gerard Hopkins was a Victorian Englishman, born in 1844, seven years after the unknown seventeen-year-old Princess Victoria ascended the throne, and he would die in 1889, twelve years before the respected Queen, Empress of India and monarch over the greatest empire the world had ever known, breathed her last.

He was the eldest child of a hard worker in City of London marine insurance, Manley Hopkins, who was just making a name for himself as an average adjuster, a new profession in which he would eventually be an authority and leading light. Gerard's mother had been Kate Smith, daughter of a fashionable family doctor with a practice by the Tower of London. Christened Gerard Manley Hopkins, though his second name was seldom used in his lifetime, he was brought up just beyond the eastern border of London, in Stratford, a town which had been a pleasant rural retreat for City businessmen. But in 1852, when Gerard was eight years old, the Hopkinses moved to Hampstead, a prosperous village on a northern height overlooking London. Stratford had been overtaken by the Industrial Revolution. Obnoxious trades which had been barred from within the City boundaries set up in Stratford – chemical manufacturers, bone-boilers, a fertiliser plant – and huge railway sidings could be seen from the Hopkins house. Besides those disadvantages, cholera had been reported nearby, and several of Kate's relatives had succumbed within living memory,

Whereas Stratford was on low marshy ground, Hampstead's highest point, Whitestone Pond, was higher than the top of St Paul's Cathedral. Although separated and protected from London by Hampstead Heath, Hampstead was within easy reach of the city by train, horse-omnibus, horse, or walking. So the Hopkins children were brought up in ideal surroundings – countryside walks, swimming in ponds on the Heath, and yet with all the advantages of the greatest city in the civilised world. Hopkins described its amenities:

I prefer London to any large town in these islands. . . . In summer its air is a balmy air, certainly in the West End. Then it – well the West End – is cheerful and quietly handsome, with many fine trees, and then there are so many resources, things to go to and hear and see and do. Everything is there. (L3. 292–3)

Hopkins boarded at Highgate School, then a minor public school with no great reputation. Although classics were taught for a larger proportion of the syllabus than was officially recommended, Hopkins benefited from the traditional concentration on Latin, Greek, and ancient history, at the same time missing modern subjects like languages and science, which had been taken up by up-to-date schools like Eton, Harrow, Winchester, and St Paul's. He gained linguistic fluency and flexibility in the use of English, but throughout his life was unfamiliar with several currents of modern thought. Until Hopkins reached the Sixth Form although always near the top he was seldom first in his class, spending a lot of time with Marcus Clarke, an intellectually lively boy, who, like Gerard, was no good at sports, preferring aesthetic interests. Clarke encouraged Hopkins in sketching and in writing poetry, and discussing artistic questions. Together with Hopkins's next younger brother, Cyril, they subscribed to *Once a Week*, a journal which, in his final year at Highgate, printed a poem of Gerard's, 'Winter with the Gulf Stream', which shows mastery of simple verse technique, Keatsian natural imagery and fanciful mythologising:

> A simple passage of weak notes
> Is all the winter bird dare try.
> The bugle moon by daylight floats
>
> So glassy white about the sky,
> So like a berg of hyaline,
> And pencilled blue so daintily
>
> I never saw her so divine.

He was rebellious, arrogant, and scruffy at school, on bad terms with the headmaster, and in his last year as a Sixth-Former his father decided it would be better for him to be a day boy. Each morning he walked past Keats's Hampstead house, over the Heath, past S. T. Coleridge's tomb, to school, and back each evening. At his second attempt, he won an exhibition at Balliol College, Oxford, which enabled him to have the best university education of the day.

Oxford University was everything to Hopkins that school was not; afterwards he always said that his moral and intellectual being had been formed there. He made deep and lasting friendships at Oxford, particularly with Robert Bridges and Mowbray Baillie. But although he was taught by some of the best and most advanced teachers and scholars of the day, including Benjamin Jowett, the Regius Professor of Greek, and T. H. Green, the well-known philosopher, in his personal philosophy Hopkins reacted against their influence and that of the dangerously modern Balliol College, and turned to the eminent High-Churchmen, Canon H. P. Liddon and Dr E. B. Pusey, who were preaching puritanical Ritualism, an updated version of J. H. Newman's teachings of a generation ago, before he had become a Roman Catholic. Hopkins became familiar with doctrines, rituals, and practices close to those of the Roman church, and, brought up in a moderate High Church atmosphere at Hampstead, which was insufficiently earnest for his tastes, he converted in 1866 from Anglicanism to Roman Catholicism, like several of his Oxford friends.

Hopkins had gone up to Oxford intending to become a painter, although his surviving drawings do not suggest a more than ordinary middle-class talent; he closely followed the precepts of drawing accurately from close observation of nature's details advocated by John Ruskin, his sketches showing intense desire to record nature. In his diaries and journals, on the other hand, he undertook a deep apprenticeship in learning about words, and building a useful vocabulary hoard while attempting poetic, if unscientific, excursions into etymology:

> Skill, discernment. To keel, to skim. Keel, that part of a ship which cuts a way through the water. Skull, an oar which skims the water. Shell (in a school) a division. Shilling, a division of a pound. School and shoal as applied to fishes, a division, company. . . . Shell of a snail, bird etc, skull of the head are from word meaning hollow and their likeness to the words above is a coincidence only. (J. 31)

He was also evolving highly distinctive verbal means of describing natural phenomena:

> The sun coming with pennons of cloud, cloud-bannerets, an oriflamme, a 'plump' or something of the sort, of spearlike rays./ The sluiced sunrise./ The fields of heaven covered with eye-brights. – White-diapered with stars. (J. 17)

Hopkins was writing many different kinds of verse, much of it derivative from the Romantic poets:

> As void as clouds that house and harbour none,
> Whose gaps and hollows are not browzed upon,
> As void as those the gentle downs appear
> Of such a season of the day and year.
> There was no bleat of ewe, no chime of wether,
> Only the bellèd foxgloves lisp'd together.
>
> *'Richard'*

At a certain stage in his Ritualist devotions, he decided to give up the prospect of becoming a professional artist, as he felt the passions would be too strongly involved (he had enquired whether it would be possible for an artist to substitute a book of anatomical drawings for drawing the nude from life). But his poetry writing continued, and several poems he wrote at Oxford show stages of his conversion to Roman Catholicism: a romantic Pre-Raphaelite picture of the life of a professional religious:

> O feel-of-primrose hands, O feet
> That want the yield of plushy sward,
> But you shall walk the golden street
> And you unhouse and house the Lord,
>
> *'The Habit of Perfection'*

or religious doubt, asking similar questions to Tennyson's in *In Memoriam*:

> God, though to Thee our psalm we raise
> No answering voice comes from the skies;
> To Thee the trembling sinner prays
> But no forgiving voice replies,
>
> *'Nondum'*

or the Church of England as a halfway house to Roman Catholicism (an image of Newman's); or self-disgust:

> Trees by their yield
> Are known; but I
> My sap is sealed,
> My root is dry.
>
> *untitled poem*

Hopkins's conversion caused his parents much anguish ('O Gerard, my darling boy, are you indeed gone from me?' wrote his father [L3. 97]), but, to Hopkins's surprise, they came to accept it fairly soon, as they did later on when his sister Milicent became a High-Church Anglican nun. He obtained a first-class degree, a good though not brilliant result; his college was noted as a well-oiled machine for producing Firsts, and, unlike some of his contemporaries, he took four years (1863–7) over a single degree, and gained no prizes. He was offered a teaching post at the Oratory School, Birmingham, by Newman, who had received Hopkins into the Catholic Church, and whose spiritual autobiography, *Apologia Pro Vita Sua* (published in 1864), had certainly influenced him. Hopkins was unsuccessful and unhappy as a teacher – the only secular job he ever had – finding the self-discipline unpalatable, with few opportunities to continue his self-education or see his Oxford friends. He decided to remedy his aimlessness and feelings of the sordidness of life by becoming a professional religious, eventually choosing the most severely disciplined of Counter-Reformation orders, the Society of Jesus.

First, however, he took a month's walking holiday in Switzerland (July 1868), following the romantic lead of Wordsworth and Ruskin; his companion on the trip, Edward Bond, had told him that Jesuits were forbidden entry into the country. There his journal writing achieved new heights of liveliness and inventiveness, including human scenes as well as descriptions of Alpine scenery:

> But Basel at night! . . . we walked about the place and first of all had the adventure of the little Englishwoman with her hat off. We went through great spacious streets and places dead still and came to fountains of the clearest black water through which pieces of things at the bottom gleamed white. We got up to a height where a bastion-shaped vertical prominence shaded with chestnut trees looked down on the near roofs, which then in the moonlight were purple and velvety and edged along with ridges and chimneys of chalk white. A woman came to a window with a candle, and some mess she was making, and then that was gone and there was no light anywhere but the moon. We heard music indoors about. . . .
>
> I never saw anything like the richness of the herbage here – one field especially, where those boys were playing tipcat, mixed of fat and gleaming dandelion and buttercup-leaf which had all its lobes like antlers . . . . The mountains and in particular the Silberhorn are shaped and nippled like the sand in an hourglass. . . . Then one of their beauties is in nearly vertical places the fine pleatings of the snow running to or from one another, like the newness of lawn in an alb and sometimes cut off short as crisp as celery. (J. 169, 174)

Such passages make one regret the comparatively limited range of journal subject once he had joined the Society of Jesus.

In September 1868 he entered the Jesuit novitiate at Roehampton, near London. There are few records of his novitiate experiences, except that for most of the two years he kept a 'weather journal', which in fact is considerably more – it kept Hopkins's writing alive. In 1870 Hopkins went for three years to the Jesuit Philosophate at St Mary's Hall, Stonyhurst, in a remote part of Lancashire. Stonyhurst people were obsessed by dampness and rheumatism, and Hopkins was soon dragged down into his own pessimism, complaining about overlong winter and lack of a proper spring: 'Early in the year they told me there wd. be no spring such as we understood it in the south. When I asked about May they told me they had hail in May. Of June they told me it had one year been so cold that the procession could not be held on Corpus Christi' (L3. 234). Nevertheless he wrote vivid accounts of scenery and weather phenomena:

> Today the river was wild, very full, glossy brown with mud, furrowed in permanent billows through which from head to head the water swung with a great down and up again. These heads were scalped with rags of jumping foam. But at the Roughs the sight was the burly water-backs which heave after heave kept tumbling up from the broken foam and their plump heap turning open in ropes of velvet. (J. 200)

And in spite of his vow before he became a Jesuit that he would write no poetry, he wrote two or three pieces of verse – uninspired perhaps because merely devotional exercises Jesuit students were encouraged to do on the Virgin Mary's feast-day.

Hopkins's most vivid writing during his three years at St Mary's Hall was his journal during two holidays in the Isle of Man. His sea descriptions are intensely creative, conveying extraordinary excitement:

> I had many beautiful sights of [the sea], sometimes to the foot of the cliff, where it was of a strong smouldering green over the sunken rocks ... which ... discolour the coast all along with a fringe of yellow at the tide-mark and under water reflect light and make themselves felt where the smooth black ones would not shew – , but farther out blue shadowed with gusts from the shore; at other times with the brinks hidden by the fall of the hill, packing the land in/ it was not seen how far, and then you see best how it is drawn up to a brow at the skyline and stoops away on either side, tumbling over towards the eye in the broad smooth fall of a lakish apron of water, which seems bound over or lashed to land below by a splay of dark and light braids: they are the gusts of wind all along the perspective with which all the sea that day was dressed. (J. 222)

In September 1873 Hopkins started a year's teaching classics and English to Jesuit juniors at Roehampton. It was intended as a holiday, and Hopkins took full advantage of being near London to visit art exhibitions; but before the end of his time there he again felt depressed and tired. In August 1874 he was sent to St Beuno's College, in North Wales, to make his theology. St Beuno's is commonly considered Hopkins's happiest time in his life as a Jesuit, but this needs to be qualified. It certainly started out optimistically, building up towards the composition of 'The Wreck of the Deutschland' in December 1875. After having been discouraged from learning Welsh he received approval and started learning the language and practising Welsh versification. He also wrote the odd piece of stilted occasional verse in English, and on receiving his rector's encouragement composed his longest and most original poem 'The Wreck of the Deutschland', employing principles, techniques, and vocabulary drawn from his early journal etymological notes, his Isle of Man seascape descriptions, his Roehampton lectures on verse, his Welsh studies, his Oxford knowledge of Pindaric verse forms, and his own poetic genius.

The poem's most successful parts are those describing the seascape and the wreck, on the one hand, and on the other, the stanzas which give an account of some of Hopkins's most powerful personal religious experiences (all literally true, he told Bridges), such as his terrible confrontation with God at his conversion:

> I did say yes
> O at lightning and lashed rod;
> Thou heardst me truer than tongue confess
> Thy terror, O Christ, O God;
> Thou knowest the walls, altar and hour and night:
> The swoon of a heart that the sweep and the hurl of thee trod
> Hard down with a horror of height:
> And the midriff astrain with leaning of, laced with fire of stress.

or his pantheistic response to nature:

> I kiss my hand
> To the stars, lovely-asunder
> Starlight, wafting him out of it; and
> Glow, glory in thunder;
> Kiss my hand to the dappled-with-damson west:
> Since, though he is under the world's splendour and wonder,
> His mystery must be instressed, stressed;
> For I greet him the days I meet him, and bless when I understand.

One of the most admired stanzas is that describing the ship meeting the approaching storm:

> Into the snows she sweeps,
> Hurling the haven behind,
> The Deutschland, on Sunday; and so the sky keeps,
> For the infinite air is unkind,
> And the sea flint-flake, black-backed in the regular blow,
> Sitting Eastnortheast, in cursed quarter, the wind;
> Wiry and white-fiery and whirlwind-swivellèd snow
> Spins to the widow-making unchilding unfathering deeps.

The poem was accepted by *The Month*, the official Jesuit periodical, before the editor had seen it, but was rejected when the editor found he could not understand it. This refusal signified more than the negative opinion of one individual; it meant that Hopkins did not have official approval for his verse making. The effect on his poetry was far reaching: we shall never know the full extent of the harm and pain. Hopkins never again tried any verse form which was long, complex, or experimental, when, plainly, in more encouraging surroundings he would have been capable, with his knowledge and understanding of verse and language principles, of developing much stranger and more wonderful creations than even 'The Wreck of the Deutschland'. Most of his subsequent poems were sonnets, a form he had practised from a long way back. In the new atmosphere of discouragement he could compose them in his head, on his half-day's recreation each week, without his colleagues knowing. There is a sense of openness and expansiveness about 'The Wreck of the Deutschland', one of the few poems that the people around him knew about, but the remainder of Hopkins's St Beuno's poetry, including the famous 'The Windhover', 'Pied Beauty', 'Spring', and 'Hurrahing in Harvest' were sonnets, and were not submitted for publication, Hopkins sending them to Robert Bridges to keep, until conditions changed and they could be put before the public.

There were several positive aspects to Hopkins's three years in Wales, particularly his blissful exploration of the countryside, his discovery of holy wells, especially St Winefred's, which came to mean so much, and his discovery and use of the Welsh language and poetry. But careful reading of his letters, journal, and especially the poems tells a more complex story, of the increasingly isolated dreamer, unsympathetically treated by the realities and restrictions of everyday life. Often there is a descent into purposeless and negative aspects of his life and observations: man's religious apathy ('Why do men then now not reck his rod?') and degeneracy ('drain fast towards man's first slime'), even, in 'The Lantern', a subdued picture of the narrator's loneliness and pessimism, while he lives in 'much-thick and marsh air'.

Around the time that his great ode was rejected, Hopkins attracted attention for his inspirational support of the downgraded philosopher Duns Scotus, against his traditional opponent, the approved theologian Thomas Aquinas. He had written an impolitic assault, masked in Latin verse, against Fr Thomas Burke, a Dominican advocate of Aquinas, who was visiting St Beuno's, and failed his important theology examination at the end of his third year, so that he could not stay on for the fourth year, which would have fitted him for higher posts in the Society. So in spite of being ordained in September 1877, at the end of his time at St Beuno's, there was a sense of failure and disappointment about his subsequent career in the Jesuits: he would not achieve the top professional grade because of his theology failure, and as far as poetry writing went he would have to guard his time carefully, knowing that he had not gained official approval for his efforts so far.

In October 1877 Hopkins went to teach, as sub-minister, at Mount St Mary's College, near Sheffield, where, during seven months, he composed 'The Loss of the Eurydice', a much cruder shipwreck poem than 'The Wreck of the Deutschland', but which *The Month* also rejected, and a 'Wordsworthian' poem 'Brothers'. He was then sent to several places in a short period; his life, he said, was only of a 'cobweb, soapsud, and frost-feather permanence'. He taught senior students at Stonyhurst College for three months in 1878, then for five months was curate at the fashionable Farm Street church, in Mayfair, central London, before being sent in December 1878 to Oxford, as curate at St Aloysius church for ten months. At Oxford he wrote 'Duns Scotus's Oxford', 'Henry Purcell', 'The Candle Indoors' and 'Binsey Poplars', a sad and hypnotic poem, in which the aspens are symbols of Hopkins's past affection for Oxford, which no longer offers hope.

At the end of 1879 a particularly low period for him began – 'so fagged, so harried and gallied up and down', as he described his lot among some of industrial Britain's worst slums: Bedford Leigh ('a darksome place, with pits and mills and foundries'), Liverpool ('I am brought face to face with the deepest poverty and misery'), and Glasgow ('wretched . . . repulsive to live in'). In spite of the occasional beautiful poem ('Spring and Fall: to a young child') there were numerous signs that Hopkins, considered by his contemporaries 'delicate' and 'aesthetic', was not the sort of workhorse priest needed for jobs like these.

It must have been a huge relief for Hopkins that in October 1881 he was due to start his Tertianship year at Roehampton. He resolved to give up non-professional writing for the ten months, but, as with every other known vow of his to give up beauty or art in his life, Hopkins's artistic and writer's compulsions would not be suppressed, and in the last three months of 1881 he wrote long criticisms of his friend Canon R.W. Dixon's poetry, an account of music he had composed, and a lecture on the sonnet form. In August 1882 Hopkins was sent to Stonyhurst College to teach classics, where he met the poet Coventry Patmore and wrote three or so poems himself. In August 1883 he heard that he had been reappointed to Stonyhurst for another school year, but late in the autumn term he received a surprise visit from Fr William Delany, President of the newly reformed University College, on St Stephen's Green, Dublin, Ireland.

Chapter Two

ENGLAND AND IRELAND

→>-<←

Since he had been visited unexpectedly at Stonyhurst in the first week of December 1883, by Fr William Delany, the Jesuit President of University College Dublin, Hopkins had known that, if all went according to plan, he would soon be leaving England for Ireland, to take up a position as junior professor of classics. Delany had enthusiastically put in Hopkins's mind the picture of a professor lecturing in his chosen field in the university college for Irish Catholics which had been idealistically founded by Hopkins's mentor, John Henry Newman, in the 1850s. Hopkins had never before in his Jesuit career had the luxury of lecturing exclusively in the classics at a university institution, and there must have been some attractions in the idea.

Hopkins and Delany travelled to Ireland that December so that Hopkins could be shown where he would live and work, in two houses on the south side of St Stephen's Green in Dublin, and Delany also took him to Clongowes Wood College, a prominent Jesuit school in the County Kildare countryside, where a photograph was taken of the community with their two visitors in prominent positions; Hopkins does not appear happy. Delany probably told Hopkins that his appointment was a foregone conclusion, but, as Hopkins told Bridges, 'there was an Irish row over my election'.

*   *   *

It was a complex row, involving opposed principles of administering third-level education for Irish Roman Catholics, as well as racial arguments about employing Englishmen, and the question of how loyal an independent body like the Society of Jesus was to the local bishops. The row was conducted at a time when the old type of conservative prelate was being replaced in Ireland by a more outspoken and politically independent, even nationalist, kind.

In 1882 the Society of Jesus had been invited to take over the remnants of Newman's old Catholic University of Ireland, whose organisational structures had all but collapsed. Fr Delany, an enthusiastic and successful secondary-school headmaster, took charge as President. Not all Irish Jesuits thought it a good idea, and their Provincial, Fr Tuite, wrote to Delany of the old college's many disadvantages – cramped living conditions, buildings full of dry rot, 'a dingy old barrack that would require a vast outlay'. But in spite of other discouragements, such as that of the Irish bishops, who, though owning the buildings, would not release money for their proper upkeep, Delany idealistically pressed ahead with his plans.

Delany tried to appoint foreign Jesuits to his staff, against the advice of his Provincial, who wrote: 'I look upon Dr Newman's selection of English professors and officials as the first cause of failure of the Catholic University [a common opinion, but not supported by the facts: see Ch. 4]. I am afraid the same might happen with regard to us. . . . We must not hurt national prejudices on any account.' Delany argued that there were insufficient Irishmen trained to a degree appropriate for a university professorship. He had decided on Hopkins for a vacant classics chair after having written to the English Provincial, Fr Purbrick, enquiring about the availability of seven scholars in the province. Delany had been advised by a friend who knew the English province's resources well, that Hopkins 'is clever, well trained, teaches well but has never succeeded well: his mind runs into eccentric ways.' Fr Purbrick replied that much as he would have liked to help 'in so great and important a work' as a new Jesuit University College in Dublin, he could not spare six of the seven, who were 'just the cream of the province'. That left only Fr Gerard Hopkins, but he warned: 'Fr Hopkins is very clever and a good scholar . . . but I should do you no kindness in sending you a man so eccentric. I am trying him this year in coaching B.A.s at Stonyhurst, but with fear and trembling.' (For a fuller account of Hopkins's appointment, see White, 'Gerard Manley Hopkins and the Irish row'.)

At this stage Delany was not certain that Hopkins was the man he needed. But he had to get a Jesuit, because with the post of Professor of Classics went a £400 Fellowship of the Royal University of Ireland. If a Jesuit were appointed then this money would be added to the college's income (there had been a loss of £700 the previous year). An influential friend, Dr James Kavanagh, advised: 'Take Hopkins, if you cannot get a better. The £400 a year you will find useful, [Hopkins] being an S.J.' Fr Purbrick agreed to let Hopkins go:

> I have no objection to your inviting Fr Gerald [sic] Hopkins to stand as a Candidate for a Fellowship. He is the only man possible. You know him. I have the highest opinion of his scholarship & abilities – I fancy also that University work would be more in his line than anything else. Sometimes what we in Community deem oddities are the very qualities which outside are appreciated as original & valuable. (Irish Jesuit archives)

Hopkins obtained references from his former tutor at Balliol, Benjamin Jowett, now Master of the College and Vice-Chancellor of the University, and from his former Oxford friend R.L. Nettleship, now a Fellow of Balliol. Neither of them had had experience of Hopkins's academic work beyond that when he was an undergraduate nearly twenty years before, nor did they have the remotest idea what teaching at University College Dublin, would be like.

The meeting to elect the RUI Fellows was held on 30 January 1884. Both of Delany's candidates, Hopkins for the Classics chair, and Robert Curtis for the Natural Philosophy chair, were opposed by other candidates. Learning of the opposition Delany went to see the Cardinal Archbishop of Dublin, Edward McCabe, who was influential in the Senate. Delany reported that the Cardinal had said:

> a propos of Fr Hopkins's name, that he disliked having Englishmen, and thought this place had had too much of Englishmen in its past history [again, the same prejudice about Newman's university]. I [Delany] replied that unfortunately there were hardly any qualified Irishmen, and that the only two whom I knew of were already engaged here – Quinn and Starkie – and that Fr Hopkins's appointment would secure my being able to keep both these men on my staff – gaining Hopkins himself in addition. I explained that I wished to have Fr Hopkins also on account of the competition with Trinity College [Dublin] which prides itself on its [classical] verse writers, this being Hopkins's strong point. (Irish Jesuit archives)

Hopkins's election was opposed by Dr William Walsh, an influential cleric of a new, nationalist type, who the following year was elected Archbishop of Dublin, in spite of pressure on the Vatican from the British government against the appointment. He opposed concentration of the Royal University fellowships in one institution, the University College, preferring their distribution among several colleges. But Hopkins was nevertheless elected, with only three votes against him, including those of Walsh and the old Cardinal, both of whom resigned from the University Senate in protest. The fellowship issue was debated in the Dublin press for some weeks afterwards, and there were several legacies of ill-feeling, such as a motion passed in the University Senate that in future only RUI graduates should be appointed to posts in that university; Hopkins was given the honorary degree of MA as safeguard. His resignation was requested by an episcopal committee, and he offered it, but the new Jesuit Provincial, Fr Brown, refused to comply. Hopkins and Walsh met on a few occasions during the next few years, and letters between the two exist, though there is no mention of controversy, and they kept to the safe topic of Loisette's system of memory recall, which both men practised.

* * *

Hopkins came over to Ireland the week following the Senate election, and took up residence on the top floor of No. 86 St Stephen's Green, in one of the best rooms in the house, with a view over formal gardens to the distant Dublin hills. He found with horror that as a teacher had been appointed at the start of the academic year to do his teaching, his main task for the rest of the year would be examining. And there were six groups of examinations each year, involving several thousand scripts to mark. Robert Curtis, appointed at the same time as Hopkins, gave 105 lectures over the same period, while Hopkins gave none.

Hopkins wrote his first impressions to Bridges: 'Dublin . . . is a joyless place and I think in my heart as smoky as London is; I had fancied it quite different' (LI. 190), probably as it had been before 1800, the second city of the British Empire, elegant life of Georgian streets and town-houses, informed literary and social circles, military displays. But Dublin had fallen into decay. George Moore wrote of 'Decrepit houses that had once sheltered an aristocracy, now falling into the hands of nuns and lodging-house keepers', incapable of appreciating the marble chimney-pieces and ceilings of sculptured plaster. The once grand Merrion Square was now melancholy – 'broken pavements, unpainted hall-doors, rusty area railings . . . how infinitely pitiful'. The souls of middle-class Dubliners, thought Moore, harmonised with their surroundings. 'Gossip and waltz tunes are all that they know. Is there a girl or young man in Dublin who has read a play of Shakespeare, a novel of Balzac, a poem of Shelley? Is there one who could say for certain that Leonardo da Vinci was neither comic-singer nor patriot? – No' (George Moore, *A Drama in Muslin*, 158).

The Industrial Revolution had bypassed Dublin, whose trade had been overtaken by the rapidly expanding industrial centres of Britain and Belfast in northern Ireland. Unemployment, poverty, bad housing, and drunkenness were profound problems. And Irish politics in general – evictions, the Land League, the campaign for Home Rule – were in a new period of militancy in the 1880s. Irish–English relations were in a combative and insensitive state. The two nations viewed each other largely as national caricatures. English newspapers, wrote the Belgian essayist Gustave de Molinari in 1880, 'allow no occasion to escape them of treating the Irish as an inferior race – as a kind of white negroes [*sic*] – and a glance at Punch is sufficient to show the difference they establish between the plump and robust personification of John Bull and the wretched figure of lean and bony Pat.' The coincidence of Fenianism with the Origin of Species debate in the 1860s had led to links being made between anthropoid apes and Irish Celts. *Punch* of 18 October 1862, for instance, had carried a fantasy called 'The Missing Link':

A creature manifestly between the Gorilla and the Negro is to be met with in some of the lowest districts of London and Liverpool by adventurous explorers. It comes from Ireland, whence it has contrived to migrate; it belongs . . . to a tribe of Irish savages: the lowest species of the Irish Yahoo.

When conversing with its kind it talks a sort of gibberish. . . . Sometimes . . . it sallies forth in states of excitement, and attacks civilised human beings that have provoked its fury.

Later in the nineteenth century a chimpanzee in London Zoo was named 'Paddy'. After the assassination of Lord Frederick Cavendish and his Under-Secretary in Phoenix Park in 1882, cartoons in London's weeklies showed the Irish as 'ape-like monsters with huge mouths and sharp fangs'. The heartless and avaricious Anglo-Irish landlord was pictured in the southern Irish press 'with thin face, drooping white moustache, monocle, and tattered clothes', while Ireland was represented by Erin and Pat. Pat was 'the epitome of Irish masculinity. His face was long but full, his forehead high, his chin square, and his nose and mouth straight and firm. There was a twinkle in his eyes and an easygoing smile.' Erin was 'a stately as well as sad and wise woman, usually drawn in flowing robes, embroidered with shamrocks. Her hair was long and dark, falling well down her back; her eyes were round and melancholy, set in a face of flawless symmetry' (Perry Curtis, 75).

* * *

Before he came to Dublin, Hopkins had spent periods of longer than a year in emotionally amenable postings – Roehampton, Stonyhurst, and St Beuno's, while the places which did not suit him had been his base for only a year at the most. But there was an unwelcome sense of permanence about the Dublin appointment – the Professorship was a permanent academic appointment, and he could move only if his superiors wished it. Hopkins had been thrust into a world that would seem foreign and strange, where an Englishman would never know for certain if he were accepted, or how far surface signs of acceptance were merely convenient gestures. Labels would be silently bestowed on him by everyone, starting with mention of his name. Both 'Hopkins' and 'Gerard' would be common in Ireland, but his voice would cause negative responses, with its usual association in Ireland – upper middle-class, southern, effete and elitist Oxonian – with the British superiors, not just the obvious label of the English man. There would be a distant admiration of the supposed Anglo-Saxon qualities – skills, training, and gifts of precision and orderliness – but close sympathy would be impossible. He was immediately associated with Newman, whose legacy to Ireland was often seen – at that time – as harmful (although Newman's image underwent a transformation within the last half of the twentieth century, so that he is now considered in Ireland as almost a saint). He was also associated – whether justly or not is another matter – with a particular type of English convert to Roman

Catholicism, one of those who had been attracted by the religion's supposed aesthetic superiority over Anglicanism; this was a charge that Hopkins was bitterly aware of, and which he fervently denied, saying that if externals were the criterion he would have preferred to stay in the Church of England.

* * *

There were practical difficulties in the running of the college. The buildings consisted of two houses, 85 and 86 St Stephen's Green. Most of the college's activities took place in 86, a square block of a Georgian mansion, called by Delany a 'neglected old barracks' (Newman was probably the first to describe it as a 'barracks', and the description stuck). It was full of dry rot, and sanitary arrangements were outdated and unhygienic; despite frequent requests the bishops would not allocate funds for repairs which the Jesuits could not afford. Because of some tenancy regulation the college could not use most of the first two floors, in which lived Dr Molloy, Rector of the otherwise defunct Catholic University. The college had to make do with the top two floors, composed of small rooms, for lecture-rooms, chapel, rooms for the Jesuit community and for one or two resident students, dining room, and kitchen. Science studies could hardly be carried on, because there were no laboratories or apparatus, and, the bishops having taken away the Catholic University library before the Jesuits moved in, there were few books, professors having to buy whatever was offered in the bookshops on the Liffey quays. As there was nowhere to house the books, they were arranged on various staircase-landings.

Another disadvantage was that the college had inherited some staff of the old Catholic University, men, sometimes appointed by Newman himself thirty years before, who through physical or mental infirmity were no longer suited to teach. Thus the holders of the two classical chairs senior to Hopkins's, Professors James Stewart and Robert Ornsby, were both in their sixties and infirm. The Professor of English was Matthew Arnold's younger brother, Thomas, who had first been appointed by Newman in 1856. Most of the other senior posts were held by Irishmen.

* * *

Within a month of his arrival at St Stephen's Green Hopkins was feeling deeply pessimistic:

> In the events which have brought me here I recognise the hand of providence, but nevertheless have felt and feel an unfitness which led me at first to try to decline the offer made and now does not yet allow my spirits to rise to the level

of the position and its duties. But perhaps the things of most promise with God begin with weakness and fear. (L3.63)

He wrote to Bridges that his appointment to Dublin was 'an honour and an opening and has many bright sides, but at present it has also some dark ones and this in particular that I am not at all strong, not strong enough for the requirements, and do not see at all how I am to become so' (LI. 190).

In March and April 1884 his depression seemed to be worsening: 'I cannot spare much time . . . . I wish, I wish I could get on with my play [*St Winefred's Well*]. . . AND WHAT DOES ANYTHING AT ALL MATTER? . . . The East wind is worse than in England. I am in a great weakness, I cannot spend more time writing now' (LI. 191–2). Other notes and letters dating from that spring and early summer tell the same story.

A holiday in the West of Ireland in early July 1884 strengthened him, but only for a short time. Soon after he wrote to Bridges:

The weakness I am suffering from – it is that only, nervous weakness (or perhaps I ought not to say nervous at all, for I am not in any unusual way nervous in the common understanding of the word) – continues and I see no ground for thinking I can, for a long time to come, get notably better of it, but I may reasonably hope that this pleasant holiday may set me up a little for a while. (LI. 193–4)

He continued to confide his poor mental state to Bridges, identifying examination marking as one of the tangible causes:

I have a salary of £400 a year, but when I first contemplated the six examinations I have yearly to conduct, five of them running, and to the Matriculation there came up last year 750 candidates, I thought that Stephen's Green (the biggest square in Europe) paved with gold would not pay for it. (LI. 190)

Hopkins was shocked by the poor standard of examination answers – most would appear to him to be of elementary-school rather than university quality – and the general standard of written literacy, particularly grammar and spelling, would have been inferior to that in England. He made notes on strange things that caught his eye. One Latin phrase which candidates were asked to translate and comment on produced the following versions:

So good a gladiator though certainly rude
Was so good a gladiator so vulgar with his food?
So good a gladiator get red so suddenly!
A good rough gladiator though hasty
Although a good gladiator yet rood on that account
As good as the caller is so the sooner his voice becomes rude
Being so good a gladiator have you become a rustic all at once?

Dublin Notebook, Campion Hall

Indignantly Hopkins wrote after this last version: 'And he alleges reasons for this rendering.' The same passage produced from one candidate the comment: 'Gladiators were those who carried the lash in front of the magistrates emblamatic of punishment.' The sentence 'Apothecae totae nequissimis hominibus condonabantur' was translated variously as 'Every apotheosis was pardoned by these most abandoned men', and 'Every cartaker was abandoned to the most worthless of men'; while another student responded to 'Quo me teste convincas? An chirographo? in quo habes scientiam quaestuosam', with 'With what experiment would you convince me? O surgeon. I seek a knowledge of the science in which you have been engaged. This means that the speaker wishes to learn surgery but before doing so wishes to see an operation.' Various papers yielded extraordinary versions or comments, such as 'What Charybdis so glutinous?', 'Then the Greeks goes and snatches the maiden', and 'So many drinking saloons are patrionised by the most wicked men.'

There are many examination marks and comments recorded by Hopkins in 'The Dublin Notebook', a battered red exercise book which also gives evidence in a most raw and direct way of his disturbed consciousness in 1884. The most vivid display of disturbance comes on folio 19v, a page forming part of a series of notes on a Caesar text, probably the comments Hopkins would make on the text in an elementary translation class. He starts to comment on the Roman coin, the sestertius; but a coherent framework disappears, he loses control, and ceases to make sense. Hopkins's mind is malfunctioning:

Sestertius = semis tertius = $1 + 1 + \frac{1}{2}, \ldots \ldots$ = as + as + semis, written IIS or HS. It represents a combination of the duodecimal (the as divided into 12 parts) and decimal (denarius = 10 asses) systems. It is then the ¼ denarius and this value it kept in spite of its name when the as was reduced from $\frac{1}{10}$ to $\frac{1}{16}$ of the denarius (which is the introduction of another system, one founded of the powers of 2)

1000 sestertii called sestertium, perhaps, but not certainly, a mistaking of sestertium = sestestiorum in mille sestertium and afterwards used as a substantive and declined, genitive sestertii etc

[then eight lines of calculations crossed through]

But take the sestertius for 2d. Then 100 sesterces = 16s 8d. and the sestertium or 1000 sesterces = £8 6s. 8d.

Bis et vicies millies sestertium = 22,000 sestertium = 22,000 (100,000) sestertii or sesterces = 2,200,000,000 sesterces = 2,200,000 sestertia 2,200,000 (£8 6s. 8d.) = £17,600,000 + (13,200,00 s. = 660,000 £) + (17,600,000 d. = 1,465,000 s. = 73,250£) = £18,333,250

[There are several other deletions not recorded here.]

Alien and lonely in Ireland Hopkins strongly needed communication with understanding, close friends. Canon R.W. Dixon was sympathetic but did not grasp Hopkins's situation: 'The prospect of reading for examining others would be a pleasant one to me: at least if it involved re-reading books that I once read with the other motive of being examined' (L2. 120). Dixon's picture did not correspond sufficiently to the reality for Hopkins to draw any comfort. The friendship with Bridges, on the other hand, had developed since their Oxford days into one of openly communicated feelings and many common interests; Hopkins sent pleasant and personal greetings on Bridges's marriage to Monica Waterhouse. He had, he revealed, 'a kind of spooniness and delight over married people, especially if they say "my wife", "my husband", or shew the wedding ring' (L1. 198). Bridges had asked Hopkins to be his best man, but Hopkins felt he had to decline.

Perhaps Hopkins conveyed to Coventry Patmore the nature of his liking for Bridges and his poetry, because in a letter to Hopkins Patmore seems to echo some of Hopkins's feelings, notwithstanding the initial wariness he felt at Bridges's lack of religious commitment: 'Personally I am attracted to him, as I am to all really poetic minds, by – may I call it so? – a sort of sanctity of intellect, a power of perceiving an immense range of things rightly. . . . A Poet, though without faith, still seems to me like the cartoon . . . of a holy picture: and I confess that I feel much more at home with such a man than I do with many a very orthodox and exemplary member of the "visible" Church, who believes all and perceives nothing' (L3. 357).

The one person in Ireland who 'rained against our much-thick and marsh air rich beams' (as Hopkins's St Beuno's poem 'The Lantern' had described the effect of close friendship) was Robert Curtis, the only person in Dublin with whom he was on close terms. Eight years younger, in fragile health (as Hopkins sometimes appeared to be, even when not ill), Curtis was also destined for a premature death, and would be buried in the same plot as Hopkins in Dublin. Both known as eccentrics, it was noticed that Hopkins often kept Curtis up late at night. Curtis's background made mutual sympathy more likely: his father was a pro-British lawyer, and he himself had studied at the anglicised Trinity College, Dublin, the only one of Hopkins's colleagues to have done so. Hopkins used to visit Curtis's parents on the north side of Dublin, and the two men went on holiday together at least twice.

Hopkins developed a hitherto dormant interest, albeit short-lived, in horticulture. He wrote to his sister 'I have a kind of charge of a greenhouse' (L3. 165), which was in the small garden at the back of no. 86. The college accounts show a sudden flurry of activity during the four days from 7 to 11 October, when a carpenter was hired to repair the greenhouse. Bartle Philips's horse and cart and a donkey-cart brought four tons of soil from the Jesuit house at Milltown Park; gardening tools were bought from Hodges, and two pounds were spent on seeds from Toole's of D'Olier Street. Labourers and a gardener were hired, probably for one day. In November an oil stove was purchased for the greenhouse, and in December a contractor was paid £12 10s. for unspecified work on it. After that, the activity which cost the poverty-stricken college well over £17 stopped. It looks like another sudden and aborted enthusiasm of Hopkins's.

But other potentially pleasurable occupations he lacked energy to start. A French Jesuit tried to persuade Hopkins to share his enthusiasm for photography, and when that failed asked to see the few sketches in chalk of cows and horses that Hopkins had done long ago in Wales. These he admired 'to that degree that he is urgent with me to go on drawing at all hazards'. But Hopkins's spirit was broken: 'I do not see how that could be now, so late: if anybody had said the same 10 years ago it might have been different' (L3. 165). During that first difficult year in Dublin he also found that letter writing was 'a most harassing duty to set to with other work on hand', and had lost touch with his brother Lionel, who had gone to China in the Foreign Service, and with his sister Grace, who complained that writing to Gerard was like throwing letters into a well. Nor did he accept his mother's invitation to spend Christmas 1884 with the family at Hampstead; he wrote to her 'You can easily understand reasons' (L3. 163).

She must have been considerably disappointed. However, he had limited success with two enthusiasms that Michaelmas term before Christmas. During the October examinations he had made the acquaintance of the two examiners in music, Dr Joseph Smith and Sir Robert Stewart. The latter introduced him to Stainer's *Theory of Harmony*, and as a result Hopkins completed a Gregorian setting to William Collins's 'Ode to Evening': 'Quickened by the heavenly beauty of that poem I groped in my soul's very viscera for the tune and thrummed the sweetest and most secret catgut of the mind' (L1. 199). 'Something like a glee', the piece was to be performed by a soloist and double choir, with accompanying organ or string band.

He also revived his flagging Ruskinian sense of observing natural phenomena. One evening he noticed a sunset glow that seemed relevant to current correspondence in the scientific journal *Nature*, about a halo or corona seen surrounding the sun. Writing a letter to the journal, he contradicted the interpretations of two correspondents, with his old Balliol self-confidence, and then described another celestial sight he had observed:

> If a very clear, unclouded sun is then gazed at, it often appears not convex, but hollow; swimming – like looking down into a boiling pot or a swinging pail, or into a bowl of quicksilver shaken; and of a lustrous but indistinct blue. The sky about it appears to swell up all round into a lip or brim, and this brim is coloured pink. The colour of the light will at that time be (though the eye becomes deadened to it) between red and yellow. Now it may be noticed that when a candle-flame is looked at through coloured glass, though everything else behind the glass is strongly stained with the colour, the flame is often nearly white: I suppose the light direct from the sun's disk not only to master the red and yellow of the vapour medium, but even, to the eye, to take on something of the complementary blue. (*Nature*, 30 October 1884)

Later that autumn of 1884, he composed a more considered study of a sunset, in perhaps the most remarkable poem he ever wrote.

Chapter Three

SPELT FROM SIBYL'S LEAVES

Dies irae, dies illa
Solvet saeclum in favilla:
Teste David cum Sibylla.

Woe to them that shall behold that day. For a dark mist shall cover the boundless world . . . the lights of heaven shall melt together into a void shape . . . And then shall all the elements of the world be laid waste, air, earth, sea, light, poles, days and nights, and no more shall the multitude of birds fly in the air . . . but he shall fuse all things together into one . . . then out of the misty darkness they shall bring all the souls of men to judgement . . . and the righteous shall be saved whole . . . but the ungodly shall perish therein . . . and all of them shall the . . . angels . . . chastise terribly with flaming scourges, and shall bind them fast above in fiery chains, bonds unbreakable. And then shall they cast them down in the darkness of night into Gehenna among the beasts of hell.

Second Book of the Sibylline Oracles

The lost now lying in hell are Devils without bodies and disembodied souls, they suffer nevertheless a torment as of bodily fire. Though burning and other pains afflict us through our bodies yet it is the soul that they afflict, the mind: if the mind can be deadened, as by chloroform, no pain is felt at all: God can then if he chooses bodily afflict the mind that is out of or never had a body to suffer in. No one in the body can suffer fire for very long, the frame is destroyed and the pain comes to an end; not so, unhappily, the pain that afflicts the indestructible mind, nor after the Judgment day the incorruptible body . . . Let all consider this: we are our own tormentors, for every sin we then shall have remorse and with remorse torment and the torment fire . . . sinners are themselves the flames of hell. O hideous and ungainly sight! which will cease only when at the day of Judgment the body and the soul are at one again and the sinful members themselves and in themselves receive their punishment, a punishment which lasts for ever.

Hopkins's notes for a meditation on hell

Hopkins felt no need after he joined the Society of Jesus to submit his journals to any censorship process – conducted either by his own conscience or, more formally, by his religious superiors. Keeping such a record of everyday observations and things he saw in nature was evidently morally innocuous. He cannot have contemplated that his journals would ever be published; although to him they were part of his 'treasury of stored beauty' he knew that to the outside world they would be considered unimportant, personal jottings, a spare-time activity. His poems, on the other hand, were a much more serious matter which opened up ethical questions of primary importance. He first recorded his feeling that the act of writing verse was morally dubious a year before he joined the Jesuits, and nine months later he burned his poems, 'slaughtered the innocents', as he called it in religio-romantic deprecation. He wrote to Canon Dixon his reasons for that act: 'You ask, do I write verse myself. What I had written I burnt before I became a Jesuit and resolved to write no more, as not belonging to my profession, unless it were by the wish of my superiors; so for seven years I wrote nothing but two or three little presentation pieces which occasion called for' (L2. 14). The serious formality with which Hopkins came to this decision shows it to be of comparable importance to the other two matters he resolved in the same short period – of whether to be a 'priest and religious', and if to be a religious, whether to become a Benedictine or a Jesuit.

Poetry writing would represent a serious interference and form of rivalry with his religious vocation. Hopkins wrote to Bridges: 'I cannot send my Summa for it is burnt with my other verses: I saw they wd. interfere with my state and vocation' (L1. 24). There was, however, a door left slightly open – the narrow but sole possible entrance for his poetry: 'I want to write still and as a priest I very likely can do that too, not so freely as I shd. have liked, e.g. nothing or little in the verse way, but no doubt what wd. serve best the cause of my religion.' Poetry was a high security risk, and only to be let out under close guard.

About the time he started writing 'Spelt from Sibyl's Leaves', Hopkins defended the Society of Jesus against Bridges's charge that they had not valued his poetry as it deserved: 'It always seems to me that poetry is unprofessional, but that is what I have said to myself, not others to me' (L1. 197). Much has been made since Hopkins's death of his over-fastidiousness about what fitted in with God's purpose; people have pointed to the lack of formal rules in the Society for making its members' works conform to the Jesuit motto 'Ad Maiorem Dei Gloriam'. But on the other side it has to be said that the Jesuits are a propagandist, not a contemplative, order. They were founded in the Counter-Reformation spirit of active soldiers in the cause of re-conversion. And Hopkins's puritanical attitude towards his poetry was certainly true to the later nineteenth-century, sometimes Jansenist mood of the Society in Britain. Rhetoric, the art of persuasion, was their prime concern, and the mere looking at, the contemplative or the aesthetic for its own sake, was certainly to be discouraged. The comparative 'Maiorem' in the motto suggests not concentration on the present state but the forceful adding on of something.

No rule was made about Hopkins's poetry because it was a more-or-less unheard of occupation – apart from conventional occasional verse – for a Jesuit of those times.

Hopkins considered his poems as (potentially) public utterances. His journals were private, whereas he sent nearly all his completed poems eventually to Bridges, who kept them pasted in a special book, with Hopkins's permission and approval. Hopkins saw and checked them occasionally, sometimes altering these fair copies, and sometimes sending Bridges later decisions for phrases or even for whole poems. The possibility of eventual publication was certainly in both Bridges's and Hopkins's minds. And therefore it was a primary condition of Hopkins's poems written as a Jesuit before the 1885 Dublin sonnets that they had as motivation and justification the Jesuit proselytising purpose.

And so there is in Hopkins's poems about nature the common pattern of a two-part structure: the first part (the octave of a sonnet, or almost so) has the poet looking at a scene, describing it and his involvement in it, while the second part (the sestet) is the poet's attempt to force this scene into a Christian context and draw a lesson out of it which could not have been predicted from the first part. The plainest examples are 'The Windhover', 'The Starlight Night', and 'Spring'. The latter poem starts with a scene of thrilling shapes ('weeds in wheels'), sounds ('thrush . . . does so rinse and wring the ear'), textures and colour ('the glassy peartree leaves and blooms, they brush/ The descending blue'); but the sestet starts with a startling contrast: 'What is all this juice and all this joy?' The narrator's voice, absent from the octave, asks the meaning of these seasonal excitements, and answers that they are left over from the paradisal delights of the Garden of Eden. The assumption that Hopkins is making is that all nature is a fable, and that as a priest he has the key and is the intermediary and interpreter.

With this background in mind, 'Spelt from Sibyl's Leaves' can be seen as one of the most distinctive and remarkable of Hopkins's poems. Its impressiveness is most curious because it does not conform to the general pattern of Hopkins's nature poems. The priestly stance here is un-self-conscious, and the moral lesson is not dragged out of unwilling natural description by a determined didactic. By taking a traditional fable in which the scene and message are already inseparable, Hopkins is able to dispense with his role of originating the link. Thus freeing himself from that role Hopkins also releases his attitude towards his material from certain constraints; he can now replace in this poem his priestly persona, so often prone to gush and patronising sentimentality, with a freer and more personal response. The Doomsday tradition within which the poem takes place is of such extreme power that the narrator-figure is subdued into quite a different character from that in, say, 'Spring', one more successfully defined and constant, dramatically more convincing in the strength of his response. The relationship between nature and the narrator is now thoroughly integrated into the poem's structure and fabric.

* * *

The date of the poem's inception (which is how Hopkins dated his poems) is probably between 15 October and 20 December 1884, but it was not finished until two years later, between 26 November and 11 December 1886. On 26 November Hopkins wrote to Bridges: 'I have at last completed but not quite finished the longest sonnet ever made and no doubt the longest making. It is in 8-foot lines and essays effects almost musical'; and on 11 December:

> I mean to enclose my long sonnet, the longest, I still say, ever made; longest by its own proper length, namely by the length of its lines; for anything can be made long by eking, by tacking, by trains, tails, and flounces [such as the three sonnets with codas which Hopkins was to write towards the end of his time in Dublin: 'Harry Ploughman', 'Tom's Garland', and 'That Nature is a Heraclitean Fire']. . . . Of this long sonnet above all remember what applies to all my verse, that it is, as living art should be, made for performance and that its performance is not reading with the eye but loud, leisurely, poetical (not rhetorical) recitation, with long rests, long dwells on the rhyme and other marked syllables, and so on. This sonnet shd. be almost sung: it is most carefully timed in tempo rubato. (LI. 246)

Despite Hopkins's repeated insistence over a period of almost twenty years on the importance of the sounds of his poems, this aspect is still often ignored. More than with any other of his poems this one cries out for a dramatic vocal reading, carefully planned to incorporate Hopkins's markings. Its sound orchestration scores the poem's major structure of a vast terrestrial movement, broken up into a variety of successive effects which build towards the terrible climax. For instance, the ponderous broken beat of the first line establishes the unexplained inexorable quality of the poem's opening; the process of casual, aesthetic Nature being forcibly strained away by the harsh forces of Doomsday ethics is directly articulated in the second line; the almost skittish nature of the third line's sounds, followed by their unexpected cancellation 'Waste', in the first syllable of the following line, shows the transitory and dispensable nature of earthly joys which are about to be replaced by the stark values of inevitable morality. Above all, the meaning is manifested by the way the varied rhythms at the start of the poem are gradually forced into an insistent, simplistic beat. This takes over with the unnatural emphasis on

'Óur . . . óur . . . óur . . . óur', which gradually ignores more and more the usual pronunciation-emphases of words, and forces them to participate in an uncomfortable tyrannic discipline, 'thoúghts agaínst thoughts ín groans grínd'.

*   *   *

This poem has been called a pagan one, whereas it was written within a Christian tradition. The early Christians were called Sibyllists because they believed that the Sibyl's writings truly prophesied Christian events; Michelangelo's 'Creation of Man' on the Sistine Chapel ceiling, and the medieval nativity plays called *Prophetae* bear witness to the long tradition in which she was ranked alongside biblical prophets. The Sibylline Books were first known for their prediction of the Messianic birth, but later and more frequently for their vision of the general Judgement Day. Hopkins was familiar with the best-known Christian examples of this – the old hymn from the burial mass, the 'Dies Irae', which brackets David and the Sibyl as prophets of Doomsday, and *The City of God*, where St Augustine quotes part of the eighth Sibylline Book and says the Sibyl clearly belongs to the City of God. In both instances man is sternly admonished to beware of Judgement Day, which will be presaged by violent terrestrial upheaval. The subject, tone, and purpose of Hopkins's poem are strikingly similar. And his 'all in two flocks, two folds – black, white; right, wrong' originated in the 'Dies Irae', where the ethical division into flocks occurs, using the same metaphor as Hopkins, 'Inter oves locum praesta,/ Et ab haedis me sequestra' ('make me a place among the sheep, and separate me from the goats'). Hopkins had probably also read those parts of the Oracles that describe doomsday apart from the one quoted by Augustine: the Apocryphal New Testament is among books he intended to read listed in his journal for Spring 1865 (J. 56).

Spelling from leaves was the method of prophesying normally used by the Cumaean Sibyl. She shuffled her palm-leaves, on each of which was inscribed an oracle, and used them for fortune-telling like a Tarot pack, by drawing some out at random. She was the prophetic votaress of Apollo, the sun god. Now in Christian times, the priest Hopkins has taken over the role of interpreting the sun god's portents. He sees the sun's portentous decline, and grasping fragments of its significance, 'Earnest, earthless, equal, attuneable, vaulty, voluminous, . . . stupendous', fits them together, until their total significance clarifies and bursts into his understanding: 'Óur tale, O óur oracle!'

Doomsday is not just an ending to the Christian era, but to all time. If one sees the whole of history as a single and purposive unfolding of God's plan, then Christ was incarnated only after a delay. He can therefore not represent all time, whereas the Sibyl can, coming before Christ, and yet predicting the end of time. The greatest pagan souls were precursors rather than enemies of faith, which was why Michelangelo was ordered by Pope Julius II to paint the Sibyl on the Sistine ceiling, as though she were a Christian prophet. The Sistine roof, according to Christian thinking, is thus representative of all time; and the Sibyl shows the faith to be all embracing and part of the original vast cosmic plan, not just an historical accident. The cosmological background to the poem, then, is scrupulously Christian, despite the pagan and classical sound of the title. The poem reiterates the Sibyl's vision in modern times. The sunset one evening seems so dramatically portentous that the poet sees it as a cosmic paradigm, of the final Judgement Day into which all evenings will be transmuted.

It was a common earnest Ruskinian habit of Hopkins's to observe sunsets; there are 56 entries under 'Sunset' in the index to Hopkins's journals, and Ruskin used to visit the sunset 'as regularly as a soldier does his evening parade'. But unlike several other poems in which the experience of looking at nature is described through the excited feelings aroused in him (for example, 'Look at the stars! look, look up at the skies', in 'The Starlight Night'), Hopkins is oddly null in this poem until line 7 – 'Heart, you round me right' – and muted thereafter, even when he comes to describe his personal idea of Hell. This powerful sunset presents itself: a portentous spectacle, whose magnificence would be belittled if the poet thrust himself forward, and so he remains untypically self-restrained, letting the words come from the sunset, gradually impinging on him.

This sunset is less a spectacle than a vast, imperspicuous event of oracular significance. Its disproportionate magnitude is suggested by the difficulty with which the seven first-line epithets are extracted: the meaning has to be 'spelt', told out, drawn out by the poet in hints and unordered pieces, rather than by a direct, continuous telling.

And so there is a laboriousness, a strain, about these epithets and the structure of the first line. Although grammatically they qualify 'evening', the adjectives are separated from their noun in several ways: by forming a line of their own distinct from their noun, and by that line being extraordinarily long and heavy; by the commas; by the adjectives having a mysterious solidity, an almost substantive entity (the substantive meaning 'a token' or 'sign' hangs about the adjective 'earnest'); and by their being established each with a distinct life before the noun comes, while the listener loses his anticipation of the noun because of the strength of the epithets. The meanings of several of these adjectives overlap, but the connections are at first less noticeable than the threat of each to the others (like the Sibylline leaves, which instead of telling a story in consecutive, interlocking parts, just gave odd fragments and left the seeker to make out what order he could or wanted to).

*   *   *

line 1. *earnest* ➻ A key word for the Victorians, who used it to describe their counter-attitude to pre-Victorian unserious ways of life. 'Earnest' was substituted for 'serious' by Dr Arnold of Rugby, who constantly referred every action to the fundamental principles of right and wrong. It was used by Victorian religious revivalists, both low church and high, to describe the best frame of mind in which to think about religious and moral issues. Hopkins used the word frequently and attached great importance to the concept: 'A kind of touchstone of the highest or most living art is seriousness; not gravity but the being in earnest with your subject – reality' (LI. 225). In sermons he uses it most often to describe prayer: 'our earnest hope and prayer' (s. 251), 'with earnest and humble entreaties' (s. 31). In his journal it and words of similar tenor describe the sky: 'the higher, zenith sky earnest and frowning' (J. 207), and 'it was a grave . . . sky' (J. 218). His most interesting other use is in a scrap of sermon, where he dwells on the meaning: 'Truth – reality or earnest and the feeling of it, earnestness: spiritual insight. This guards chastity and temperance . . . it cuts off the flowing skirts of idleness and worldliness' (s. 234).

Hopkins strikes the keynote of 'Spelt from Sibyl's Leaves' with this word, describing the evening tone with a word more appropriate to the human mind than to nature, thus predicting the human application of nature's message. The poem is a warning for earnestness about the Four Last Things in the Catechism – Death, Judgement, Hell, and Heaven.

earthless ➻ The earth, with its associations of unspiritual clay and variegated dapple, no longer has its usual nature or is distinguishable from heaven. As darkness increases so the sight of the earth decreases and the mind concentrates on spirituality, on the unearthly black and white. The necessary preliminary to the Four Last Things is the nullifying of all earthliness (Jeremiah [4. 23] foretells the day of God's vengeance: 'I beheld the earth, and lo, it was without form and void').

Looking at the Northern Lights, Hopkins wrote in his journal for 24 September 1870: 'This busy working of nature wholly independent of the earth and seeming to go on in a strain of time not reckoned by our reckoning of days and years but simpler and as if correcting the preoccupation of the world by being preoccupied with and appealing to and dated to the day of judgment was like a new witness to God and filled me with delightful fear' (J. 200). This journal extract helps also to clarify the meaning of 'tíme's vást . . . night', the vaster cosmic night which the sight of a particularly portentous dusk suggests.

equal ➻ Applies both to the visual scene, following after 'earthless' – earth and heaven are now uniform in colour and tone, without variation – and also to the portent of the scene foretelling the equality of Judgement Day, when all are equal and justice will be dealt impartially. In this sense it connects with the 'becoming even' of 'evening'. Compare 'That Nature is a Heraclitean Fire':

> Manshape, that shone
> . . . death blots black out; nor mark
> Is any of him at all so stark
> But vastness blurs and time beats level.

attuneable ➤ Follows 'equal' with something of the same meaning, probably 'bringing into harmony or accord', and refers to the evening's bringing to one tone the dapple of daytime earth and sky. This is essentially an aural image, and there is a suggestion of spheral music. Each sphere of the seven main planets of classical times sounded its own note of the seven-note scale. Visualising the evening scene as the long night, which existed before and will exist after the life of our universe ('womb-of-all, home-of-all, hearse-of-all night'), Hopkins suggests that, rather like the ancients' spheres, the parts of the cosmos, including the earth and its 'dapple at end', have lost their characteristic individual tunes and are now all of one note. This would be an obvious sign of cosmic breaking-up and the end of time.

vaulty ➤ Hopkins wrote to Bridges in October 1886: 'when anything, as a court, is uncovered and roofless strictly speaking, a dome is just the one kind of roof it may still be said to have and especially in a clear sky and on a mountain, namely the spherical vault or dome of heaven' (LI. 244). 'Vault' is the common poetic visual image of something vast, arched and hollow, having associations with burial chambers and death, and connects with 'hearse' in line 2. Compare Sidney's 'Well (me thinkes) becomes this vaultie skie/ A stately tombe to couer him deceased'. It is also used by Hopkins in Caradoc's soliloquy from Act II of 'St Winefred's Well', the part written about the same time as this poem: 'heaven-vault fast purpling portends'; and in 'The Blessed Virgin compared to the Air we Breathe': 'The thick stars round him roll . . . / In grimy vasty vault'.

voluminous ➤ Note the concealed 'luminous'. Vastness on a three-dimensional scale; the container of this volume is the vault of 'vaulty'. Compare Milton, *Paradise Regained*, IV. 382:

> . . . if I read aught in Heaven,
> Or Heav'n write aught of Fate, by what the Stars
> Voluminous, or single characters,
> In their conjunction met, give me to spell.

. . . stupendous ➤ The first six adjectives are kept at a distance from their noun 'Evening' by the one-beat stressed pause after 'voluminous',

indicated by the three points, and the summarising adjective 'stupendous'. The pause incorporates a standing away by the speaker from the preceding adjectives, a gathering of enough breath to collect together his scattered impressions, and emphasises the force of the word 'stupendous' when it comes and its meaning. The three points indicate the process of emerging from the stupefaction, while 'stupendous' describes and summarises not the six words, which represent qualities emanating from the sunset, but the effect the qualities and the whole sight have on him. The apparent syntactical incoherence of the six adjectives, with their noun 'evening' hidden away and the expectation of it lost, is thus explained by 'stupendous'.

Like many words in this poem, 'stupendous' has several functions. It stresses the overwhelmingly sensuous nature of the scene, and is also the intermediary between the two states of the poet – the poet as sensitive yet impassive receiver of impressions, and the poet as interpreter, having sorted the impressions into order, showing how the previous portentousness is justified. It is the climax to its line in the same way as the final words of lines 4, 5, and 8 are: it contains 'end us'. The word is also appropriate for a Sibyl's spell – the Sibyl often used to pass out, be stupefied, at the height of her pronouncements, in her oracular frenzy.

line 2. *Evening* ⇥ Hopkins brings out the not usually distinguished difference between 'evening', the coming on of 'even', and 'night', the completed process, reminding us of the original meaning of 'evening' (a usage still common in Ireland). The original participial meaning of 'becoming even' describes the period when things are still as uncertain as the equivocal adjectives; evening is becoming a definite noun, thus connecting with 'equal'. There is almost a birth process – 'strains to be'; and evening becomes the night in which time finishes, the vast night of eternity, in which are wrapped like a body in a hearse all events of time.

strains ⇥ In this purification process the colour is filtered off until only black remains. The movement to discovery is a strain (cf. 'The midriff astrain with leaning of, laced with fire of stress', 'Wreck', stanza 2). The word is partly onomatopoeic; and the single-syllabled feet, 'time's' and 'vast', continue the associated effect of tension and weight.

time's vást, womb-of-all, home-of-all, hearse-of-all night ⇥ Nature is shown by the syntax in the first line to be pieces of a puzzle; these pieces come together in the second line, which finishes with the first overall view, 'time's . . . night'. Hopkins has divined from the Sibyl's leaves what Calchas, best of the Greek prophets (in *Iliad* I and II) could divine – what is and what shall be and what was before. The day of General Judgement for both pagans and Christians meant the end of time, with all events wrapped up in the night of Eternity:

'the soul [on Judgement Day] will see time as God sees it – all at once, past, present, and future embraced in a single moment of perception' (Watts, 225). Compare Fulke Greville, Lord Brooke, 'Sonnet 87', from *Caelica*:

> But when this life is from the body fled,
> To see it selfe in that eternall Glasse,
> Where time doth end, and thoughts accuse the dead,
> Where all to come, is one with all that was . . .

This epigrammatic method of representing life by its three, or sometimes two, common prominent characteristics, is one of the several apocalyptic features of this poem: '"I am the Alpha and the Omega", says the Lord God, who is and who was and who is to come' (Revelation 1. 8).

The rhyme 'womb . . . tomb' is an almost irresistible poetic metaphor for the beginning and ending of life, used by, for example, Tennyson (*Lucretius*, 243–4), Swinburne (*Ave atque Vale*, xviii), Joyce (*Ulysses*, 61), and Auden ('At the Manger', *For the Time Being*, section 2). Hopkins used it in 'Thee, God, I come from' (lines 29–30), and the question arises why he chose 'hearse' here? It is probably because he wanted to suggest a progression in the vowel pattern of the three words, making a smoother gradual lowering of the voice from 'womb' to 'night' in a recitation of the poem. Whereas both the vowel and final syllable of 'tomb' would be voiced, the voice is cut off after the vowel of 'hearse' by the sibilant, producing a further falling-off effect. Also 'hearse' is a vehicle moving towards, while the tomb is the destination, the ultimate end of the process.

tíme's ⤞ In an early version of 'On the Portrait of Two Beautiful Young People' Hopkins brackets as alternatives in line 7 'time's' and 'fate's'.

vást ⤞ In the early journals Hopkins wrote: 'Above/ The vast of heaven stung with brilliant stars' (J. 43).

womb-of-all ⤞ This expresses both shape, connecting with 'vaulty' in the sense 'a hollow space or cavity, or something conceived as such (e.g. the depth of night)', and is also a metaphor for place of origin. The same combined meaning occurs in *Paradise Lost* I.150: 'swallowed up and lost/ In the wide womb of uncreated night'; and in John Norris of Bemerton's 'Hymn to Darkness': 'Thee [Darkness], from whose pregnant universal womb/ All things, even Light thy Rival, first did Come.' There was an ancient allegory of Eros, or Divine Love, producing the world from the Egg of Night, as it floated in Chaos (see Erasmus Darwin, 'Botanic Garden', note to lines 693–700). Hopkins's first version on the 'A' manuscript had 'woom'.

hearse-of-all ⤞ Compare Henry King, 'Midnight Meditation': 'Night is thy Hearse, whose sable Canopie/ Covers alike deceased day and thee'.

night ⤖ Night is not here just a symbol of birth, life, and death; it is the container of all beginnings, lives and deaths, and all time once time has come to an end.

line 3 ⤖ The two halves of this line are parallel in sound pattern and syntax structure; the first half gently declines, like the sun, towards its end, while the second half hangs on the height and is suddenly let down by 'Waste' at the beginning of the next line.

fond ⤖ The most fitting meaning seems to be 'clinging as if reluctant to go' (Leavis, 132), but Hopkins seems to have an additional idea, which is perhaps expressed by the word 'tipsy' in a similar context from his journal: 'westwards lamping with tipsy bufflight, the colour of yellow roses' (J. 236), where he uses a word which can have a similar meaning to 'fond' in the sense of 'foolish'. But again, perhaps he is implying something he is trying to capture in another journal phrase 'shade-softened grey in the West'. R. K. R. Thornton suggests it 'seems to mean something like loveable, familiar, so that both the human, domestic light of the sublunar world and the frighteningly alien insubstantial light of the Milky Way are both irrelevant – "waste"'.

yellow ⤖ Hopkins often noticed and recorded yellow in sunsets: 'It was a glowing yellow sunset', 'steelgrey at sunset, with yellow lustre in the West', and the 'sundown yellow' (J. 210, 144, 196), and in an early poem: 'After the sunset I would lie,/ And pierce the yellow waxen light.' He often used 'lamp' to describe this yellow, with the same picture of 'yellow hornlight': 'In the sunset all was big and there was a world of swollen cloud holding the yellow-rose light like a lamp' (J. 201), and see also the journal extract under 'fond' above.

hornlight ⤖ This is a coinage. Although the first tendency is to associate it with the moon, as does OED, the light plainly described here as fading in the west must be that of the setting sun. Hopkins often used 'horn' to describe the sun: 'the sun put out his shaded horns' (J. 141), and 'the crown of horny rays the sun makes behind a cloud' (J. 200). And there are several journal entries to show what he means when he applies the word to a sunset: 'Sunset over oaks a dapple of rosy clouds blotted with purple, sky round confused pale green and blue with faint horned rays' (J. 146). Hopkins is concerned with the appearance of the sun reminiscent of the light from a horn-lamp or a horn-pane of a window. Compare J. 163: 'On the same evening the fields facing west glowed as if overlaid with yellow wax.'

wound ⤖ The sun's winding down, as of a winch, towards the west. OED quotes *Cursor Mundi* 8968: 'Prophesy . . . ho talde . . . of domys-day/ How al þis werlde sal winde a-way'.

west ⤖ As the quarter of the sun's declension west often metaphorically represents death, as in Donne's 'Hymne to God my God, in my sicknesse': 'As

West and East/ In all flatt Maps (and I am one) are one,/So death doth touch the Resurrection'. In church architecture it is the area of the flesh, where the font (the womb) is situated, whereas the East, where the altar is, represents that of the spirit. There is a phonal and sense connection with 'waste' in line 4.

    hollow ⇥ Again the idea of the firmament's shape, as in 'vaulty' and 'voluminous'; it suggests the void left by dapple's departure.

    hoarlight ⇥ Not the stars, but the white-grey semi-light everywhere in the sky except at the place of the sun's setting, and suggests the complete Old English meaning of *har*, old and venerable, as well as grey like rime, rather than just its more limited modern meaning.

    to ⇥ 'hung to the height' parallels 'wound to the west'; but whereas the first 'to' conveys 'down to', the second implies 'up to'.

    height ⇥ OED 13, 'The regions above; the heavens. obs.', as in the hymn 'Hail to the holiest in the height/ And in the depths be praise'.

line 4. *Waste* — See 'The times are nightfall':

> The times are nightfall, look, their light grows less;
> The times are winter, watch, a world undone:
> They waste, they wither worst.

The word describes sight ('getting fainter'), with the sense of use and validity having passed; also desolate, fatigued, and decline/diminish.

    earliest ⇥ The first to appear that night.

    earlstars ⇥ 'Earl' is the oldest noble title, with similar words in Norse and Old English, and so conveys both the ideas of age and nobility to the stars. Stars as people also occur in 'The Starlight Night': 'the fire-folk sitting in the air'.

    stars principal ⇥ This combines the two ideas of 'earl' (first in rank), and 'earliest' (original, OED 'principal', 8). Compare J. 50: 'A star most spiritual, principal, preeminent/ Of all the golden press'.

    overbend us ⇥ An astrological image: the stars 'govern' men's lives; but also denotes the stars leaning over, continuing the sense of 'vaultiness'. Suggests the growing sense of superhuman power as man's earth loses its being. There is a sense of threat and growing seriousness.

line 5. *Fíre-féaturing* ⇥ With features of fire twinkling: hence the present participle. Also the purgatorial torment of fire, and the flames of hell.

    her béing has unbound ⇥ Compare 'Binsey Poplars': 'strokes of havoc unselve the sweet especial scene', and J. 124: 'an idea is our thought of a thing as substantive, as one, as holding together its own parts and conditions; an ideal is the thing thought of when it is most substantive and succeeds in being distinctive and one and holding its parts or conditions together in its own way'; also J. 128; 'for absence cannot break off Being from its hold on Being: it is not a thing to scatter here, there, and everywhere through all the world'.

dápple ⇥ Vari-colouredness. OED's first meaning of the noun is 'One of many roundish spots or small blotches of colouring by which a surface is diversified'. Hopkins pictures these spots of *haecceitas* breaking away from the shape which decides their being – the aesthetic equivalent of breaking down a physical object into atoms; these become an invisible part of the container of all things, Night. The peculiar attraction and significance the Ruskinian concept of 'dapple' had for Hopkins may be judged from 'Pied Beauty' and 'On the Origin of Beauty: A Platonic Dialogue', J. 88–9.

Compare 'Just as the light makes things and their visible qualities stand out, so the night swallows them up and threatens to swallow us up, too. What is drowned in it is not just nothing: it continues to exist, but indistinctly, invisible and without form, as the night itself, or like a shadow or a ghost, hence it is threatening . . . . The night deprives us of the use of our senses . . . . It is a foretaste of death' (Stein, 27). Hopkins sees this night and its depriving of the senses as a foretaste of death and final judgement. St John of the Cross induced in himself 'the Dark Night of the Senses' so that he would be prepared for his ultimate night.

line 6. *throughther* ⇥ Adverbial phrase: '(Mingled) through each other or one another; promiscuously; indiscriminately; in disorder' (OED). Compare Evans, 30: 'The word that best fits the untidy house cluster [in Irish villages] is one often heard in Ireland – "throughother" – which is properly applied and probably owes its origin to the scattered plots of the openfield.' Note that 'all through' indicates everything finished, done, tired out.

throngs ⇥ EDD notes meanings of 'bustle, confusion', and 'a multitude of petty cares'.

lines 6–7. *self ín self stéepèd and páshed – qúite/ Disremembering, dismembering all now* ⇥ There is an ancient tradition of violence associated with Judgement Day, both the pagan one (the breaking up of the heavens at the twilight of the gods), and the Christian. See the *Dies Irae*: 'Dies irae, dies illa/ Solvet saeclum in favilla' ('Day of wrath, that day when the age dissolves in glowing ashes'); and the Responsory, *Libera Me*, from the absolution in the Roman Catholic burial service: 'Deliver me, O Lord, from eternal death in that awful day, When the heavens and the earth shall be moved . . . . When the heavens and the earth shall be shaken'. Although Hopkins has an idiosyncratic view of the details, the theological background is traditional.

line 6. *self ín self* ↠ 'What has departed from 'this' life has become divinised, though . . . the death is that of "self" rather than of the physical body' (Watts, 196).

Compare 'To what serves Mortal Beauty?', where the 'world's loveliest' things are 'men's selves'; the destruction in 'Spelt from Sibyl's Leaves' is especially terrible – the best of the world is disintegrating violently.

steeped ↠ OED 3, 'permeated'. See 'páshed' below.

pashed ↠ Commonly used in northern England of beating clothes, in the washing process of which 'steeping' is the preliminary action. Compare J. 233: 'the sun sitting at one end of the branch in a pash of soap-sud-coloured gummy bim-beams'. 'Self in self' then is a process similar to clothes being turned in on themselves in the washtub. This is a harsh bleaching process though, rather than a mere washing. All the dappled selfhood is knocked about and strained out until, in line 14, the blanched self is wrung out and strung up.

line 7. *Disremembering, dismembering* ↠ The paring down of 'disremembering' to 'dismembering' enacts the process going on of losing definition. The uneasy rhythm emphasises the physical violence.

Disremembering ↠ 'Consigning to oblivion', not just 'forgetting'. A widespread dialect word, picked up by Hopkins in Ireland, where it is still used. See L3. 165, a letter to his sister Kate from Dublin (9 December 1884, about the time of this poem): writing humorously in phonetic Irish, using Irish words and pronunciation, he says: 'but for ivery word I delineate I disremember two'. Used by the Irish peasant student Davin in *A Portrait of the Artist*.

dismembering ↠ A further description of the breaking down process which will occur at Judgement Day; 'disremembering' pared down to 'dismembering' enacts the process of losing definition.

Heart, you round me right ↠ To Hopkins, as to Newman, the heart often discovers the significance of phenomena: see 'The Wreck of the Deutschland', stanza 7: 'What none would have known of it, only the heart, being hard at bay'. In stanza 29 of the same poem the heart reads the message of the Deutschland disaster: 'Ah! there was a heart right/ . . . / Read the unshapeable shock night/ And knew the who and the why'. Similarly, in 'The Handsome Heart': 'What the heart is! . . . / To its own fine function, wild and self-instressed,/ Falls light as ten years long taught how to and why.'

round ↠ OED, 'To take (one) privately to task'.

line 8. *Óur évening . . . óur night* ↠ The interpretation of the oracle's phenomena. Not *any* night, but the one which especially concerns us. The stress mark on 'Óur', like that in line 10, is important. Again Hopkins distinguishes between 'evening', the continuing process, and 'night', the final result of this process, by using the present tense with 'evening' and the future with 'night'.

Compare the close of Hopkins's early poem 'Winter with the Gulf Stream': 'Into the flat blue mist the sun/ Drops out and all our day is done'.

whélms ⇥ OED 'trans. . . . to submerge, drown', EDD 'to cover over with a large vessel' (thus continuing the 'vaulty . . . hollow . . . overbend' image).

ánd ⇥ Compare the emphatic affirmative 'and' in 'Their ránsom, théir rescue, ánd first, fást, last fríend' ('The Lantern out of Doors'), and 'Buckle! AND the fire that breaks from thee then' ('The Windhover').

line 9. *beakleaved boughs . . . damask* ⇥ The leaves look like birds' beaks. The boughs and leaves are black against the grey light. The grey background appearing alternately with the black leaves gives the branch the appearance of a damasked sword, or the common household cloth (originally from Damascus, which has scrolls of foliage patterns on), except that in this poem the leaves end in a point, like a beak.

Compare J. 151: '[Appletree] sprays against the sky are gracefully curved and the leaves looping over edge them, as it looks, with rows of scales.' This helps to explain 'dragonish' as well, the leaves being like a dragon's scales.

dragonish ⇥ An image of menace and portent, as in Shakespeare, *Antony* 4.14.2: 'Sometime we see a cloud that's dragonish/ . . . thou hast seen these signs;/ They are black vesper's pageants'. OED also has an archaic (from Greek) usage of 'dragon' as an appellation of Death and of Satan. Hopkins thought of a dragon as 'a type of the Devil' (s. 199).

damask ⇥ Hopkins probably knew Ruskin's recommendation to amateur artists (*The Elements of Drawing*, Letter I, para. 61): 'the dead leaf-patterns on a damask drapery, well rendered, will enable you to disentangle masterfully the living leaf-patterns of a thorn thicket or a violet bank'. Compare J. 207: 'But such a lovely damasking in the sky as today I never felt before. The blue was charged with simple instress, the higher, zenith sky earnest and frowning, lower more light and sweet'; and J. 228: 'Where the snow lies as in a field the damasking of white light and silvery shade may be watched.'

tool-smooth bleak light ⇥ Compare J. 144: 'steel-grey at sunset'. 'Bleak' is a word of both colour and tone, both 'pale' and 'cheerless'.

lines 9–10. *black,/ Ever so black on it* ⇥ Black is one of the 'colours' most frequently written of by Hopkins. It is often intensified in his poetry, as 'pitchblack ', 'blackest', 'coffin-black', and 'blear-all black'. Compare J. 137: 'Beautiful blackness and definition of elm tree branches in evening light (from behind)'; and J. 141; 'Aspens blackened against the last light seen seem to throw their scarcer leaves into barbs or arrowheads of mackerel patterns'. There is a note of childish dread in 'ever so'.

line 10. *tale* ⇥ 'Reckoning' or 'account' (OED, 6), besides simply 'story'.

    oracle ⇥ Our sign of divine import (that is, the various phenomena of the sunset which Hopkins has been describing). It refers back to the title.

lines 10–14. *Lét life, wáned . . . ín groans grínd* ⇥ An admonition to that part of man's mind which appreciates the world's stress to yield to the final, ethical (more important than aesthetic), dichotomy. The all-seeing poet-seer is speaking to the tender and fearful part of himself which cannot see beyond the terrible destruction of that part of the earth most dear to him – its dapple – to the scene's cosmic, moral significance. The poet describes the process of division into moral alternatives which occurs at the Last Judgement; the sunset gives premonition of the general tone and also of the replacement of non-ethical, aesthetic, issues (represented by earth's individuality and colour) by the blanket ethical alternatives of right and wrong, symbolised by evening's black and white.

line 10. *life* ⇥ The discovery implicit in the exclamations 'Our tale, O our oracle!' is that the fading light is a symbol of our earthly life.

    wáned ⇥ Again, describes both the decrease in colour and strength, and the drawing to a close of a period of time (OED, 6).

lines 10–11. *wínd/ Off . . . on twó spools* ⇥ OED, 15: 'to wind off' in the sense of 'to unwind'. Here winding off from a skein, the large loose knot of wool or thread, into smaller units, into balls, or onto 'spools', that is, bobbins. OED quotes a figurative use from Clare (*Village Minstrel*, I. 170): 'Short is the thread on life's spool that is mine'. This idea developed from the Greek legends of the Fates or Moirae, often described as the daughters of Night and Time, one of whom, Clotho, spins the thread of life. Its winding off from the skein of life onto two spools is Hopkins's own imaginative completion of the life-death spinning process, which to the Greeks ended with the cutting of the thread by the third sister Atropos.

    The image of a huge colourful skein uncompromisingly wound off onto two spools, of black and white, is a brilliant metaphor connecting the two parallel processes of the colour of day being replaced by the black and white of evening, and the replacement of the generous aesthetic values of earthly life by the stark ethical values of heavenly Judgement Day.

line 11. *hér* ⇥ A stressed syllable according to Hopkins's marks, but there is no special meaning brought out by the emphasis. However, the last three lines are of an inexorable chanting character, and the unexpected stressing of some of the syllables which are less significant in meaning (also 'ín', line 14) suggests that all individual meaning is swallowed up by the greater, solely important 'bláck, white'.

skéined . . . véined ⇢ Coupled by Hopkins in a scrap of verse from the early journals, J. 50: 'Although she be more white,/ More white,/ Than a skeined, than a skeined waterfall,/ And better veined than pea blossoms all'.

stained véined variety ⇢ Welsh rhyming and alliterative device of *cynghanedd sain*: the first two words connected by rhyme and the second and third by alliteration.

stained ⇢ Coloured with pigment; once 'stained', as opposed to her present chiaroscuro. Also 'sinful': beauty but also sin, which the stark division into black and white will sort out.

veined ⇢ Geological term, recalling Ruskin again, and suggesting 'there lives the dearest freshness deep down things' (in 'God's Grandeur').

varíety ⇢ Absence of uniformity (not all black-or-white).

párt, pen, pack ⇢ 'Pen' and 'pack' are farming terms; to 'pack' is to collect into a pack of animals.

line 12. *twó flocks, twó folds – bláck, white* ⇢ Not the biblical comforting, paternal shepherd of Psalm 23, but the inhuman, strict divider into two flocks; in the *Dies Irae* these are of sheep and goats. 'Flocks' denotes groups and 'folds' the enclosures the two groups are in, defined and cut off from the other.

reckon ⇢ Double meaning of 'to count over', as of flocks, and 'to consider'.

réck ⇢ OED 1.b.' 'to take heed . . . of some thing . . . so as to be . . . troubled thereby, or to modify one's conduct . . . on that account'. This definition might have been written with Hopkins's usage in mind. He uses it similarly in two other poems, with reference to the power of God and the After-Death: 'Ah, the heir/ To his own selfbent so bound . . . / And none reck of world after' ('Ribblesdale'), and 'Why do men then now not reck his rod?' ('God's Grandeur').

line 13. ⇢ Hopkins wants to emphasise both the words 'these' and 'two', so he repeats them, stressing a different word each time.

ware ⇢ Obsolete and dialect 'to take care, be on one's guard', and combining 'aware' and 'beware'.

world ⇢ The world where moral judgements are the only valid ones; the rack is Hell, the world of those already morally judged to their detriment.

tell ⇢ (1) Matter, have weight or significance. (2) Are enumerated. (3) In a painting one colour tells off another.

eách off the other ⇥ Good and bad are each recognisable, definable by their opposite.

line 14. *selfwrung* ⇥ 'Wrung': that has suffered distress, grief or pain; racked. Medieval paintings picture Hell's torments as physical, whereas the Hell that Hopkins always pictures (as in the Meditation on Hell, s. 241–20) is of mental pain. As Hopkins says, 'We are our own tormentors, for every sin we then shall have remorse and with remorse torment and the torment fire'.

    selfstrung ⇥ 'Strung': in a state of nervous tension; a Victorian term, at the birth of modern psychology. But note also the completion of the washing/ bleaching process of the self, started in line 6, 'self in self steeped and pashed', and continued with 'selfwrung'.

    thoúghts agáinst thoughts ín groans grínd ⇥ Hopkins's personal idea of Hell; his worst earthly experience (see 'not live this tormented mind/ With this tormented mind tormenting yet' in the 1885 poem 'My own heart let me more . . .').

*   *   *

In superficial ways 'Spelt from Sibyl's Leaves' resembles twilight poems of the 1870s and 1880s, which formed a sub-genre stretching back to songs in Tennyson's *The Princess*. Alongside sections predictably headed 'Parting and Absence', 'Home and Fireside', and 'Echoes of the Past', a typical anthology, *The Humbler Poets. . . 1870 to 1885*, has one called 'In the Twilight', with poem titles such as 'Growing Old', and 'Twilight Dreams'. Most of these poems sentimentally exalt faith over reason, but a few recall the old tradition, close to the sternness of Donne's Holy Sonnets. This is part of 'Twilight Hour', by W. F. E. I.:

> It is the hour when mankind hears,
>   Amid earth's mingled moans and laughter,
> Chords which will swell when unborn years
>   Are buried in the great hereafter.

But Hopkins's poem is a genuine experience earnestly created, and the more remarkable when compared to hundreds of other sunset poems written about the same time. 'Spelt from Sibyl's Leaves' ultimately does not resemble any other Victorian poem. Hopkins had not merely seen one sunset and written down what occurred to him, but had strung together pieces of his hell-like experiences during the recent past to spell out his inner autobiography (the Sibylline framework providing sufficient indirectness to mask its personal significance). His observations of external nature have become painfully transformed through disproportionate moral scrupulosity. His personal hell of incessant moral thoughts grinding against others had made him neuroti-cally indecisive, unable to externalise his thoughts or see anything outside himself objectively.

The poems written before 1884 had advocated different aspects of a unified moral code: the chief good is nature, in both countryside and man, the chief evil those forces which ignore and pervert it. But the narrator-figure who presents and interprets the tableaux in the pre-Dublin poems according to this code does not retain a consistent emotional tone. The St Beuno's poems of 1876–7 displayed an enthusiast, who shook and shouted a dull listener without reactions to the natural scene into looking at it with fresh eyes; and with a jerky change of voice ('What is all this juice and all this joy?') sometimes laboriously, at other times obscurely ('these are indeed the barn' in 'The Starlight Night'), explained its religious import. In contrast, the persona of the Oxford poems of 1878–9 was less shrill, more settled and convincing as a priest figure; but he had an unrooted melancholy, regretful and wishful ('Let me though see no more of him, and not disappointment/ Those sweet hopes quell'), connected with Hopkins's unhappy comparison of this second Oxford stay with his earlier undergraduate days. In the transitional poems of 1878 to 1883 there was no awkward change of attention halfway through, from demon-stration objects to audience. The narrator no longer exhorted an imaginary audience, but pondered wistfully; the emotional tone darkened, and the clear focus subtly fogged. Ideal solutions, no longer a possible achievement, had become merely a distant picture. With the withdrawal of shrill confidence in an over-wide viewpoint, his poems were becoming more unified, although at the cost of ego-shrinkage into a muted, uncertain self.

By the end of 1884, when this poem had been conceived and was being gradually moulded, Hopkins had experienced one of his most prolonged and profound periods of pessimism, to which more factors than ever before had contributed. His physical and mental powers were, as usual, unreliable; and the factor for which he had given up so much and staked everything – his religious profession – was anything but efficacious. For the first time since his reception into the novitiate sixteen years earlier his professional duties, in Dublin, seemed of doubtful value, and the local church at ethical odds with his religion. He now lacked almost every kind of deep comfort.

In 'Spelt from Sibyl's Leaves', for the first time since he became a Jesuit, Hopkins's poetry has become a vehicle for his pessimism; the sonnet form has now gathered other things into its net than a pictured natural scene and its doctrinal message. It is not just that the subject matter has developed beyond hope and melancholy to the ultimate fatalism of Judgement Day and Hell, nor that the sonnet line has been painfully lengthened out from five feet to the ponderous octameter. The persona of the Dublin poet is now irrevocably changed from the St Beuno's or Oxford or Stonyhurst figures.

In times of prosperity and happiness the religious person believes that virtue will be rewarded on earth. But traditionally, in times of persecution or pessimism which make earthly rewards unlikely, the religious have found it necessary to focus on rewards and punishments in the afterlife, if their base of divine justice is to be sustained. Hence the strain in the Bible of revengeful against benevolent ethics, and the inconsistencies found generally between the religious forms into which unhappy and happy people have traditionally focused their emotions. Should sinners be punished or forgiven? In this first of his Dublin poems, alienated from his surroundings, Hopkins obscures his ego and finds some sort of refuge for his terrified self in the medieval traditions of Doomsday. His own sense of helplessness finds both promotion and support in the *Dies Irae* from the Burial Mass. But although other Catholics, both medieval and modern, might have found compensation for their dissatisfaction with the present world in these myths of the afterlife, 'Spelt from Sibyl's Leaves' shows that the pill did not work for Hopkins. His psychological make-up was unorthodox – it refused, against his will, to conform to the programme. Here, there is no martyr's serene confidence in immortality. (Another racked exiled Jesuit martyr, who had once been the flower of his generation at Oxford University, as well as a peculiarly skilled writer, Edmund Campion, possessed a relieving gaiety and certainty of purpose which Hopkins usually lacked in Dublin.)

The psychological pressures he is up against have weakened him so much in Dublin that he has now fled from the world of here and now, which in Wales had seemed to reflect God's grace to him, into the medieval world of the inescapable hereafter, which overwhelmingly reflected God's justice and punishment. In Dublin he lacks the earthly things he finds invaluable – the human scale, home, beauty, art, aesthetics; the light of these personal encouragements has been replaced by the bare values of his profession, stripped of any soft modulations or compensations. He is on the morally right side, but that is all. It is a predominantly harsh world, darker even than Liverpool, which, four years earlier, he had considered the ultimate hellhole.

In going back to an orthodox medieval text of the Requiem Mass, his particular psychological need has made him fasten, not on the predominantly pitiful tone of the *Lacrimosa*, not on the weary plea for rest and mercy of the *Agnus Dei*, but on the psychic terrorisation of the *Dies Irae*, with its extreme animal fear of irrevocable pain. Hopkins can no longer find the psychic strength to observe and experiment with reality. Weakness has made him discard these Protestant characteristics, to reject disquieting enquiry, to revert to the orthodox, mystical, Catholic certainties, supported by the prestigious prophets of antiquity: the Sibylline foretelling of Doomsday violence, the Pythagorean ideas that Earth was tainted and irrevocably opposed to divine Heaven, that the body was alienated from the mind. This bleak twilight will not be followed by a rejuvenating dawn, because this is the ancient cosmology, not the newfangled Copernican: the sun is not at the centre of the solar system, the earth does not turn; this sunset's finality is not temporary but ultimate.

For Hopkins the price of this certainty is morbidity. There is no optimistic metaphor to convey the idea of immortality, merely the inescapably pessimistic image of the setting sun which will never rise again. Creativity and wonder have been replaced by fear, openness of rhythm by an ever-more cloistering beat which eventually sweeps all sorts of protesting ill-fitting words into its scheme ('thoúghts agáinst thoughts ín groans'), which only suits the strictly, morally correct words of 'bláck', 'white', 'ríght', 'wrong', 'but', and 'two'. The poet's diction is gradually drawn in, his choice of words becoming controlled and repetitive, forced within the limits of the narrow dogma he is expounding.

At first no words are repeated, although the fatalistic 'end us' has appeared disguised in 'stupendous' at the end of line 1; then 'stars ... stars, stars' in line 4 concentrates the mind which had been wandering over a limitless range of evening phenomena with a variety of rhythms and degrees of importance. Soon afterwards the violence builds up and 'end us' becomes obsessively repeated as the rhyme-words, but concealed until it finally stands forth stark at the end of line 8. Then repetitions gradually increase: 'self ... self' in line 6, 'member ... member' in line 7, 'óur ... us ... óur ... us' and 'whélms, whélms' in line 8. 'Black' becomes a rhyme-word in line 9, with similarly vicious echoes in its rhymes of 'pack' and 'rack', and is itself repeated in both lines 10 and 12. 'Óur' is repeated twice more, in line 10. And in line 11 a rocking rhythm, which until then had been threatening, is properly started with 'two', which is repeated four times in lines 12 and 13, and has as tock to its tick the word 'but', which is similarly obsessive in lines 12 and 13. The end of the poem is dominated by the sound-patterns which take over the word-meanings from the words themselves. On top of the repeated syllables, longer particles with the same sound keep on recurring: 'But thése two; wáre ... where bút these twó ... off ... of'. There is an important insistent harmony in this poem, but instead of being lyrically supportive of the imagery, as was the music of the St Beuno's poems, it now gradually establishes complete domination, so that eventually the dogmatic beat replaces the variable images, just as black/white has overcome and replaced variegated dapple. The metaphor-bank is closed down, taken over by the simplistically limited but all-powerful forces of orthodoxy.

Within the mind a battle is taking place with an inevitable conclusion: the idiosyncratic is being suppressed. Although the poem's ultimate subject is the poet's mind, nothing about the poet is explicitly mentioned until 'us' at the end of line 4, and then that 'us' is weakened by being pluralised, and its force is also minimised by the suppressing 'overbend', which squashes it by meaning and by heavy stress. Whenever 'me' and 'us' occur in the poem they are weak-syllabled, slaughtered by stressed and powerful words: 'end us', 'over us', or the nasty sandwich 'round me right'. 'Our' always precedes a noun which pushes it on to the next dire stage – 'evening', 'night', 'tale', 'oracle' – signifying the inevitable capitulation and destruction of the personal. Not only is the narrator being suppressed by cosmic power, but he is forced to participate in the self-overwhelming process, when his heart (in previous poems the inspirational, benevolent sage) hurts him into subservient fatalism – 'Heart, you round me right'. This division of parts of his being against one another forms one constituent of the personal plot of the poem, as opposed to the cosmic. In the wash preliminary to the bleaching process of Judgement Day, different parts of the self are whirled uncontrollably around in one another to become merged, so that only the poet's thoughts remain after the wringing out and stringing up, and they are in a state of division against themselves.

This is a poem of deep autobiographical significance. There is no hearer, just the narrator, although the poem is didactic; whereas in the St Beuno's poems the narrator and hearer are side by side in a teaching situation, with the narrator exploding in feeling and then nudging the hearer when he has calmed down. The essential common ground between the narrator and the listener in the St Beuno's poems is that the image the world sees and the one the narrator feels are the same; whereas in 'Spelt from Sibyl's Leaves' the narrator rarely brings in the observed world, and on those few occasions the parts are either cancelled out (line 3, with its individual tripping and balanced rhythm is cancelled out by its solitary but all-powerful controlling verb 'Waste', that starts the fourth line), or serve the purpose of a more powerful didactic thrust ('the beakleaved boughs dragonish damask'– form the black/white visual sign which tells of the moral pattern).

Before this poem God was all-powerful, 'mastering me', *and* benevolent. He showed His care for His creatures by creating intrinsic idiosyncratic aesthetic properties. When inscape was discovered there was a new recognition of God. But now in Dublin, Hopkins is saying with horrified regret that he has been forced to not just reject but destroy his dearest, liveliest observations, which were the most original part of him, and which, potentially (although his Church never realised it until after his death) were the greatest service he could do for his Church. By denying his St Beuno's gifts (rejecting for publication 'The Wreck of the Deutschland', failing him in his theology examination because of his Scotism – the vital spiritual sanction for his poetic credo – two acts of rejection which symbolise many more) his superiors cut off what might have proved an invaluable new proselytising method and force: a new way to find God, a contemporary propaganda light issuing from a traditionally minded teaching order, through Hopkins's religious adaptation of Ruskinian aesthetics.

But in this poem such a new didactic has been explicitly overruled.

Chapter Four

TO SEEM THE STRANGER

-+->-<-+-

No one knows but myself the desolateness in leaving
Birmingham, and being thrown among strangers
Newman, on leaving for Ireland, February 1854

... the foreseen estrangement which must happen ...
*Manley Hopkins, 15 October 1866, six days before his son
was received into the Roman Catholic church*

All things ... strange/ He fathers forth ... / Praise him.
'Pied Beauty', St Beuno's, 1877

To seem the stranger lies my lot, my life/ Among strangers.
Dublin, 1885

By his ill-judged posting to Ireland Hopkins had been unwillingly and painfully caught up in the never-ending battle of two civilisations. Roman Catholicism, the religion of the majority, was increasingly linked with Gaelic culture to feed a nationalism which reacted 'primarily against England – English manners and morals, English influences, English Protestantism, English rule'. There was no halfway house 'between the rejection of the English Culture and the restoration of the Gaelic culture' (Lyons, 82, 58).

The lives of English people who went to live in Victorian Ireland were circumscribed to a degree unimaginable in England, their choices of interest and action suddenly limited. Often they thought themselves seen as largely unwelcome national caricatures, rather than normal human beings, and had to guard their tongues, being forced to take part in debates on national, if not racial, issues not of their choosing. Ireland to English people would be in many ways uncomfortable and wearisome, a country where at times bullying seemed to be understood better than polite deference, which was considered weakness, where procrastination and inexactitude sometimes appeared more common than efficiency, where politics was less a matter of providing for society practical services (in a lamentable state compared with most of Britain) than making rhetorical points in never-ending ideological argument, where – so it seemed – straightforwardness and hard-won precision of language were devalued and often answered by evasion and impenetrability. They were forced to bond with people of their own national assumptions, either in Ireland or in correspondence back home, and this, of course, made matters worse.

Very different from John Henry Newman, Hopkins was nevertheless indebted to him in many ways, and in Dublin in the 1880s he again trod in Newman's footsteps, in spite of the thirty-year gap between their exiles in Ireland, and the differences in their roles there. 'No one knows but myself the desolateness in leaving Birmingham, and being thrown among strangers', Newman had written to Edward Caswell in February 1854, concerning his departure for Ireland. In the 1850s vast difficulties had confronted Newman, more experienced, resilient, and widely gifted than Hopkins, and more prepared through goodwill to adapt to its realities. The reason for his presence there was that the Queen's Colleges, of Belfast, Cork, and Galway, which had opened in 1849, had been branded Godless by Irish Catholic authorities because their 'permissive recognition' of all religions meant that Catholicism could not be taught as the basis of university education, and so it appeared penalised and diminished. Pope Pius IX urged the establishment of a Catholic University in Ireland, and the Archbishop of Armagh, Dr Cullen (later Archbishop of Dublin), invited Newman to become Rector.

As McGrath states (103), vision and courage were needed for 'a mid-Victorian Irish prelate to enlist in his cause an Englishman and a recent convert'; on the other hand, critical hindsight suggests that, as with Hopkins's appointment thirty years later, more imagination might have been used in envisaging difficulties. The famous lectures on the 'Idea of a University', for instance, originated in an invitation to Newman not to work out radically the philosophy for a new kind of university, but to attack 'Mixed [-Denomination] Education'. Another, more negative and pettier, reason for the invitation was that: 'people complained bitterly of not being able to get at Newman. He would not dine out, he would not preach Charity Sermons or any sermons' (McGrath, 105). There were implications here about a clash of purposes and personalities. Newman's St Mary's sermons had been unforgettably effective in 1830s Oxford. The Oxford Movement would have foundered without them, and fifty years afterwards Matthew Arnold remembered Newman's 'breaking the silence with words and thoughts which were a religious music – subtle, sweet and mournful' (*Macmillan's Magazine*, May 1884, 1). But an Irish student recalled a very different reaction – in fact a deep national gulf – in the university church on St Stephen's Green in the 1850s:

> When the Rector preached, the church was crowded, yet, sooth to say, we youngsters were not enamoured of his sermons. The language was polished and perfect, the thoughts elevated, the reasoning without a flaw; but they had that fatal drawback in our boyish judgments – they were read.

This response suggests a deep gulf, though after the first lecture Newman sensitively wrote: 'I have just discovered *how* I ought to have written the lecture, what would have been the true rhetoric, and how I have plunged into a maze of metaphysics from which I may be unable to heave myself. When this broke upon me, I half thought of lecturing extempore, quite a different lecture – but I am not equal to it'. A Birmingham Oratorian aptly replied: 'it is to be considered that you are *writing* for the world and for posterity, though speaking to an audience' (McGrath, 160).

Delany's appointment of Hopkins had also been insufficiently thought out. At a time of stronger and more organised nationalist and anti-English feeling than in the 1850s he had chosen an Englishman whose home and educational background, quite apart from his delicate constitution, were obviously unsuitable, and who had no experience of Ireland (though he had had Irish Jesuit colleagues in England and Wales, and emigrant Irish parishioners in Liverpool and Glasgow). Not known as an effective teacher in the English province, Hopkins's pedagogic reputation had not been imaginatively explored: what would he be like in front of a class of typical Irish students of that time and place? Among English-speaking Jesuits there must have been some with practical Irish connections (one has only to look at the names of Jesuits in the English province to realise the large proportion with Irish roots). With his experience of Irish education, Delany knew the vast difference between Oxford's and Catholic Ireland's standards of classical education, but had chosen Hopkins for the Oxford and Balliol connection, a snobbish and impractical gesture. Hopkins was wretchedly out of place in the Dublin post, useless for the students, his religion, and to himself. Delany's incompetence in bringing him across the Irish Sea, and in not replacing him once his unsuitability had been established, is amazing.

The case for choosing Newman as university Rector had at least been supported by his international reputation as educationist, writer, thinker, and fighter for Catholicism. At the root of many of Newman's difficulties in Ireland had been the bishops' inability to form or express a consistent decision on the nature of the university and of Newman's role, and, particularly in the case of Dr Cullen, their constant lack of elementary practical support. Several times Newman had been about to resign when urgent requests for replies to his letters were ignored:

> I had now been appointed Rector for two years, and nothing had been done . . . For two years Dr Cullen met my earnest applications for information, or a settlement of particular points, or the expression of my views and wishes, by silence and abrupt acts. He had written to me, I think, once. He did not even correspond with me through a secretary. He made a stranger to me my

secretary, and obliged me to pick up the crumbs of his words and doings by means of him . . . . His presence at [my Dublin lectures] had been . . . the only public recognition of me, since I had been appointed Rector. If, in the coming January, I went over to Ireland, as I proposed, I should seem to be coming on my own hook. I should be an Englishman, taking upon himself to teach the Paddies what education was, what a University, and how it was their duty to have one with me for a Rector. I should seem to be carrying, not a great Council's resolve, but a hobby of my own, a propagandist, not a authoritative superior, a convert, without means, looking out for a situation, and finding and feathering a nest from the pockets of the Irish. . . . That I intended to make a good thing of it, was actually said. (McGrath, 212–13)

Cullen went against Newman's wishes in many other ways, such as having a Dr Taylor appointed as Vice-Rector, contrary to Newman's clearly expressed desire to choose for himself, and 86 St Stephen's Green was bought without consulting Newman. There are many examples of Cullen's ill manners in doing things behind Newman's back: 'Officials were appointed without my knowledge, not only Dr Taylor, but Mr Flannery, whom Dr Cullen made the Dean of the University. . . . Dr Cullen meant these men to advise and control me, and to be at once his own informants' (McGrath, 197–8).

The atmosphere of episcopal uncertainty, wary politicking, hints rather than statements, unreliability as to who was on which side, had not changed by the time Hopkins came to Ireland. In the 1880s it was the Jesuits at St Stephen's Green who were the victims of procrastination and politicking by the Irish bishops, now led by Dr (later Archbishop) Walsh. Hopkins's death from typhoid was probably due in the main to the bishops having refused to pay for the overdue renewal of the drainage system in the building they owned.

But perhaps the most insidious and constant unpleasantness experienced by the two Englishmen in Ireland was racism. Just as one Archbishop, McCabe, had opposed Hopkins's appointment in 1884 because of his nationality, so another, MacHale, in the 1850s, had constantly raised the crude charge that Newman's main purpose was to expand English influence in Ireland. Before his first visit to Ireland, Newman had been warned about the agitation against things English, even to the extent of whether he should stay at an English friend's house in Dublin or take a lodging. 'There is no doubt that you will find [the national jealousy towards Englishmen] a considerable difficulty in your way. They will not like the idea of an influx of Englishmen, filling up first one office and then another. They know they cannot do without them, at present at least, but still there will be a secret dislike of . . . the gradual formation of an English set, the nucleus of which would be the University' (McGrath, 141, 147).

In Newman's time Dr MacHale was the centre of the circle of anti-English feeling, but also involved were the Dublin newspapers (as they were in the controversy after Hopkins's appointment), and American Irish asked to contribute funds for the new university. In the United States, particularly, there was strong anti-English feeling, caused by the large-scale immigrations of recent famine and eviction victims: 'Both priests and people here think that the Irish prelates and people are too favourably disposed to English rule. . . . Even a rumour has reached us . . . that the Primate was influenced by Dr Wiseman [a cardinal in England, although Irish by birth] and was about appointing the President (an Englishman) with full powers to appoint all the Professors, English, of course' (McGrath, 187, 188).

Dr McGrath dismisses the suggestion that Newman deliberately set out to foster English culture in Ireland, and adds that there were many indications that Newman 'applied his mind to the history of Ireland and of her cultural achievements with that almost painful anxiety which he always displayed to understand the point of view of others' (McGrath, 186). He frequently acknowledged the part played by Ireland in the University's foundation: 'The funds come from the Irish, and the Irish poor. . . . While the Irish support the University, it must be an Irish concern. . . . Ireland . . . has contributed the great bulk, and contributes yearly' (McGrath, 435). Newman was anxious to appoint to his staff Irishmen, not Englishmen, wherever possible. His first report to the bishops emphasises that 'out of twenty-one Professors and Lecturers hitherto appointed, all the resident and salaried teachers but two are of the Irish nation' (McGrath, 361). Also Newman was indifferent to the political beliefs of his professors, 'since it was no longer likely to be translated into any form of violent action' (McGrath, 362), and in fact he aroused Cullen's wrath by appointing three former members of the Young Ireland movement, including John O'Hagan, who in the 1880s, as Judge O'Hagan, was a much valued supporter of Delany's college, and befriended Hopkins.

Unlike Newman, Hopkins became obsessed with Irish politics, one of those areas in which he was neither knowledgeable nor thoughtful, seeming to have escaped sophistication by relying on commonplace, conservative English reactions. Irish political reaction to distant and unsympathetic English domination appeared to Hopkins simplistically as disloyalty, whereas Newman replied to Hopkins's account of Irish rebellion: 'There is one consideration . . . which you omit. The Irish patriots hold that they never have yielded themselves to the sway of England and therefore never have been under her laws, and never have been rebels. . . . If I were an Irishman [and here Newman echoes Sir John Moore] I should be (in heart) a rebel' (L3. 414).

Newman's mature judgement, in spite of his shorter stay in Ireland, was well beyond Hopkins, and there is a certain justice in Fr Darlington's crude comment 'Gerald [*sic*] Hopkins was . . . a thorough John Bull incapable of understanding Rebel Ireland' (HALB, 384). The impressions of Hopkins in Dublin that Humphry House collected, forty years after Hopkins's death, nearly all refer to his being out of tune with his political surroundings. One ex-student recorded that he was 'very strongly anti-Home Rule and no doubt regarded his students as wild Irish barbarians', which, though wrong in detail, conveys the impression he made when talking about Irish politics. Two reported classroom sayings of his suggest his voice and sentiments: 'I see that fellow O'Brien [the Land League leader] has been lying again', and, when it was being claimed that Kitchener was Irish, 'You Irish – you drag everything into your net over here' (HALB, 384).

Both Newman and Hopkins disparaged or made fun (at times) of Gaelic mythic tales, which would become so important to Yeats and Irish people generally. Newman opposed Thomas Arnold's inclusion in the Catholic University's English syllabus of literary works with English subject matter, on the grounds that (he told Arnold) 'the Irish will think it hard that the English rebellion or Civil War has the precedence of the raid of Fergus MacDiormad [*sic*] into Munster in revenge for the dun cow which was stolen from the pastures of his great-uncle Thrady in the second century before the Christian era' (McGrath, 433). Similarly, Hopkins criticised Yeats's 'The Two Titans' for being 'a strained and unworkable allegory about a young man and a sphinx on a rock in the sea (how did they get there? what did they eat?)', and with dull English literalness, told off Katharine Tynan for choosing to write on subjects from Irish legend: 'They have their features of interest and beauty, but they have one great drawback: it is the intermixture of monstrosities (as of a man throwing a stone one hundred others could not lift or a man with a leaping-pole over-vaulting an army)' (HALB, 434).

Funny in England, these examples may well have caused offence in Ireland. It is the same with some of Newman's and Hopkins's would-be jocular accounts of Irish strangenesses, as though they were picaresque travellers in primitive parts writing to amuse the folks back in England:

When I [Newman] got here, I found that the house-keeper, who would not let any of the other servants do it, had arranged, not only my clothes, but all my papers for me. I had put my letters in various compartments according to my relations towards them in my Discourse papers. . . . She had mixed everything, laying them most neatly according to their *size*. . . . . And so of my linen; I had put the linen in wear separate from the linen in reserve. All was revolutionized. I could find nothing of any kind. Pencils, pens, pen-knife, tooth-brush, 'twas a new world – the only thing left, I suppose from a certain awe, was (woe's me) my discipline. . . . She then came in to make an apology, but was so amused at her own mischief, as to show that she had no deep sense of its enormity. (McGrath, 160–1)

It is much less easy to find examples of Hopkins's sensitivity and patience towards Ireland than it is of Newman's. I find Hopkins's collection of Hiberno-English words and expressions which he made for Joseph Wright's *English Dialect Dictionary* the great exception to his short temper and irremediably English responses, and these will be considered in Chapter 13. The most visible existing sign for me of Newman's deep feeling towards Ireland is his underestimated (because small, cheaply and quickly built, and not gothic) church, with its wonderful basilica interior, and the country's most colourful display of many varieties of Irish marble:

> Naturally . . . in an institution like ours, yet in a state of infancy, and designed to draw out and deepen the heart and intelligence of the nation, we wished to set the example of developing, as far as our resources went, the natural capabilities of Ireland; and geologically, the most valuable of these are the various veins of marble so plentifully compacted under and over the soil, on every coast and in every county. (McGrath, 408)

In Hopkins's day the Jesuits in University College were not allowed to use the so-called University church, having instead to paint over Buck Whaley's vulgar plaster nymphs in one room of number 85 with thick chocolate paint, and use that as a chapel.

Both Newman and Hopkins suffered in Ireland because of their Oxford connection. Newman had used Oxford as a model for some of his ideas about the Catholic university and its education since, though no longer Roman Catholic, Oxford retained large parts of its original Catholic structure and ideals, while Hopkins was appointed because of his Oxford background. But in Catholic Ireland 'Oxford' did not convey to the majority a definite or necessarily praiseworthy picture. Part of the Irish lack of enthusiasm for an English-style university was due to vagueness about what it would mean in practice. In Hopkins's day an 'English' university was distinguished in some Irish minds by its emphasis on cramming for examinations (as Joyce describes the Jesuit institution in *Stephen Hero*). And a friend of Newman's, Robert Ornsby (still a professor at number 86 in Hopkins's day), recorded that, in reply to his remark that Oxford gave a 'general finish and refinement of manner', an Irishman said 'Oh, that seems to me like a set of little girls – finicking preciseness', which showed, added Ornsby, 'that the idea was wanting in his mind, as of the special studies of a University, so of the general outward cultivation' (McGrath, 146). It is not inappropriate to connect this with two of Hopkins's Jesuit colleagues' remarks on his appearance: Fr Tom Finlay, an Irishman, considered Hopkins 'the typically "Oxford" man', with prejudices towards Ireland of 'the Oxford type', while the Englishman Fr Darlington, who had studied at Oxford, said that Hopkins 'brought Baliol [sic] and Oxford into our College', was 'feminine', and wore slippers of 'the kind little girls of 10 or 12 used then to wear: with ancle straps' (HALB, 383).

Another similarity between Newman's and Hopkins's Irish experiences is that many fewer reminiscences exist in memoirs of contemporaries than one might expect. There are several pen-portraits of all of Hopkins's Irish colleagues, but – apart from those drawn out in interviews in the 1930s by Humphry House, all examples of memorably *exaggerated* behaviour of his – almost none of him, except for one or two lines each from W.B. Yeats and Katharine Tynan (both picturing him as a caricature aesthete), although he was continuously there for over five years. And Fergal McGrath remarks: 'It is curious that the impressions made by Newman on his Dublin students and acquaintances are to be gathered only from . . . passing references. . . . Contemporary memoirs . . . contain no mention of him, and the omission is remarkable in view of his outstanding intellectual position and of his continual activity' (McGrath, 429). It can be added that, unlike Hopkins, who was sometimes pictured walking alone, or as a man of lonely study, Newman could not be called a recluse, and that there are many garrulous memoirs of that period to be found in Dublin's secondhand bookshops. Existing references are superficial, written in pompous clichés, rather than genuine observations:

> His was a striking figure as he walked with short, rapid step from Harcourt Street to the Green, tenuous and angular, his head bent forward, his ascetic features shrouded in meditation, and his keen eyes looking neither to the right nor to the left, but introspectively as it were, with a contemplativeness far removed from things of the thoroughfare. . . . Dr Newman . . . was regarded by the students with a sort of awe-struck worship. They were very proud of him, yet, to be candid, they did not rise to the understanding of his genius. It was too cold, dry, and self-contained for their young minds. (O'Shea, 2: 114)

It is as though Newman and Hopkins were invisible to Irish eyes.

Newman had many advantages over Hopkins in Ireland. He was able to relieve his frustrations by finally returning to live in England, whereas Hopkins was doomed to be buried in the same cemetery as the Irish patriots he so disliked. Newman had sensibly kept up his intimate relationship with the Edgbaston Oratory, and while in Ireland had used fellow Oratorians as constant confidants, whereas Hopkins's pen-relationships, excepting those with Bridges and Baillie, were less intimate and inefficacious. Newman had proved a remarkable survivor by the time he reached Ireland, whereas Hopkins had lost heart, acknowledging that he was 'Fortune's football'. The Oratory had not demanded the surrender of Newman's independence, whereas Hopkins was a slave to superior decision. But Hopkins's desperate situation in Ireland allowed poetic composition to emerge as an unorthodox, personal resource, in a way that could be predicted from no previous poem of his.

*   *   *

Hopkins saw himself as – and in many ways was – a stranger. The first estrangement Christ caused Hopkins was over his reception into the Roman Church on 21 October 1866. Some of the over-intensity and anguish caused by Hopkins's conversion is conveyed in letters of that time, particularly those to and from his father, the heavy emotionalism of whom must have been an additional weight on Hopkins's mind – 'the deepness of our distress, the shattering of our hopes & the foreseen estrangement which must happen, are my excuse for writing to you so freely & so pressingly; but even these motives do not weigh with us in comparison of our pity for our dear son, and our distress at the future life to which he is in such danger of committing himself' (L3. 435). The intellectual and emotional elements are hopelessly intertwined. At first all parties assumed that the alienation in religious thought had to lead to alienation of affection. In one letter to his father Hopkins wrote: 'My only strong wish is to be independent [in thought]', but some sort of compromise was reached over the external procedures of family relationships. His father would allow him to use the family home as long as he promised not to try and convert his brothers and sisters. After six months there was no trace of an awkward relationship in the affectionate letter Hopkins wrote to his mother, and in the same letter he acknowledges a gift of twenty pounds from his father. Even when he took a further step away from his family in religion by entering the Jesuit novitiate, he wrote chatty letters to his mother, like a boy away at boarding school, thanking her for sending him a second jersey, and asking about members of the family. He wrote to his friend Urquhart: 'It is surprising – at the kind and contented way my parents have come to take the prospect' (L3. 51).

A far more serious alienation for Hopkins was in religious relationships – between himself and his family (according to the theology of the time his family, as Protestants, could not enter Heaven after death), and between himself and his native country. As a Roman Catholic, and even more so as a priest, he was an outsider in English society. There was a common prejudice, to which many English Roman (note the apparent clash) Catholics were sensitive, that 'a servant of Rome was not quite an Englishman'. Cardinal Manning wrote that converts passed 'from the broad stream of the English Commonwealth into the narrow community of English Catholics', and Manning's successor Vaughan said 'What a number there are who every day enter the fold of the Catholic Church and find themselves shy and self-conscious, as foreigners in a strange land'. A common journalistic term for converts to Catholicism was 'perverts'.

The compensation for these deep permanent estrangements lay in philosophical consolidation and sanction, both religious and aesthetic, although the two kinds did not always satisfactorily cohere. But by July 1883 he felt that he had 'long been Fortune's football . . . the impulse to do anything fails me or has in it no continuance'; and by the end of the following year what he had seen spelt from the Sibyl's leaves was no longer the prominent distinction of self but the exact opposite: 'self ín self stéepèd and páshed – quíte/ Disremembering, dismembering all now'. This Fate of his had been spelt out irrevocably, now that he was stationed in Ireland. A frequent source of unrest before he went to Ireland had been the fact that he was continually being shifted about Britain: 'permanence with us', he wrote to Bridges, 'is ginger-bread permanence; cobweb, soapsud, and frost-feather permanence' (LI. 55). Having at last reached a post from which he was unlikely to be moved, ironically it was in a place, Ireland, where he felt most foreign.

He would feel that talk was often purposely superficial, while a deeper level of meaning, which everyone knew existed, would remain unexpressed. The effect could be quite hurtful: a feeling of exclusion from close human contact and from common reactions and language. The cause was largely colonial division into two estranged nations. Hopkins would be put in the role of colonist, even though no previous member of his family had ever been associated with Ireland. He would be forced into English responses, yet would have to be constantly on guard against expressing his immediate reactions in case he caused offence, at a time of extreme nationalist sensitivities. Innocent sayings would be misinterpreted and remembered; opportunities to make fun of him would be seized by students unprepared to sympathise with an effeminate Englishman unable to keep order, and without apparent means of retaliation.

Not surprisingly he became much more of a loner than he had been in his previous postings, although he had always been seen as intellectually separate ('eccentric'). The Irish saw him as preferring the company of pro-British 'Castle Catholics' to that of the incumbents of 86 Stephen's Green, although he was careful when writing to his mother to give the impression that he fitted in well with the people he lived with; there are serious discrepancies, for instance, between his account of a dear old French father, and a witness's report of the fierce antagonism between Fr Mallac and Fr Hopkins. Hopkins needed sympathetic inter-communication with someone of similar background and assumptions. His old Oxford contemporaries Bridges and Baillie were the obvious candidates, and, to a lesser extent, his mother, Canon Dixon, and Coventry Patmore. The local Irish people who shared much of his English educational and cultural background were at Trinity College, Dublin, but contact with them was limited, because – though only a short walk away from his college in central Dublin – they were almost all Protestants, and friendship beyond professional politeness would be discouraged. There was a gulf in prestige: TCD was a prosperous Elizabethan foundation, traditional home of pro-British sympathisers, housed in fine old purpose-built architecture, and with an academic reputation comparable to that of the best English universities, while University College was an evidently poverty-stricken, much smaller, very recent, makeshift institution, in two dismal, decayed dwelling-houses, and academically not in the same class, intended for an unsophisticated, underdog people without any tradition of third-level education.

Hopkins's Newmanite conversion, his Oxford background, his effeminate build and bearing, his known interests in art, architecture, nature, and poetry, and his constant efforts to promote the work of his English friends – Bridges, Dixon, and Patmore – all seemed parts of a well-known caricature; Katharine Tynan compared him with Lionel Johnson, an effete aesthetic English poet. Hopkins's reason for being in Ireland, his role of professor at the University College, St Stephen's Green, would reinforce the barrier rather than lower it. The College's teaching was a matter of cramming for examinations, and formal impersonal lectures – on a level which would seem to Hopkins incredibly elementary – to students who mainly lived in their own homes, rather than the more intimate atmosphere of Oxford college life and tutorials. A professor at Stephen's Green was a high and distant person seen occasionally at the front of the lecture rooms, or passed in the gloomy corridors or on the stone stairs, or glanced at when you attended Mass.

Hopkins's oddnesses and strangenesses were even more exaggerated by his position as priest. Priests in Ireland are cut off from ordinary intercourse 'in a way that seems unknown in other countries', wrote Frank O'Connor (127). And he quoted a parish priest as saying 'I can't go into a living room without knowing that all ordinary conversation stops, and when it starts again it's going to be intended for my ears. That's not a natural life.' Priests in the professional orders would be further cut off, partly by their unattractive puritanical image, and the cruel practices, sometimes perversion, associated with some of the teaching orders, and only in the 1990s brought into the open. It is rare to find warm references to Jesuits in Ireland: they are probably associated mainly with three things: their extraordinarily lengthy and rigorous training, with which there was nothing comparable in Ireland; the 'snob' secondary schools, where they educated for comparatively large fees the sons of the Catholic upper and professional classes, and which had become noted for their systematic training for and success in competitive examinations; and with gracious living as befitted the gentlemen of the Church.

*　　*　　*

In 1885, in the poem which in many ways gives the emotional background to the other sonnets of its group, Hopkins stated the substance of his lot. He has reached a mature conclusion about his Fate, and makes a calm summary of it: 'To seem the stranger lies my lot, my life/ Among strangers'.

Fate's die is cast, so that he will always be separate from those around him, the lone individual among a strange community. 'The strangers' is commonly used in Ireland to refer to the English, in the hostile sense of incomprehending invader: 'The strangers tried to teach us their ways', as a patriotic song puts it. So the poem relates specifically to Ireland in more than merely the reference in line 9. But the fatalistic tone of the whole poem, from the first line onwards, implies that Hopkins is summarising years of memories and experience. The simplicity of 'lies my lot' expresses the inescapableness of the poet's conclusion, and yet the role itself, 'to seem the stranger', is *not* compensatingly clearcut; there is uncertainty, even a degree of untrustworthiness, in people's impression of him. He is the stranger, the foreigner, the eccentric. The objective summary yet expresses dreadful sadness in the realisation that the card drawn for the poet by Fate, 'my lot', means in human terms 'my life'. In 'Spelt from Sibyl's Leaves', all past, present and future had telescoped into one resultant fate; now Hopkins states what this fate is: to be a stranger among strangers. There is no sense of personal strength or firm identity here, merely passive acknow-ledgement of his fortune-cards being played out by Fate, combined with a sad self-pity which lurks in the progression 'my lot, my life'. He is condemned to the lonely reality of 'among strangers', without domicile. Fatalism had taken him over when 'Spelt from Sibyl's Leaves' had shown the destruction of positive possibilities. The pattern for the rest of his life was now fixed.

There is not a word about external nature in this poem – in 'Spelt from Sibyl's Leaves' the lesson had been drawn from unvisualised, already concep-tualised leaves, not the leaves themselves. This poem is concerned instead with people, with human relationships: but with *lack* of contact. The nature poems written in Wales had been about the two rays of feeling – of natural object and human subject meeting in joyous recognition; the inscape of parts of the natural scene giving out, and meeting with, the alert sense-tentacles of the observer, the inscape becoming instressed at the meeting, and thus forming the perfect benevolence/recognition relationship between man and God. But now, in early 1885, he finds himself emotionally thwarted by the double impasse of being strange to other people and of finding other people strange.

While still an Oxford student, Hopkins had written out John Clare's lines, 'I am: yet what I am who cares or knows', composed in isolated madness in Northampton asylum. Lines 11 and 12 of this poem were: 'And e'en the dearest – that I loved the best – / Are strange – nay, rather stranger than the rest'. There is the suggestion in both poems that the second 'strange' has a different meaning from the first, that the repetition intensifies the second usage, and that the word's field of meaning is large and ambiguous, stretching from 'estranged' – separated from the known – to 'odd' – harsh and different from the expected. This imprecise usage emphasises each poet's lack of fixed roots in his exiled position. Though not alone, both poets recognise that their near-relatives are furthest away, a poignant paradox – 'Father and mother dear,/ Brothers and sisters are in Christ not near'. It was ominous that Hopkins identified with Clare's position twenty years before it was fully realised as his own.

This poem is often considered one of the simplest of Hopkins's maturity, but too often annotation loosely describes the Irish background of ideological difficulties, while ignoring problems of the surface meaning. There have been many alternative identifications of the three 'removes' ('I am in Ireland now; now I am at a third/ Remove'). The solution is straightforward if one trusts Hopkins's words and follows the patterning. The first sentence (lines 1–2) is statement and description of the position of strangeness, the two-sided barrier surrounding the alone person. Then, opposed to this strangeness, the poet takes the three large loves, emotional roots, of his life, towards which he should not feel strange, and yet which are the foundations of that strangeness: family (2–3), religion (3–4), country (5–6). The three loves which come out from his heart – of family, of Christ, of England – are not complete, because they are not reciprocated. His family are separated from him by their religion; his religion imposes barriers between him and others; and his country would not return his affection nor reward his efforts if he did act on her behalf. By some blockage he is thus cut off from his three greatest potential sources of affection and affiliation.

This is the first poem in which Hopkins displays puzzlement and pain over discrepancies between words and their referends, a characteristic of several Dublin poems ('Comforter, where, where is your comforting?'), which culminates in the complex paradoxes in the three last sonnets ('thou my enemy, O thou my friend'). Besides showing the destruction of the poet's self-confidence and confidence in nature, 'Spelt from Sibyl's Leaves' had also signalled his disillusionment with the naive linguistic theory that words directly represented things, 'speaking self'. At the end of that poem the insistent maledictory and spellbound rhythm (indicated by Hopkins's grotesquely distorting stress-marks in lines 10 to 14) had become more important than word meaning; and 'thoughts against thoughts' (14) indicated on one level that the protagonist lacked control of mental concepts. In 'To seem the stranger' the imprecision of the repeated 'stranger', referring to two opposed referends which cannot meet, is followed by further examples of finding disrupting paradoxes. The members of the poet's blood family are 'dear' and yet, contrarily, not close to him in Christ. The second 'strangeness' and 'estrangement' is the poet's relationship with Christ, who is Hopkins's peace and yet the opposite of peace. The third example is the relationship with England, the wife of his creating persona; despite the poet's passionate advocacy on her behalf she does not hear him, does not respond with wifely support. Three potential love-relationships are incomplete; something prevents the proper culmination, juncture, and reciprocation.

The change in subject does not occur at the end of the octave – 'where wars are rife' (8) flows smoothly into 'I am in Ireland now' in line 9 – but starts with 'were I pleading; plead nor do I' (7), having been signalled by the conditional 'would neither' (6), which has ousted the expected 'does not hear'. And as in the three 1889 poems after a wandering, tentative start this poem consolidates, having found its true subject, the poet's lack of creativity.

The poem also changes at that point from a summary of the poet's past to a description of his present state; the landscape of lines 1 to 6 is composed of elaborate static patterns which form the setting for the protagonist who, from lines 6 to 14, wanders pathetically in the foreground. 'My lot, my life' (1) represents the fatalistic ego sandwiched between 'stranger' and 'strangers'. Similarly in lines 2 to 3, word positions form a diagram of the situation. Father, mother, brothers and sisters are established around their familial connecting emotion, 'dear'; but suddenly Christ is added to the group and destroys the relationship with the unexpected negative and deflation: 'are in Christ not near'. The shock discontinuity of the flowing line 3 is carried a stage further in both meaning and sound by the halt called in line 4 by the slash / and the paradox 'my peace/my parting', the alliteration showing the incomprehensible fact that opposed parts are nevertheless embodied in one concept, Christ. (Similarly in 1889, 'thou my enemy, O thou my friend' in 'Justus quidem'.)

After the family group has been cut off, in correct order of precedence, and replaced as the poet's emotional centre by Christ (at Hopkins's conversion), then line 4 continues the chronological account of his progress. 'My parting, sword and strife' conveys what has happened since the conversion; that event was the 'parting', but was followed by the symbolic sword, expressing the antagonism which devotion to religion brings, and finally by 'strife', the fight against the infidel.

The three statements of the first quatrain all constituted the pushing forward of an idea in appropriate rhythm, followed by a reversal, a discovery of hollowness and rejection: the flow of ' . . . stranger . . . my lot' is ebbed into 'my life . . . strangers'; the long 14-syllabled wave 'Father and mother dear,/ Brothers and sisters are in Christ' suddenly expires when it meets the monosyllable 'not'; and the measured tranquillity of 'And he my peace' is brutally stopped by the slash / and soured by its mocking alliterative echo 'my parting', which then rises to an angry crescendo which mocks the tone of 'and he my peace'.

The second quatrain starts with 'England' in glorious isolation from the rest of its sentence, which does not continue until the second half of line 6. In between is an indulgent emotional paean provoked by the name of England. This overripeness is then counteracted by the pathetic 'would neither hear me', the conditional further deflating it by emphasising that it existed only in heart and mind, not in external reality. The stages of the poet's realisation of his pathetic lack of creation are re-enacted in the deflating progression from paean ('whose honour . . . creating thought') to conditional tense ('would . . . were I pleading') to final despairing inversion and death ('plead nor do I'). The lonely 'I' is then focused on in its weary isolation, its circumscription emphasised by its three usages in line 7.

The patriotism of the second quatrain is focused by the Irish problem, although that is not the basic concern, which is Hopkins's creative poetry. Poetry-writing could be a patriotic act: 'We [all true poets]', he wrote to Bridges from Dublin in March 1886, 'must then try to be known, aim at it, take means to it . . . . Besides we are Englishmen. A great [artistic] work by an Englishman is like a great battle won by England. It is an unfading bay tree. It will even be admired by and praised by and do good to those who hate England (as England is most perilously hated), who do not wish even to be benefited [*sic*] by her. It is then even a patriotic duty τη ποιησει ενεργειν ["to be active in producing poetry"] and to secure the fame and permanence of the work' (LI. 231). Similarly he had written to Patmore four months earlier: 'Your poems are a good deed done for the Catholic Church and another for England, for the British Empire' (L3. 366).

Until Hopkins came to Dublin he had regarded his own poems as patriotic acts. From 'The Wreck of the Deutschland' until 'Spelt from Sibyl's Leaves' his serious poems are all in some large degree didactic, urging the unaware Englishman to change from a dull, heretical viewpoint to an aware, correct one. 'The Wreck of the Deutschland' had the grand aim of re-converting England to Roman Catholicism ('Our King back, oh, upon English souls!'), Hopkins seeing the wreck not as a horrific accident, but as a martyrdom planned by God to open England's eyes to the truth. Hopkins saw himself as the intermediary seer between God and his country, 'More brightening her, rare-dear Britain' ('Britain' because he was then in Wales, but elsewhere in the poem he focuses more narrowly on England). He had been in Dublin less than a fortnight when he wrote 'Wish to crown him [Christ] King of England, of English hearts'. In Dublin he feels himself, as this poem describes, prevented from assuming the didactic stance, which depends on ability to communicate.

'To seem the stranger' is the first Dublin poem to be primarily egoistic rather than didactic, and therefore ironically the first in which England is *not* wife to the poet's creating thought, *not* the reason for whose honour he creates. Describing his Dublin state of catalepsis, he is also describing the emotional mechanics of putting one kind of poetry behind him and creating another. At the end of his life, the poem 'To R.B.' expressed a different, more closely imagined generative diagram for his poems – 'the fine delight', the 'sweet fire', is the father and the mind the mother. In the meantime he had produced a poem which was 'patriotic' in a more obvious sense, 'What shall I do for the land that bred me?', which he described as 'a recruiting song for soldiers', an exercise within a popular convention, intended for a different, vulgar audience.

In lines 6–7, 'would neither hear/ Me, were I pleading' signals Hopkins changing from the precisely diagrammatic opening of the poem with a certain uneasiness: why complain so passionately of England's lack of response to a plea, when that plea remained silent in the poet's heart and thought? The conditional ('would') has changed the complaint from a logical one to one of peevishness, further emphasised by the pleading tone of 'were I pleading, plead nor do I', which belies his profession of *not* pleading. The stage of universal issues – family, religion, patriotism – is reduced to mental mono-logue, with the process completed by the reversal of 'were I pleading' into 'plead nor do I', and by the possibility suggested by conditional 'were' changing to the negative. Having dismissed the objective world by negatives, he has nothing left to say of it, and is left with the repeated 'I': 'Me, were I pleading, plead nor do I: I', the single capital emphasising the loneliness and the egotism.

Behind Hopkins's complaint 'would neither hear me were I pleading' lies the official rejection by *The Month* of 'The Wreck of the Deutschland' and 'The Loss of the Eurydice', his two longest works, which probably caused Hopkins's regression to the sonnet as his staple verse form, when he was keen for and capable of radical invention, with his classical training and enthusiastic fluency in practical experimentation. Although the aim of the Counter-Reformation Society of Jesus in England was identical with Hopkins's in his poetry, they could not understand his unique means of trying to achieve it; he was continually dubbed an 'eccentric'. In the previous year Hopkins had written to Bridges that he did not know 'how anything of mine on a large scale would ever pass' the censors (LI. 200), and in 1887 would write to him: 'Our institution provides us means of discouragement, and on me at all events they have had all the effect that could be expected or wished and rather more' (LI. 248).

The octave described Hopkins's plight since his conversion, whereas the sestet starts with the false calm of loneliness: 'I am in Ireland now'. Ireland is the third 'remove', its physical distance from England epitomising England's emotional distance from him. Lines 10–11, 'Not but in all removes I can/ Kind love both give and get', are often thought a diplomatic correction of the previous impression of something wrong, the two-way process of mutual recognition having been denied the poet in the three great loves of his life, causing the separation of others from him, and him from others, while in the fourth type of emotion, 'kind love', this process is achieved: 'give and get'. But that type is, he says, inferior; it is not the wisest, it is not bred in the heart. 'Kind' is merely superficial, patronising custom. 'Kind love' results from judgement, and is a surface emotion compared with words which would emanate from the deepest source, his heart. This poem is about *large* emotions, and the petty 'kind love' is put in to enlarge them by comparison.

But his heart-originated words cannot emerge into proper patriotic pleading; he is merely 'a lonely began', partly through the Jesuit censors' ban (representing heaven's will) on his most ambitious creative works, whose success would have provided encouragement to continue. 'Heaven' is a vaster and more imprecise ('baffling') source than Christ who had been responsible earlier in life and this poem for the clearcut division between the poet and his family.

The second cause of Hopkins's creative idleness is psychological – 'hell's spell'. Before he came to Ireland, even in his happy Oxford student days, he had often announced projects which never took off, but in Dublin there is a fatalistic hopelessness that he will ever create anything worthwhile:

It is so doubtful, so very doubtful, that I shall be able to pursue any study except the needs of the day (and those not enough) at all. I have tried and failed so often and my strength serves me less.

I am struggling to get together matter for a work on Homer's Art. I suppose like everything else of mine it will come to nothing in the end. (L3. 257)

The fatalistic vision at the core of 'Spelt from Sibyl's Leaves' originated not with Hopkins, but with the pre-Christian prophetess, the Sibyl, and so the poet avoided accusations of pessimism. But now in 'To seem the stranger' the authorities to be blamed for the negative vision are the alternatives 'dark heaven' and 'hell'. The poet's inability to judge between the two points to the lack of definition of his malady and treatment for it.

The poem finishes with a noteworthy summary which is partly a re-statement in more intensely dramatic form of lines 6–7. 'Hoard unheard' is wooing silently in the heart, while 'heard unheeded' succinctly paraphrases 'would neither hear/ Me, were I pleading'. The word by word logical description of his creative dual impasse in lines 6–7, is now, in lines 13–14, poetically expressed in tightly bound form. 'Hoard unheard,/ Heard unheeded' shows his problem's intensely reiterated insolubility, the difficult rhythms of lines 12–13 yielding to the subtly plangent 'leaves me a lonely began'; the lonely stranger motif combines with that of the thwarted idler. Hopkins's suffering had opened up a new range of material and expression for his poetry.

Chapter Five

NO WORST

Du musst herrschen und gewinnen,
Oder dienen und verlieren,
Leiden oder triumphiren
Amboss oder Hammer sein.
[You must either conquer and rule or lose and serve,
suffer or triumph, and be the anvil or the hammer.]

Goethe, 'Der Gross-Cophta', Act 2

With an anvil-ding
And with fire in him forge thy will

'The Wreck of the Deutschland', st.10, St Beuno's, 1875–6

My cries heave, herds-long; huddle in a main, a chief-
Woe, wórld-sorrow; on an áge-old ánvil wínce and síng

Dublin, 1885

For most of 1885 depression was a usual part of Hopkins's life. On New Year's Day that year he had written to Bridges that he should have taken up his mother's invitation to spend Christmas at Hampstead; he badly needed a change from Ireland – 'at all events I am jaded' (LI. 202). Later that week, on retreat at Clongowes Wood College, he made attempts to analyse and find remedies or consolation for his unhappiness. The example of the Magi suggested that he should 'pray to be on the watch for God's providence, not determining where or when but only sure that it will come'; and he recommended to himself that he should apply this 'to all your troubles and hopes', including his preoccupation with the relationship between England and Ireland. But the following day he wrote in a private note 'it seems a spirit of fear I live by'. His spiritual advisor at Clongowes, Fr Peter Foley, suggested that he try to replace this spirit of fear by one of love (s. 258–9).

In a meditation (s. 259) later in January 1885 he compared his own case to that in the Synoptic Gospels' story of the Gadarene swine and the demoniac who was tormented by devils. He assumes that the demons are, literally, still alive and wreaking havoc: 'Where then did they continue to live, what did they possess?' He considered himself a similar victim, and wrote 'pray not to be tormented'. He noted that 'the man did not kill himself': it was the swine into whom the devils were driven by Christ who had committed suicide. Hopkins thus mentions almost in the same breath the possibility of a tormented person, unable to withstand the pain, killing himself, and the fact that he himself was tormented. The significance of modern suicides was constantly on his mind, as so many friends sharing the same age and background to himself had been victims. He wrote to Baillie: 'Three of my intimate friends at Oxford have thus drowned themselves, a good many more of my acquaintances and contemporaries have died by their own hands in other ways'. And he added, 'It must be a dreadful feature of our days'. Hopkins had painstakingly found out details of two of the suicides whom he had known particularly well. Martin Geldart, a Unitarian minister, had been forced to resign early that year, because of 'socialistic' opinions, and had jumped overboard from a night boat to Dieppe, while Nash's death, shortly before Geldart's, was also (so Hopkins thought) suicide, although, like Geldart's, it was not officially recorded as such. Geldart, wrote Hopkins, was 'a selftormentor, [his mind] having been unhinged, as it had been once or twice before, by a struggle he had gone through', while Nash's death was 'certainly too done in insanity, for he had been sleepless for ten nights' (L3. 254).

'Self-torment', 'suicide', 'unhinged mind', 'struggles', 'insanity', 'sleepless': all were central causes and themes of the 'dark' sonnets Hopkins would compose in spring and early summer of 1885. In an essay on Duty Hopkins wrote about this time, after defining Right and Sin, he used self-preservation and self-destruction as examples:

> We feel that self-preservation is right and so a duty, self-destruction wrong and so a sin, the sin of suicide, a case of murder. . . . If the Eternal, as Hamlet says, had not fixed his canon gainst self slaughter, it might be unreasonable, wrong in the sense of perverse or crooked, to take our own lives, but who could forbid it? Only that same legislator, ourselves . . . But as it is we feel a higher will than either our own or any other will whatever forbidding the unreasonable deed. (HRB, 7, 1976)

The continual drudgery of marking examination scripts was what overwhelmed him most, he told an old friend, Mandell Creighton (L3. 424), and much of January 1885 was taken up with the marking of scholarship papers. But once that task was over 'my heart is light', and he wrote a long, entertaining letter to his mother. Among the amusing accounts of life at number 86, however, was the odd flaring against parts of his surroundings: 'these unspeakable nationalist papers, which call any man that shews common respect to authority, a flunkey and are ready, none so ready, to play the flunkey themselves'. And he contrasted the flamboyance of one newly decorated room in the college with 'the rest of this shabby and dingy establishment' (L3. 166). He also mentioned at three places in the letter the fact that he could not get rid of a cold. He was soon 'in a low way of health', and 'could do (indeed how gladly I could) – as they say – with more life' (LI. 208).

Hopkins was suffering deeply from dwelling on the Irish political situation without being able to do anything about it. A brief letter to the old Cardinal Newman on his birthday was largely about the parlous state of Ireland, and sending birthday greetings to his mother, a correspondent whom he usually tried to cheer with bright anecdotes, he mentioned 'the grief of mind I go through over politics, over what I read and hear and see in Ireland about Ireland and about England, is such that I can neither express it nor bear to speak of it' (L3. 170). He had become disillusioned about Irish literary expression, always so different from his own and that of his English friends: 'the Irish, among whom I live, have no conception of this quality [what Hopkins called 'individuation', precisely appropriate diction]: their ambition is to say a thing as everybody says it, only louder' (LI. 210).

The English political situation offered no hopeful contrast, with the death of General Gordon in the Sudan, murdered, so jingoist opinion had it, by the tardiness of the Liberal Prime Minister Gladstone. Hopkins recorded that 'Khartoum fell Jan. 26', and on the same sheet of paper guiltily tried to moderate his excessive reaction against the Grand Old Man: 'Let him that is without sin etc – Pray to keep to this spirit and as far as possible rule in speaking of Mr. Gladstone' (s. 260). Yet only a week later, he wrote to Bridges: 'There is no depth of stupidity and gape a race could not fall to on the stage that in real life gapes on while Gladstone negotiates his surrenders of the empire' (LI. 210); and at the beginning of April, he expressed to Coventry Patmore, a fellow right-wing reactionary, 'the mortification and grief the policy (or behaviour) of the [British] government have been costing me' (L3. 360). He asked his mother not to talk politics, as 'it kills me, especially under the present Prime Minister' (L3. 171). and agreed with Mowbray Baillie that 'Mr. Gladstone ought to be beheaded on Tower Hill and buried in Westminster Abbey', adding 'Ought he now to be buried in Westminster Abbey?' (L3. 257).

In the same letter (which had taken him three weeks to write, in April and May of 1885), he revealed that the accumulation of worries about his health and constitution, his daily surroundings and work-drudgery, English politics, and various Irish disloyalties to the Crown, had brought him to a very low mental state, which he summarised to Baillie (who, together with Bridges, was the only friend to whom he could express such intimate feelings):

The melancholy I have all my life been subject to has become of late years not indeed more intense in its fits but rather more distributed, constant, and crippling. One, the lightest but a very inconvenient form of it, is daily anxiety about work to be done, which makes me break off or never finish all that lies outside that work. It is useless to write more on this: when I am at the worst, though my judgement is never affected, my state is much like madness. I see no ground for thinking I shall get over it or ever succeed in doing anything that is not forced on me to do of any consequence. (L3. 256)

On 17 March he had appealed to St Patrick for help for Ireland 'in all its needs', and for himself in his position, and had also sought the aid of 'the patron of the hidden life' and 'of those . . . suffering in mind and as I do', St Joseph (s. 260). He told his mother, as though it were a novelettish trifle: 'I am in a sort of languishing state of mind and body, but hobble on', wistfully adding 'I should like to go to sea for six months'; but he wrote to Bridges of 'that coffin of weakness and dejection in which I live, without even the hope of change' (L1. 214–15).

*　　*　　*

Not the least of his problems was his unsatisfactory history of verse composition. As he told Baillie, after having written almost nothing for seven years, 'it being suggested to write something I did so and have at intervals since, but the intervals now are long ones and the whole amount produced is small. And I make no attempt to publish' (L3. 256–7); he does not mention that it was only after the official disapproval of 'The Wreck of the Deutschland' that he retired into his shell. By 1885 he had reluctantly concluded that any poetry of his should not be broadcast in the open, but would be sent to the loyal and sensitive Bridges, for him to keep until a suitable time, almost certainly after Hopkins's death.

But Hopkins was a compulsive artist. The poetic articulation of his mental desolation and pain in Spring and Summer 1885 took the form of a small, intense group often called the 'desolate' or 'dark' sonnets, which revived the over-used and outmoded sonnet form, and enlarged the range of language and art by expressing previously mute mental areas of extreme emotion. In the first sonnet, the prologue to the group, 'To seem the stranger lies my lot', he had stated and assigned causes for his estrangement in Ireland, but had also implied a psychological disturbance so uncontrolled, so indefinable and untreatable in presently known and available terms, that a creative search for new avenues and means of expression would be needed in future.

Although based on personal events and feelings, 'No worst, there is none' cannot be said to deal with a particular experience, in the way that, for instance, 'I wake and feel' describes a particular event ('*this* night', in line 3). The scape of grief feelings is established in the first two lines impersonally; it is in the nature of such pangs not to take any notice of the sufferer's identity, and to depersonalise and nullify him, so that they engulf him. This impersonality generalises the account – this is what happens with pangs of grief, so the poet has discovered. Lines 3 and 4 dramatise the fact that in the direst periods no comfort or relief can be obtained from conventional outside sources. This is done by imitating the cries of an individual, but the sources are universal, applicable to all cases ('mother of *us*'); and by implication their inefficaciousness is not selective but universal.

The solitary explicit personal reference in the poem is the 'My' which starts line 5. But this line so quickly extends away from this small dimension into human impersonality ('herds-long') and vastness ('wórld-sorrow') that 'my cries' represents any lost personality rather than the poet. Then in the sestet comes the generalised discovery drawn from the previous experience: a generalisation achieved by the metamorphosis of the feeling into metaphorical landscape. This generalised expression of the poet's bitter discovery in the octave is so powerful and memorable that at least two of its phrases – 'O the mind, mind has mountains', and 'cliffs of fall' – have become widely known and used outside purely literary contexts, as classic succinct images of the uncontrollable turmoil in the modern psyche. 'Never, I think,' wrote Aldous Huxley, 'has the just man's complaint against the universe been put more forcibly, worded more tersely and fiercely' (*Mirage and Truth*, 1935: 199). There could be no better tribute to Hopkins's ability to transcend and widen his immediate emotional experience; and Hopkins is a poet who has had to fight harder than most to achieve general currency.

The poem is about the reconstruction and verbal realisation of an archetypical – rather than single – experience. A hearer is not conducted into the poem's strange realm with a guide explaining the history and nature of every occurrence; that would separate the hearer from the protagonist too much. Hopkins is attempting to find the verbal equivalents of the most intensified parts of his experience, so that the poem is a version and limited exposition of that experience, not merely a framed picture.

The poem's opening words, 'No worst, there is none', suggest its subject: the limitlessness of the protagonist's mental pain, the essence of which is that it has no apparent containment which would act as a major turning-point back towards recovery. The poet is not offering his audience a more traditional sonnet package containing all the stages of the now-resolved experience.

The pain is of such an all-consuming and apparently continuous nature that the relief looked for is not its cessation but a first sign that it has limits at all, the definition of its extremity. But it will not reveal its limitations, and with horror the protagonist realises that this is because the dimension is limitless ('there is *none*'). Because there is no nadir, no worst, the dimension provokes uncertainty: the two negatives, 'No worst', make a positive 'is', but that is itself a negative, 'none'. The attempt at definition paradoxically only results in worse confusion, by the discovery that the dimension expands limitlessly. His first attempt at controlling – by definition – what is happening is ineffective.

In the half-line, 'Pitched past pitch', the poet states and shows how the conventional stages of intensification – simple state to comparative to superlative – do not apply to his case; the dimension of his pain is new and so unchartable that the comparative extends indefinitely without finding the limitation of a superlative. 'Pitch' was one of the earliest and most valuable key words which Hopkins selected from general currency, redefined, and placed in his peculiar word hoard. A typical usage is to describe waves: 'the white combs on each side run along the wave gaining ground till the two meet at a pitch' (J. 223); its essence is the zenith of something vertically mobile caught, frozen, at the climactic split second. Even at an apparent extremity ('pitch'), the grief will not settle into a verbal mould where the poet can look and get hold of it, and so subdue it by definition and accustomisation; it can be adequately represented only by an unlimited ascending scale – 'pitched past pitch' (the meaning of 'pitch' being so comprehensive in Hopkins's usage that it suits the musical analogy perfectly). Before a particular level of pain has been completely realised by achieving its proper note ('pitch'), it has already been invalidated and replaced by the next higher note (the 'pitch' part of the verb 'pitched'); the action of moving beyond the first 'pitch' is at the same time mimicked by the noun being transformed into a verb ('pitched'), the noun representing a static quality while the verb denotes movement beyond it. The noun is additionally devalued by the derogatory half-echo word 'past'.

The diagrammatisation in line 1 of this limitless upwards scale is then continued and more dramatically realised by line 2, 'More pangs will, schooled at forepangs, wilder wring'. Just as the similar nature of each successive temporary height of pain had been indicated by the repetition of 'pitch', so the similarity between the different fragments of pain beyond those pitches is recognised in 'forepangs' containing a recapitulation in sound of 'more pangs'. Again, just as the first element of the grief in line 1, 'pitch', was preceded in the poetic line by 'pitched', which in the experience succeeded it, so here 'more pangs' precedes 'forepangs', showing how the impossibility of ending on any particular note was anticipated in the earlier notes. There are two comparatives in line 2, 'more' and 'wilder', emphasising the 'no worst', the lack of a finalising superlative.

'Schooled' is noticeably followed not by the expected 'by' or 'with', but by the unusual 'at', which is more impersonal and which particularly locates the forepangs, thus implying a scale. Schooling – in the sense of his arduous Jesuit training – as well as the prescribed self-curbing, was of course a constant in Hopkins's life. In this poem the word is restricted to an impersonal harsh discipline: giving a lesson by punishment. These precisely positioned, inevitable and autonomous pangs provoke the cry of the lost protagonist in line 3, 'Comforter, where, where is your comforting?' The first 'where' suggests the search for a dimension whose likeliness recedes as the second 'where' hollowly echoes it. 'Where' is more prominent than the rhyme word 'comforting', which feebly and ironically echoes the direct address 'Comforter', at the start of the line. 'Comforter', a standard translation of the Greek Paraclete and Latin Consolator, usually applied to one function of the Holy Spirit, as a resort to call on in moments of anguish. In 1873 Hopkins had recorded a nightmare:

> I thought something or someone leapt onto me and held me quite fast . . . The feeling is terrible; the body no longer swayed as a piece by the nervous and muscular instress seems to fall in and hang like a dead weight on the chest. I cried on the holy name and by degrees recovered myself as I thought to do. (J. 238)

In December 1879 Hopkins had preached a sermon on the prescribed way to find Comfort as an antidote to distress:

> If we feel the comfort little, there, my brethren, is our fault and want of faith; we must put a stress on ourselves and make ourselves find comfort where we know the comfort is to be found. It *is* a comfort that in spite of all, God loves us; it is a comfort that the sufferings of this present world (St. Paul says) are not worthy to be compared with the glory that is to be revealed in us; such thoughts *are* comfort, we have only to force ourselves to see it, to dwell on it, and at last to feel that it is so. Cheerfulness has ever been a mark of saints and good people. (s. 47–8)

In this poem he describes the significant discrepancy between the cold translation 'Comforter', and 'comforting' used to represent a warm and human act. Why does the one word have two irreconcilable meanings?

An alternative official prescription to cure despair was to appeal to the Blessed Virgin Mary; and so Hopkins's second cry, following the want of a reply to his first, rhetorical question, is to the 'mother of us'. These are not cries for help, but utterances from a stage beyond; already in despair he asks why the two major sources of comfort have not provided any, and do not even seem to be present. Having given up his actual mother as a source of comfort when he joined the Jesuits he finds the Church's metaphorical replacement has not brought the relief he needs. Whereas the two 'wheres' in line 3 had been desperate cries asking for an answer (the repetition suggesting that there has been no reply), this third 'where' is quietly poignant and lonely, a sad reproach rather than a question. By its parenthetical nature, 'mother of us' gives some relief from the poem's insistent pressure of repetition, questioning, and stabs of pain, but turns out to be merely a subsidence into pathetic loneliness, rather than a step towards recovery.

The protagonist is not just injured by the pain, but mentally disordered. The three personae in the scene are playing wrongly allocated roles. The pain, the alien and *im*personal force, is incomprehensibly irresistible, and of the two agencies who should combine to fight it, the protagonist's inner strength and the holy relief forces, the latter do not respond when summoned. The weak 'my' forces should be reinforced by the 'your' forces; but the call of the two question-marks in lines 3 and 4 is unanswered, and so in line 5 the focus of the poem shifts from 'your' to the solitary 'my'.

In line 5 the poem's audience experience, as from within the protagonist, the discharge of his cries, which 'heave, herds-long; huddle in a main, a chief-/ Woe, wórld-sorrow'. These abrupt changes of metaphor which so disconcert readers represent a disconcerting experience; wild, unrooted attempts to place the violent emotions, which because of their burgeoning instability cannot be tied down into any category of interplaying metaphors. The intransitive use of 'heave' gives it the force of the passive mood, so increasing its suggestion of involuntariness, almost vomiting. The cries are progressively enlarged while being projected into vast emptiness, without encountering any hindrance. Then there is the inordinate further expansion into 'herds-long', and thence, via a major sorrow ('main') which develops to a principal ('chief-') woe, into the poetical superlative 'wórld-sorrow'. Hopkins commonly used 'world' to picture an all-encompassing extreme ('world's loveliest − men's selves' in 'To what serves Mortal Beauty?', and 'drunkenness . . . is a world of woe' [s. 42]); but his coinage 'world-sorrow' is a literal translation of the German romantic term *Weltschmerz*, a certain type of melancholy; thus the large-scale word is still rooted in an *individual* person's emotion through this German origin.

The inequity of the combat is emphasised by this progression from the victim's minute 'my' through several magnifications to 'wórld', and this comprehensiveness of 'world-sorrow' (extent in space) is continued in line 6 in the parallel construction 'áge-old' (extent in time). Here the syntax becomes fittingly ambiguous: the thing which winces on the anvil should be, grammatically, 'my cries', and yet it makes more straightforward sense if the protagonist-victim is the subject. 'Wince' reinforces this ambiguity, embracing the two constituents − the protagonist's involuntary movement and the metallically piercing cries. Hopkins's mark ˘ over the word 'wince' encourages an appropriately diptych pronunciation. The insistent high-vowel sounds in 'anvil wĭnce', climax in the rhyme-word 'síng', from which pressure and pace are suddenly released by 'Then lull, then leave off', a progression mimicked in corresponding positions of the next two lines – 'shrieked "No ling-/ Ering"' – but with an increase in dramatic violence suitable to its agent, Fury.

Hopkins's pagan minister of vengeance, 'Fury', is appropriate to the protagonist's mental turmoils, since appeals to Christian resources have failed (cf. Hopkins's similar reversal to pre-Christian mythology in 'Spelt from Sibyl's Leaves'). The poem explodes dramatically at this point, the personification putting blood and flesh onto mental action. 'Fury' was a common anglicisation of the Greek Erinnyes, the angry ones, known to Hopkins especially in the Oresteian trilogy. Predating Zeus and the Olympian dynasty, the Erinnyes represented less humanoid motivation and actions, wreaking blind vengeance without reference to judgement or morality. They drove victims, gods or men, mad. Their ruthless yet poetic presence in this sonnet is dramatised by the fierce squat monosyllables and Jacobean archaisms of line 8, 'Let me be fell: force I must be brief'. The pluperfect 'had shrieked' takes the shrieking back to before 'lull' and 'leave off', and explains why the cries have stopped – Fury had decreed sharp and short ('fell' and 'brief'), that it should leave off. Hopkins's clever manipulation of sound and rhythm in '"No ling-/ Ering! Let me be fêll"' corroborates the meaning. The poetical 'fêll', suitable for the ruthless Fury, also suggests quickness, emphasised by the poet's mark over it.

This sonnet has the minimum four rhymes, each enhanced by similar sounds in preceding syllables: the most obvious examples are 'anvil wince and sing', and 'steep or deep. Here! creep'. The frequency of these four sounds suggests the defeated protagonist dully playing out a Fate-ordained role. The intense activity of the protagonist's suffering is conveyed by forceful dramatic devices, while its predestined outcome is ever present in the constantly signalled restrictions of the Italian sonnet form.

The exclamatory 'O' signals the sudden contrast of the lyrical lines 8–9, and the repeated 'mind' emphasises the musing and commentary nature of the sestet. It is difficult and destructive to assign precise referends to the mountains and cliffs of the mind (let alone the cliffs of Moher in the west of Ireland, as has been seriously suggested). The mountains are insurmountable obstacles rising in front of one's path, and the cliffs perilous disasters into which it takes a single step to fall irretrievably. Just as he avoids 'madness' in the octave so here Hopkins avoids a needless closer definition, although letters from Dublin easily fill the space. Three more facets are then added to the account of the mind's agitations: that experience, not intellect, is the only way of knowing them (a further hidden criticism of the official antidotes to depression); that man's ability to protect himself is limited and unreliable (again, implied criticism of remedies which assume indefinite amounts of will power); and that the only consolation is the partial, muted, and unChristian one offered in line 14.

There are remarkable devices in the sestet where sound and sense interweave and interact. 'Mind has mountains' does not convey feeling, only fact, and so 'O' adds a human voice with an emotional charge; the obstinate repetition of 'mind' prevents the word being passed over thoughtlessly on the path to 'mountain', and makes it an obstacle. 'Cliffs of fall' suggests height and a falling down, and 'frightful' is similarly a panic syllable followed by a fall. By its native particles 'no-man-fathomed' adds a dimension of amazement, which the more obvious 'unplumbed' would have lacked. 'May' in line 11 augments the previous cliff imagery, being 'hung' there by the surrounding rhythm, while the smallness of our durance is ironically mimicked in the immediate contradiction of 'long' by 'small'. The poem finishes not triumphantly, but with an ironic climax which is a conclusion but no solution – 'death' and 'dies'. This ambiguity is heightened by the march-beat certainty of line 14 being incorporated not in the rhyming couplet of an English sonnet form, but in the drawn-out reticence and complexity imposed by the Italian form.

'No worst' is also remarkable for its varieties of uncertainty and instability. The location of the scene, the images, the perspectives, and particularly the nature of the different personae in the poem, all disrupt by changing. The pain-pangs are so impersonal that they depersonalise their victim in lines 1–4, although something left of him cries to the 'your' forces. In line 5 comes 'My', but subsequent images are again impersonal, until completely replaced by personified Fury. The sestet opens with the generalised 'the mind', but in the following line a narrator expresses bitterness at those who lack his experience, and in line 11 is no longer on his own, but representative of men, 'our'. Then in the final two lines there are two personal characters – the poet (at last a comforter) who gives the small consolation and the protagonist-wretch to whom it is offered. The predictability of the sonnet form contains all this unpredictable turmoil, as the protagonist feels himself a lonely sufferer battered in turmoil by the disciplined forces of cruelty. The poem deals with boundaries, limits. There is *no* limit to the suffering ('past pitch') of the depths of the mind ('no-man-fathomed'), but there *are* the desperate limits of day (sleep) and life (death). We are incapable of suffering for long – Fury has to be brief and our small durance does not last long.

*   *   *

The parallels and echoes in the storm scenes of *King Lear* are often pointed out. There is no proof that they are sources of the poem, but the similarities justify an account which leaves readers free to make their own judgements.

→ 71 ←

At the opening of 4.1 of *Lear* Edgar congratulates himself (1–9) on the meagre comfort that as his fortune is now at its worst, it is bound to change for the better: 'The wretch that thou hast blown unto the worst/ Owes nothing to thy blasts' (8–9). But a 'strange mutation' comes when he sees his blinded father; and he comments on his previous words, giving them, as Hopkins does with 'worst', a conceptual personality of their own, distinct from his utterance of them:

> O Gods! Who is it can say 'I am at the worst'?
> I am worse than e'er I was.
>
> . . . .
>
> And worse I may be yet; the worst is not
> So long as we can say 'This is the worst'. (25–8)

This is the most notable close parallel, but there are deeper conceptual and thematic resemblances, signalled by the frequency in the play's storm scenes of key words and concepts shared by Hopkins's poem, 'grief', 'comfort', 'mind', and 'wretch'. The pain undergone by the poem's protagonist is mental, and both poet and playwright emphasise that the mind's pangs are severer than the body's, partly because they threaten the selfhood of their victim, who lacks the usual fixed points of reference, and partly because the sufferer lacks the sympathy commonly extended to physical suffering.

Continually nagged by Kent and the Fool to shelter his body from the storm, Lear shares, but overtly, something of the poem's indignant avowal that hidden mental woes are greater than physical, plainer ones. For instance, in 3.4. 11–14:

> . . . this tempest in my mind
> Doth from my senses take all feeling else
> Save what beats there.

This motivation is submerged in the octave of the poem, but surfaces plainly in lines 10–11: 'Hold them cheap/ May who ne'er hung there'. Two scenes later, Edgar's observation 'Who alone suffers, suffers most I' the mind' (3.6.107) indicates the striking similarity between the lonely situation of the mind-sufferer in both works.

In *Lear* the storm's powers are magnified by the night; the two combine 'What? I' th' storm! I' th' night?' asks the horrified Cordelia (4.3.29). The night deprives the protagonist of another of his combative and protective senses, his sight, and this is underlined in the sub-plot by the blinding of Gloucester. The power of the attacking forces thus becomes impersonalised, and less easy to be counter-attacked. In 'No worst' the protagonist's questions in lines 3 and 4 issue forth into a void; the whole octave is sightless. Both Shakespeare and Hopkins emphasise this impersonality of the furious agency by ironically personalising it; they picture it at the same stage of its attack, the calling-off of the force, and at this moment create dialogue for it:

> Fury had shrieked 'No ling-
> Ering! Let me be fell: force I must be brief.'
>
> *Hopkins lines 7–8*

> Gloucester: henceforth I'll bear
> Affliction till it do cry out itself
> 'Enough, enough,' and dies.
>
> *Shakespeare 4.6.75–7*

Apart from a few identical words ('hung' on Hopkins's cliff, 'hangs' on Shakespeare's, 4.6.15), the main similarity between the landscape images is that both authors emphasise that the mountains/cliffs are in the mind, not in physical reality, and that, because of it, they are more terrifying. In his 'nighted life' Gloucester sees the cliff plainly in his mind; while the poet exclaims dramatically 'O the mind, mind has mountains', and continues the picture into 'cliffs of fall' and beyond, so that we have no doubt of their reality.

Earlier in the play the duality of Edgar/Poor Tom's role enables his references to the physical storm to apply equally to the mind's storm. His cry 'Fathom and half' (3.4), suggesting an extreme measurement of rain, could apply to both the stormy mind and the weather; and Hopkins's 'no-man-fathomed' (10) similarly refers to mental and physical scapes. But a more convincing similarity comes in the scene of Gloucester's fall (4.6.50, 53–4): 'So many fathom down precipitating/ . . . / Ten masts at each make not the altitude/ Which thou hast perpendicularly fell'.

In lines 11–12, Hopkins describes in one sentence both the limited endurance of man's mind, and the division of his mental burden into two parts: 'Nor does long our small/ Durance deal with that steep or deep'. Kent's fearful consideration of the physical storm in *Lear*, 2.2.48–9 deals in a similar tone with the same subject and final division: 'Man's nature cannot carry/ Th'affliction nor the fear'. If 'affliction' represents the attacking force, and 'fear' its effect, then parallels can be drawn with parts of the octave and sestet of the poem: '-ing' may be said to represent the attacker (particularly 'wring' and 'sing'), while '-ief' (especially 'grief') is the effect on the protagonist. In the sestet these are replaced by 'mountains' and 'cliffs of fall', opposed yet complementary parts of the same.

Two other minor alleviations of mental pain are treated similarly in the two works. 'A comfort serves in a whirlwind' (13) resembles Gloucester's opening words to Act 3, Scene 6: 'Here [a chamber in a farmhouse] is better than the open air. . . . I will piece out the comfort with what addition I can.' And the hovel later provides a similar comparative shelter from the storm. The noticeably sudden change of image in 'whirlwind' (13), from cliffs to storm (the only specific storm reference in the poem), might be said to show Hopkins's unconscious preoccupation with images from *King Lear*, although an alternative reason might be that Hopkins had changed to this from his original 'at worstwhiles' because that would contradict the first words ('No worst') of the poem. Hopkins then follows through this image to champion sleep as the alleviation: 'all/ Life death does end and each day dies with sleep'. Similarly both Kent and the Doctor prescribe sleep in the play:

> Kent: Oppressed nature sleeps.
> This rest might yet have balm'd thy broken sinews
> Which if convenience will not allow
> Stand in hard cure. (3.6.100–2)

> Doctor: Our foster-name of nature is repose,
> The which he lacks; that to provoke in him,
> Are many simples operative, whose power
> Will close the eye of anguish. (4.4.12–15)

Hopkins's consciousness of Jacobean literature at this time is shown in the stilted mock-Shakespearean line 8: 'Let me be fell: force I must be brief'.

It should be added that Hopkins does not mention madness explicitly in the poem, whereas in *Lear* the word and idea are both frequent. But in letters written in 1885, which certainly refer to the experiences out of which all the 'dark' poems grew, 'madness' is often mentioned in conjunction with Hopkins's fits of melancholy:

8 May: The melancholy I have all my life been subject to has become of late years not indeed more intense in its fits but rather more distributed, constant, and crippling . . . when I am at the worst . . . my state is much like madness. (L3. 256)

17 May: I think that my fits of sadness . . . resemble madness. (LI. 216)

1 September: . . . soon I am afraid I shall be ground down to a state like last spring's and summer's, when my spirits were so crushed that madness seemed to be making approaches. (LI. 222)

The landscape images of this poem, now used to describe his inner geography, tell us why there are no true landscapes and joy in Hopkins's Dublin poetry. For the next year, his poems would portray the mind rather than external nature, and the striven-for emotion would be comfort out of despair.

Chapter Six

WORSE

➜➤◄◄

I see
The lost are like this, and their scourge to be
As I am mine, their sweating selves; but worse.
'I wake and feel the fell of dark'

The times are winter, watch, a world undone:
They waste, they wither worse.
'The times are nightfall'

the departed day no morning brings
Saying 'This was yours' with her, but new one, worse.
'To his Watch'

Reason, selfdisposal, choice of better or worse way,
Is corpse now, cannot change; my other self, his soul
Life's quick, this kind, this kéen self-feeling,
With dreadful distillation of thoughts sour as blood . . .
Caradoc's soliloquy, 'St Winefred's Well'

Within a month of arriving at 86 St Stephen's Green Hopkins had written a letter to Bridges in which he said that Dublin was 'joyless', not as he had fancied it, and 'as smoky as London is'; that he had mislaid books and poems in packing; that there had been 'an Irish row over my election'; that he was 'unworthy of and unfit' for his post; that he had contemplated the examination marking he would have each year with disbelief; and 'I am not at all strong, not strong enough for the requirements, and do not see at all how I am to become so'. Six weeks later, he could not find time to read Bridges's plays or write a letter, the East wind was worse than in England, he was 'in a great weakness', and – what may have disturbed Bridges even more – in the middle of the letter he suddenly wrote, in capitals, 'AND WHAT DOES ANYTHING AT ALL MATTER?' And his letter in mid-April 1884 congratulating Bridges on his engagement to Monica Waterhouse had as postscript: 'I am, I believe, recovering from a deep fit of nervous prostration (I suppose I ought to call it): I did not know but I was dying' (LI. 193). Bridges's anxious enquiry resulted in this reply from Hopkins, showing already how limited were his ideas and resources for remedying his depression:

The weakness I am suffering from . . . nervous weakness . . . continues and I see no ground for thinking I can, for a long time to come, get notably better of it . . . . there is no reason to be disquieted about me, though weakness is a very painful trial in itself. If I could have regular hard exercise it would be better for me. (LI. 193–4)

The pressure of examinations, the standstill of his writing, 'wearifully tired', 'jaded': until the end of 1884 there are further signs of depression, although his letters are otherwise nearly full of their customary liveliness, no matter what the state of his mental health. Somehow he can still joke about his low state: 'I am in a low way of health, indeed I always am, but especially now in Lent . . . [Fr Mallac] will have it that I am dying – of anaemia. I am not, except at the rate that we all are; still I could do (indeed how gladly I could) – as they say – with more life' (LI. 208). On 1 April 1885 a letter to Bridges starts: 'Holidays are begun, but I am not in the frame of body or mind to avail myself of them for work, as I should wish'. In spite of that it is a lively letter, but at the end of a long paragraph about his musical compositions he returns to 'that coffin of weakness and dejection in which I live, without even the hope of change' (LI. 212–15). A six-week delay before the next letter to Bridges is excused by 'work, worry, and languishment of body and mind – which must be and will be. . . . I think that my fits of sadness, though they do not affect my judgment, resemble madness. Change is the only relief, and that I can seldom get' (LI. 216). That letter took twelve days to write, and there is then a gap of three months. The next, of 1 September, includes the well-known paragraph:

> I shall shortly have some sonnets to send you, five or more. Four of these came like inspirations unbidden and against my will. And in the life I lead now, which is one of a continually jaded and harassed mind, if in any leisure I try to do anything I make no way – nor with my work, alas! but so it must be.

Later in the letter he describes his pessimism about his lack of creativity:

> I can scarcely believe that . . . anything of mine will ever see the light – of publicity nor even of day. . . . if I could but get on, if I could but produce work I should not mind its being buried, silenced, and going no further; but it kills me to be time's eunuch and never to beget. . . . soon I am afraid I shall be ground down to a state like this last spring's and summer's, when my spirits were so crushed that madness seemed to be making approaches. (LI. 221–2)

But Hopkins had not been uncreative during his first fifteen months in Dublin.

'I wake and feel the fell of dark' is closely related to 'No worst, there is none', and written out of the same group of experiences. Both poems concentrate on the world within the protagonist; by the insistent power of its pain, that world compels his foreground attention, and is more real than the external world. But because it is internal its nature and structure are 'dark'. The protagonist's wish to end the pain merges with the artist's compulsion to dramatically define it in sonnet form. The strength of these complementary motivations is plain in both poems.

Because the pain's power is beyond definition, the poet is forced into unconventional expression. Pain triumphs over the protagonist, but the truthful chronicling of the conflict makes for greater poetry than if he had won. In 'I wake and feel the fell of dark' there is no disruptive, final congratulation, which had cheapened earlier sonnets.

Arising from the same experience, the poems have other similarities. Both tell that traditional sources of comfort ('Comforter', 'Mary', 'dearest him') have been ineffective, and thus account for their initial compassless venture into the unknown. This explains also why both poems proceed not by argument but by less confident devices of reiteration, reinforcement, and alternative successive images. In both poems the narrator needs to augment the impression he gives of his own inadequacies by insisting on his truthfulness ('Hold them cheap/ May who ne'er hung there', and 'With witness I speak this'). In both poems the protagonist's cries extend limitlessly in some way, not clearly perceived or articulated ('My cries heave, herds-long', and 'my lament/ Is cries countless'). In 'No worst' the poet is obsessed by limitlessly expanding progressions –'pitched past pitch', 'more pangs will . . . wilder', 'main . . . chief . . . world', while in 'I wake' there is a similar quick development from dimension to further dimension and beyond, imitating the mental experience of losing control of an image and its scape: 'more . . . yet longer', 'hōūrs . . . years . . . life' (where the effect is heightened by the omission of the expected 'days'), 'bones built . . . flesh filled, blood brimmed'.

Hopkins's desperate lack of self-confidence at this time, exacerbated by so much instability in his life, was probably also the main factor in deciding the common verse form of these two sonnets. In the past his most ambitious formal experiment, 'The Wreck of the Deutschland', had been the most negatively received; after its rejection he never regained confidence for similar formal inventions. For these two poems he therefore fell into the Italian sonnet form which since his undergraduate days had been second nature to him.

Differences in form and content between the two poems arise because one seems to precede the other. 'No worst' described areas emanating from, or adjacent to, the mental pain experience, which, however, remained elusive. Although the precise 'sights' and 'ways' of 'I wake' are still self-consciously

Revd William Delaney sj

Archbishop William Walsh

*Thomas Arnold (Jr), Professor of English
at University College Dublin*

A. W. M. Baillie

St Stephen's Green (West)

Phoenix Park, the Wellington Memorial

Katharine Tynan, by John B. Yeats

Monasterevin

The Cassidy house, Monasterevin

Stonyhurst, the boys' bathing place (the Epithalamion)

Lord Massy's de-
main, Co. Dublin
April 22 1889

Hopkins's last known sketch

Glasnevin cemetery, late 1960s

Monasterevin, statues of Miss Cassidy and Hopkins

undisclosed, the pain arising from them is tackled: attempts are made to register its taste, cause, and consequences. The argument of 'I wake' therefore seems more confident, its protagonist more visible and characterised, his struggle more precisely labelled, and the sonnet form more distinctly gripped. The agent of the pain in 'No worst' had been the externalised, unconvincing 'Fury', while in 'I wake' the source and object of the pain is the self, Hopkins expressing here a variation on the pain's origin in 'Spelt from Sibyl's Leaves': 'Selfwrung, selfstrung . . . thoughts against thoughts'.

'No worst' had closed with a line of magisterial monosyllables: 'all/ Life death does end and each day dies with sleep', implying a climactic conclusiveness; but the meaning of the words showed something at odds with this pompous machinery. The climax of the line lay in its first words, 'Life death', the head-on clash of opposed elements in the human condition (the stress on 'death' showing its outcome), while the remaining eight syllables are not just a succession of anti-climaxes, but a dilution of those two strongest words: 'all/ Life' is lessened to 'each day', 'does end' becomes merely the metaphor 'dies' (a devaluation from the real death of the line's second word), and 'sleep', mock death, is substituted for real death. The poem's conclusion seems to be purposely moderated, so that instead of ending the story it merely closes a chapter; sleep provides a lull during which the artist can gather his strength to take up the story's next episode in another sonnet. After the life-death generalisation the focus narrows to a single day which closes banally, 'sleep' tailing off after the secondary echo-climax of 'day dies'. Despite its grandeur the last line is the crust disdainfully thrown to the crawling wretch, as promised by the 'Here! creep,/ Wretch' of lines 12–13.

* * *

'No worst' finished with the implied closure 'each day dies with sleep'. As if to invalidate that, 'I wake and feel' starts with an awakening into an incontrovertible consciousness ('more must in yet longer', line 4); and it finishes with another problematical anti-conclusion, more ambiguous and self-contradictory than that of 'No worst', but reinforcing with 'but worse' (line 14) the 'No worst' message.

The opening of 'I wake' could be the continuation of 'No worst'. The ponderous iambic march continues with 'I wake and feel the fell of dark, not day', while 'day dies with sleep' is answered by 'I wake', invalidating the proferred comfort. Yet the protagonist does not wake to 'day' but into another dimension, that of a palpable darkened consciousness, 'the fell of dark'; this is a new chapter, signalled by the sudden jerking into action of the ego, 'I wake', which thus impressively claims dominance over the rest of the poem.

'I wake' is a protagonist's poem of self-expression: there are eight 'I's, two 'my's, three 'me's, a 'mine', and a 'we'. The opening of 'No worst, there is none' had provoked immediate questions in the bewildered reader about specifications ('to whom is this happening, if to anyone? no worst of what?'). In 'I wake', on the other hand, the setting is immediately and succinctly defined ('the fell of dark') by the protagonist, unambiguously present ('I wake'), who suggests that the exploration ('feel') of the imperspicuous mysteries ('dark') within this limited ('fell') setting will be the poem's procedural method.

The long 'feel' and the short, ironic imitation 'fell' suggest the protagonist's waking awareness suddenly stifled by realisation of the thick dense covering of darkness. 'Fell' signifies the 'having fallen' covering of darkness, nightfall. It simultaneously conveys qualities of 'fell' – ruthlessness and suddenness (cf. 'Let me be fell' in 'No worst').

There is to be no place in 'I wake and feel' for the 'mountains' and 'cliffs' of 'No worst': the deliberate contradiction 'dark, not day' emphasises that a restricted and negative scape will be explored. The protagonist of line 1 is prone and in darkness within a severely limited physical space; because of this confinement and inactivity his mind becomes the arena for action, for the relating of sights seen and ways went. 'Black' used in the senses of 'night' and 'horrific' intensifies the passage of time and the protagonist's perception of its quality. The exhausting protraction of physical and mental night is conveyed by the repetition of 'What hours' lengthened into 'O what black hōūrs', with the second 'hōūrs' carrying the weight of two syllables. Coming at the end of the wearily drawn out line 2, 'spent' acquires the force of 'expended wastefully' as well as merely 'passed'.

With the protagonist's mind established as the stage, the dramatisation starts with 'I' of line 1 dividing in lines 2 and 3 into two personae (announced by the startling 'we'), one being the inert body, while the other is the agent which experiences feeling, the heart, functioning separately from the rest of the body, without the protagonist's voluntary participation: 'what sights you, heart, saw; ways you went!' This pointed melodramatisation of lines 2–3 insists that the experiences were more powerful and alive than could be conveyed by mere narrative. (Hazlitt had written: 'The seat of knowledge is in the head; of wisdom, in the heart. We are sure to judge wrong, if we do not feel right'.) Another emphatic kind of dramatisation is in the lengthening of line 4 by its broken rhythm, the comparatives 'more' and 'longer' with the words 'and' and 'yet' stretching them further, and the long, final 'delay' further still.

The second quatrain verifies the images of lines 1 to 4, as though the poet feared that the hyperbolic images of 'No worst' be judged too wild to be trustworthy. 'With witness I speak this' is Hopkins's means of connecting the co-personae of lines 1 to 4 (the protagonist and the heart) with the narrator, the one who expresses the events in lines 5 to 8 ('I say', 'my lament'); the two are one. Lines 5–6 are impressively honest in their Hopkinsian scrupulosity: 'I insist on the veracity of this, on any audience taking it seriously. This is my testament, truth, not art. Nevertheless I need art to demonstrate the literal truth'. The opposition of 'say' to 'mean' again suggests that his experiences lie beyond normal rational statement, so that only art, the heart's agent, can adequately represent. The expansion from the literal 'hours' of line 2 to the figurative 'years' and then 'life' in line 6, dramatises the depressive's compulsive urge to protract disproportionately the perspective of a particular experience so that it becomes generally representative; hence 'my lament' is not just this poem's complaint but a general lament, an elegy, for all his life. 'Cries countless' also seems to encompass complaints from the present into the past, just as did 'my cries heave herds-long' in 'No worst'; 'countless' suggests that the cries have spread beyond numerate control, a control which might have been effected by 'dearest him', of line 8.

This expansion is only superficially of time-length; on a deeper level it is through degrees of sorrow. Similarly in 'No worst' 'my cries' had expanded into eventual 'world-sorrow', after appeals for relief had gone unanswered by 'Comforter' and 'Mary'. In 'I wake' this order is reversed, 'hõurs . . . years . . . life' is followed by unanswered cries to 'dearest him'. Without dramatic addresses to the Comforter and Mary, the protagonist/ poet of this poem uses the Post Office term for unclaimed mail, 'dead letters', to represent Christ's lack of acknowledgement of his pleas.

'Dead letters' means, literally, pleas without life, the life bestowed by an audience; this and the other desolate sonnets are dead letters. The confidence of the St Beuno's poems had been partly due to the poet's expectation of an audience at some unspecified future time ('Look at the stars! look, look up at the skies', he had exhorted someone). 'The Windhover' had been addressed 'To Christ our Lord'; a letter to Christ and to every man capable of Christlike action, of appreciating the Church's teaching in Hopkins's poem. In Dublin, on the other hand, there is no audience of Christ or readers; these poems were not sent to Bridges, but lay in a desk drawer until after Hopkins's death. The audience for this poem is only inside the poet's head.

The depression is so extreme that 'life' becomes not just all the protagonist's time on earth, but slides in the sestet into his physical constituents, 'gall', 'heartburn', 'bones', 'flesh', and 'blood'. (Cf. the similar progression in Psalm 69 [*The Book of Common Prayer*]: 'I looked for some to have pity on me, but there was no man, neither found I any to comfort me. They gave me gall to eat'.) But Hopkins intensifies the use of 'gall', a self-secreted bitter fluid, which becomes a self-denigration (similar to 'wretch' in 'No worst'); self-induced mental rancour is suggested by the physical fluid and its taste. The source of 'ways' and 'sights' undergone by the heart in line 3 is now diagnosed as internal putrefactive processes, 'heartburn' representing a failure to produce anything fresh. Both gall and the heart have salutary refreshing potential, but gall churning around bodily channels without outlet induces pain and worsening general health, Hopkins implying that heartburn is similarly caused by the heart's morbid stagnation. 'My taste was me' (line 10) is another process of expectation thwarted by a sudden cutting-off, which was first dramatised in line 1's 'I . . . feel the fell of dark, not day', with the thwarting agent, ridiculously, the same as the subject who needs to progress beyond. The protagonist's world, limited within his own emotional and mental processes, excludes objective, external nature, and he has become both subject and object of his own world, fatally habituated to the treadmill of self-concentration.

The anastrophe of 'bitter would have me taste' conveys the bursting pre-cipitance of self-bitterness, lacking the softer quality of the normal word order 'would have me taste bitter'. As though the self-putrefaction is eating ever more deeply into the poet's consciousness, the 'decree' of line 9 has degenerated into a 'curse' by line 11, and further into a 'scourge' two lines later. Hopkins's nature, judged by other people (his father, teachers, friends, Jesuit colleagues) to be highly unusual from schooldays continuously to his death, he himself judges a curse from God; line 11, 'Bones built in me, flesh filled, blood brimmed the curse', with its dire Anglo-Saxon maledictions, must be Hopkins's most powerful expression of self-disgust. The expression of self-torture, with no outside resources inspiriting his flaccidity, is continued with line 12, 'Selfyeast of spirit a dull dough sours', suggesting strong feelings churning over what is already inside him, producing acidic sourness rather than healthy nutrition.

As in 'Spelt from Sibyl's Leaves', he assumes a prophetic stance and visionary language, 'I see . . .'. That poem had signalled his fatalistic preoccupation with eschatology: decay, self-searching and -sapping, and inevitably, malign judgement. He has repeated, in stronger imagery, the kind of discovery of his nature turned in on itself which he had expressed in 'To seem the stranger . . . my life among strangers'. In that poem inner and outer worlds were interrelated in a new, ominously unhealthy way; he doubted his existence to other people, and the outer world did not exist for him.

Lines 12 to 14 are a condensed and poeticised version of some of the most powerful points he made in a Meditation on Hell (s. 241–4); there are other parts also of this and other Dublin poems which bear close resemblances:

> The lost now lying in hell . . . suffer . . . a torment as of bodily fire. Though burning and other pains afflict us through our bodies yet it is the soul that they afflict, the mind . . . No one in the body can suffer for very long, the frame is destroyed and the pain comes to an end; not so, unhappily, the pain that

afflicts the indestructible mind. . . . we are our own tormentors, for every sin we then shall have remorse and with remorse torment. . . . <u>taste as with taste of</u> <u>tongue</u> all that is bitter there . . . the worm of conscience, which is the mind gnawing and feeding on its own and miserable self. . . . their sins are the bitterness, tasted sweet once, now taste most bitter; no worm but themselves gnaws them and gnaws no one but themselves.

Hopkins's concept of Hell may be compared to *Paradise Lost* 4. 20–3:

> for within him Hell
> He brings, and round about him, nor from Hell
> One step, no more than from himself can fly
> By change of place.

The ending of the poem is problematic, a nadir, ending in 'worse', rather than a climax; and while its *tone* of mystic intuitive disclosure is conclusive, more questions are raised than settled. To compare himself to the lost seems a traditional eschatological conclusion, but he is like them in merely one respect, that of similar torture: he is suffering the mortal, worldly version of what will be far worse. This is some comfort, and also a dire warning not to go down that road for eternity – at least he can repent.

Hopkins's experiences demonstrate here that the justice of the Christian cosmos is meaninglessly contradictory; this thematically unstructured work nevertheless represents a profoundly Victorian mental chaos.

*   *   *

The unfinished state of 'The times are nightfall', its unstable focus, and its imbroglio of images, suggest a work still in the workshop, and yet it is a central biographical document of Hopkins's Dublin despair.

The success of line 1's powerful rhythm can be judged by comparing it with the first version's 'The times are nightfall and the light grows less'. The second version's device of the pivotal word, 'look', a device repeated in line 2 with 'watch', impressively links two halves of the line with different functions. The first half is a dramatically overdone synecdochic metaphor, an almost consciously literary figure uttered by the poet-seer. The difference between 'times' and 'nightfall' is extreme, underlined by disturbing confrontation of plural 'times are' by singular 'nightfall'; and yet the link is uncompromisingly raw and direct – an irreducible convergence. An objective observation and a subjective vision are said to coincide, and yet there is a violent schism. The first four words are a worthy opening from a master of the blitz start, prominent in all the desolate sonnets of 1885. 'Look', a living full stop in mid-line, enforces a sensuous confrontation between the listener and the physical scene. After the climax of that imperative the line declines, mimicking the meaning of 'their light grows less'.

The mimetic techniques of lines 1 and 2 are strongly effective and yet, as the poem develops, its listener becomes aware of clumsiness out of keeping with the initial technical control. The argument loses direction. Similar things fight rather than reinforce each other – 'grows less', 'undone', 'waste', 'wither worse'; and there seem to be alternative visions in lines 1 and 2, of 'winter' and 'nightfall'. In Hopkins's great other Dämmerunglied, 'Spelt from Sibyl's Leaves', the two elements of waning light and dissolution of earthly variegation were coherently incorporated with other images of waste and breaking up into a monotone duskscape. Technical infelicities then increase: 'grows less' was an odd clumsiness in line 1, and in line 4 'blazon' cannot avoid a confusion with 'blaze', contradicting the prevailing imagery of lessening light.

The second quatrain shows why 'Spelt from Sibyl's Leaves' was the Hopkins sonnet 'longest in making', and how hard won was its unity. The poetic persona of that poem keeps to the role of visionary, the only suspicion of special pleading being its uncanonical vision of Hell as a place where 'thoughts against thoughts in groans grind'. Line 5 of 'The times are nightfall' signals by 'And I not help' a transference of the narrator's role from poetic visionary to a hang-dog, self-absorbedly contemplating death and oblivion – a gloomy position for a priest who once hoped to convert England.

The poem's pentameter seems to break down in line 7, which can be scanned more easily as tetrameter, whether one considers the feet to be anapaests or dactyls. The following line scans as pentameter only because Hopkins has shortened 'endear' to 'dear', so making an unhelpful ambiguity. Subsequent rhythms become simplistic in keeping with the deadening banality of lines 9 to 11. Hopkins seems to have given up any idea of continuity here, while his confidence has petered out. Lines 9 and 10 rhyme, suggesting that 11 to 14 would have rhymed *d c c d*, as frequently used by Hopkins in Dublin. Such an ending would be a more gradual release of the sonnet's concluding energy than a final couplet, and suggests that Hopkins was thinking in muted personal terms, rather than of a generally applicable climax.

Biographically the poem shows the breakdown of the priestly control over phenomena, caused by the peremptory precedence of his mental depression. In 'Spelt from Sibyl's Leaves' the breakdown had been disguised as traditional Christian altruistic vision, and in this way 'The times are nightfall' gives a more honest picture of Hopkins's despair. In a more bald way than any other poem, this shows how desperately Hopkins needed psychological help, and the gap between his needs and what his religion could provide. His anachronistic faith-world did not contain adequate concepts, means of expression, or flexibility to deal with the reality of his troubles. He is on his own, powerless: the space unfilled by the poem's last three lines makes its own poignant conclusion.

*   *   *

'To his Watch' is also unfinished and in an unsatisfactory state, a pathetic representative of Hopkins's many Dublin projects given up through lack of the strong, confident will to persevere, and the mutually supporting encouragement from within and outside himself which his constitution needed.

The anachronism of the main image makes its own comment on Hopkins's lack of contact with contemporary reality. To many early Victorians, following the famous opening argument of William Paley's *Natural Theology* (1802), a watch poetically symbolised the physical universe, leading to the optimistic conclusion of an almighty clockmaker; but by the time of this poem this picture of the Newtonian mechanical universe had been replaced by the new symbol of the steam engine. Hopkins, however, goes back even further to the fatalistic tradition in which the watch symbolises man's limited time span.

The initial method of procedure, from the limitations of which the poem never escapes, seems a lazy and unpropitious choice. Needing to explore his desolate preoccupation with mortality, Hopkins takes a traditional metaphysical conceit, which had been employed most notably in Lord Herbert of Cherbury's 'To his Watch, when he could not sleep', and in Baudelaire's 'L'Horloge'. But he is too weighed down by the implications of mortality to develop the initial analogy with the sparkling and ingenious wit and control for which it calls. The conceit is lengthened by dragging appendages rather than organic development, and there is a feeling of tiredness about the whole exercise. There is no philosophical development, no power behind the admonition, and after 'Mortal my mate' no exact imagery. In contrast, the opening lines of 'No worst, there is none' and 'I wake and feel the fell' are genuine curtain raisers. It was a strange misjudgement of Hopkins's to have selected such a poetic vehicle.

In passing, the pathetic irony can be noted of 'lie/ The ruins of, rifled, once a work of art' in this wreck of a poem, and the muddle, which had almost successfully been masked in 'Spelt from Sibyl's Leaves', but openly present in the finale of 'I wake and feel', between personal fatalistic feelings and the inevitably inhuman values of cosmic eschatology.

Both 'The times are nightfall' and 'To his Watch' have an octave which lacks a working-out in the sestet. As I said earlier, the sestet is often the place where Hopkins tries to force the pace, but here he seems unable to find the way out of the problem.

*   *   *

While Hopkins was undergoing the frightful experiences documented in his letters from Dublin and the desolate sonnets, he occasionally took up his unfinished drama about the holy well that had meant so much to him while he was studying theology at St Beuno's, in North Wales. Like his Epithalamion, which described 'Paradise', the beautiful bathing place near Stonyhurst College, in Lancashire, *St Winefred's Well* is in part an attempt to recapture good times in the past, but it is essentially light writing, and does not approach the intensity of personal involvement and earnestness of Hopkins's writing in his Welsh period.

Act II of *St Winefred's Well* was probably written between October 1884 and April 1885. There are two sections, Beuno's paean of thirty lines, and Caradoc's soliloquy of seventy-one, of very different character. Act I reads like a mixture of Hopkins's undergraduate Jacobean style and imprecise sentiment from a virgin-martyr poem, and Beuno's unfinished address in Act II is scarcely more attractive, with its faint echoes of earlier, more powerful nature imagery, its lack of urgency and purpose, and its quaintly medieval picture of lyricised disease and infirmity:

> While cripples are, while lepers, dancers in dismal limb-dance,
> Fallers in dreadful frothpits, waterfearers wild,
> Stone, palsy, cancer, cough, lung-wasting, womb-not-bearing,
> Rupture, running sores, what more?

The other extant part of Act II, the villain's soliloquy after the murder, was also written in the lifeless Jacobean style, without any strong conception of time or place or character. There is no knowledge of dramatic action, and, like many contemporary playwrights, he is unsuccessful at putting life into a vanished age. Unsurprisingly, Caradoc's motivation for killing Winefred is stated mildly and indirectly. A Victorian priest of limited experience, who professionally avoided sexuality, would find difficulty in attempting to portray a sexually motivated murderer's mind and emotions. (In the Epithalamion he had also experienced difficulty in describing the prevailing sexual happiness.) The legend had already suffered Christian censorship in that Winefred was said to have been deprived of her head, rather than the maidenhead of tradition, although Caradoc's sexual pursuit of the maiden had been retained. In Hopkins's piece Caradoc's personality has to fit in with puritan conventions of speech and narrowly Christian interpretations of the roots of his crime, rather than be the man of primitive violence and whim he obviously was:

> Reason, selfdisposal, choice of better or worse way
> Is corpse now, cannot change. [61–2]
> Not hope, not pray; despair, ay, that: brazen despair out. [67]

The nearest Hopkins can portray to sexual attraction is lines 22–7:

> Her eyes, oh and her eyes!
> In all her beauty, and sunlight to it is a pit, den, darkness,
> Foamfalling is not fresh to it, rainbow by it not beaming,
> In all her body, I say, no place was like her eyes,
> No piece matched those eyes kept most part much cast down
> But, being lifted, immortal, of immortal brightness.

There is no human sensuousness here; Winefred becomes yet another unindividualised and unrealistic conventional virgin-martyr on Hopkins's list.

But occasionally and fragmentarily Hopkins finds he can use his own recent experiences of mental abnormality to portray parts of Caradoc's mind, where certain themes and expressions resemble parts of the desolate sonnets and other Dublin poems: 'My heart, where have we been? What have we seen, my mind?' (line 1) resembles 'What sights you, heart, saw; ways you went!' in 'I wake and feel', while 'darksome' and 'comfort', in several desolate sonnets, also appear in lines 47–9 of Act II of *St Winefred's Well*: 'we must weary/ And in this darksome world comfort where can I find?/Down this darksome world comfort where can I find?'. There is also common imagery in 'I wake and feel' and lines 63–4: 'Life's quick, this kind, this keen self-feeling,/ With dreadful distillation of thoughts sour as blood'.

How disenchanted Hopkins must have felt with himself to knowingly have shared some of his lowest feelings with a psychotic murderer. Part of his trouble was that his vocabulary was limited by his ideological framework and its history. After a certain amount of analysing his mental problems according to the precepts and vocabulary of his order, he had found himself repeating words and concepts, with no apparent escape. The words 'Comfort' and 'Patience', for example, now sounded hollow.

Chapter Seven

NOW DONE DARKNESS

-+->-<+-

That night, that year
Of now done darkness.

Hopkins's depressed mental condition over the spring and summer of 1885, 'when my spirits were so crushed that madness seemed to be making approaches' (LI. 222), connects directly with the dark sonnets. But it would be giving a false impression of those eight months to ignore their positive aspects. Hopkins was always a serious enthusiast, and even such markedly low spirits as he endured in 1885 did not completely stop him from indulging in pleasures and artistic compulsions which to some extent had been continuous from his Oxford years in the mid-1860s: 'in all that toil, that coil . . /. . my heart lo! lapped strength, stole joy, would laugh, cheer'.

Not that his fellow teachers at University College were much involved in such interests, which concerned English culture, people, and attitudes, as though that were the real, positive world, into which he would one day wake from his nightmare life in Ireland. The sole Irish person that Hopkins wrote about in 1885 as a close friend was Robert Curtis; he wrote to his mother: 'I should like you to see Mr Curtis some day – to see him (or know him) is to love him' (L3. 170). Otherwise he mentioned Fr Jacques Mallac, a Mauritian philosophy teacher at the college, with whom he attended the monster meeting in Phoenix Park of William O'Brien, editor of the fiery nationalist paper *United Ireland*, who a few years before had been clapped into 'cold Kilmainham jail' with Parnell and other leaders of the Land League agitation:

> It was not so very monster, neither were the people excited. Boys on the skirt of the crowd made such a whistling and noise for their own amusement as must have much interfered with the hearing of the speeches. . . . There were bands – it gave them an outing – and banners, including the stars and stripes and the tricolour. The people going were in Sunday clothes when they had got any, otherwise in their only suit, which with some was rags. (L3. 169)

Hopkins looked through opera glasses at O'Brien speaking from an open wagon, and 'got near enough to hear hoarseness, but no words'. O'Brien was bareheaded and, as the wind was from the east, must, Hopkins thought, have developed 'a terrible cold'. The crowd was 'quiet, well behaved, and not jocular (which the Irish in public are not). . . . Excitable as the Irish are they are far less so than from some things you would think and ever so much froths off in words'. It may have been the influence of the older Fr Mallac, which provoked this mildly patronising, almost benevolent tone of Hopkins's, although the outing was, he fancied, 'rather compromising'. Mallac had witnessed the revolution of '48 in Paris, and told Hopkins that 'there the motions of the crowd were themselves majestic and . . . they organised themselves as with a military instinct' (L3. 170). But in the same letter Hopkins expressed unbearable 'grief of mind' over Irish politics.

This account was given in a letter celebrating his mother's sixty-fourth birthday, and was designed to be entertaining. His letters to her had always been of this nature, friendly and loving, yet with a, usually well-hidden, patronising tone, selecting subjects suitable for domesticated female consumption, and conscious that she would read out entertaining passages to her daughters and friends. Thus in two letters earlier that year Hopkins had conveyed to her the scene in the non-academic part of University College when

we are expecting as a student and boarder AN IMPERIAL PRINCE or at least a prince from the Austrian Empire. He has four names tied together with hyphens besides Christian names. . . . I do expect Fr Delany will have been a little fluttered and the imperial sitting-and-bedroom-in-one has been got up in a style gayer than the rest of this shabby and dingy establishment. . . . And as our windows, when they open at top at all, as mine did not, till, by gentle but continued pressure, I got a carpenter to it, open by the pulling of a rope, the imperial tackle has been made of crimson cord like a girdle, with an acorn knop, the size of a big fircone, at each end, which is a thing of beauty and will be to the prince a joy for ever till he pulls it off. (L3. 166)

Count Maximilian Walbourg (or Waldburg – the College documents vary the spelling) Wolfegg arrived on the anniversary of Hopkins's arrival in Dublin. Kate and Julia had been hired especially to polish his room, new feather brushes were purchased, hardware was bought from Dockrell's, together with his own new set of delf (china); a gasman came to repair the lamp, and another to attend to the heating apparatus. The college cash books became clogged by entries concerning Count Max and his brother Count Joseph, who arrived two months later. 'Did I tell you of our German count?' Hopkins asked his mother. 'He is a splendid sample of a young nobleman, especially on horseback' (L3. 166, 170). He further told his mother about the Countess Mary, sister in her teens to the Counts, who wanted to read 'some good English storybooks'. Fr Mallac had bought some 'Catholic tales', but on reading them discovered that 'unfortunately . . . children were born in the first chapters . . . . This, for a young countess of fifteen or eighteen, he found too strong'; and so he appealed to Hopkins to name books 'in which the personages should have got their birth completely over before the story begins'. Fr Mallac also wanted the books 'not to be lovestories'; Hopkins found this another difficult condition, as 'the most highly proper English stories have love in them', and so, having rejected *Alice in Wonderland*, as an unfunny book which he had never admired, he begged his mother's help (L3. 167). (The Austrian noble family were not mentioned in his letters after April, and their names mysteriously disappeared from the college's accounts).

Hopkins never described to his mother in detail his negative feelings towards Ireland, for fear of upsetting her, but they were frequent features of his 1885 letters to Baillie and Bridges, his twenty-year-old friendships with whom had lately grown stronger and more confiding. Perhaps because Baillie, unlike Bridges, was not a writer nor especially interested in literature – he said after Hopkins's death that he much preferred his friend's undergraduate poems, written before he became too serious – his correspondence with Hopkins could be more personal and more directly express their mutual affection. There is only one letter written to Baillie in 1885, a moving and emotional one (starting 'My dearest Baillie', and finishing 'always your affectionate friend'), which besides describing Hopkins's melancholy and preoccupation with suicide, expresses his deep gratitude for Baillie's letters 'overflowing with kindness', and recalls their initial meeting at Balliol in 1863:

> the first thing . . . I can remember your saying was some joke about a watering hose which lay on the grass plot in the Outer Quad; a small spray was scattering from it. I stood watching it and you, coming in from a walk, waving your stick at it quoted or parodied either 'Busy curious thirsting fly' [a misquotation from the eighteenth-century poet William Oldys] or the Dying Christian to his Soul. (L3. 256)

In spite of his torpor, Hopkins wrote nine letters to Bridges that year, plus in mid-May an apology for a six-week delay in their correspondence 'due to work, worry, and languishment of body and mind':

> which must be and will be; and indeed to diagnose my own case (for every man by forty is his own physician or a fool, they say; and yet again he who is his own physician has a fool for his patient . . .) . . . I think that my fits of sadness, though they do not affect my judgment, resemble madness. (LI. 216)

This would not have completely surprised Bridges. Two years before he had received a letter which began: 'I have been in a wretched state of weakness and weariness, I can't tell why, always drowzy and incapable of reading or thinking to any effect' (LI. 168). Although almost every letter to Bridges expressed Hopkins's 'low way of health' and 'jaded' feeling, the major subjects are nevertheless their two main common interests – verse and music.

It was not until 1874, when they had been friends for almost ten years, that Hopkins knew that Bridges wrote poetry; until then he had thought him a composer of music. This could have been because on poetry, always Bridges's favourite art form, Hopkins was dogmatic and overbearing, while Bridges lacked his self-confidence and ready self-justification. Although being more practical and knowledgeable about music and composition, Bridges still remained deferential to Hopkins's face, reserving his private opinions; after Hopkins's death he was more openly critical, writing to Hopkins's sister: 'Gerard had a notion of starting music, as everything else, on new lines, and I cannot without great difficulty follow his intentions so as to do them justice.' And he added, 'Honestly I think that his ingenious inventions do not lead to anything, and I have not myself the delicacy of ear to fully understand them' (Phillips, *Robert Bridges*, 168). Undeterred by his complete lack of technical training (unlike at least four members of his Hampstead household who had had music lessons), and the fact that 'he could not play the piano at all' (Fr Darlington), Hopkins nevertheless, as Abbott says, 'obviously felt that he could make a contribution of importance to [music] . . . based on new theories. So absorbed is he in this pursuit, so enthusiastic . . . that the reader of his poetry expects to find that he has brought to music a similar genius and freshness of approach' (L3. 168).

He 'occupied a good deal of his leisure', said Fr Darlington, 'in writing original musical accompaniments for Songs. . . . He would sit at a piano and spell out the air with one finger' (letter to Fr G. Lahey, Farm Street archives, 13 July 1928). In the 1880s Hopkins wrote musical settings for several of Bridges's poems; his sister Kate recalled: 'Sometimes he would come home [to Hampstead] with an air he had composed, humming it to my sister Grace, get her to write it down & set an accompaniment to it – usually the words were one of Dr Bridges' poems – altogether a rather difficult task' (Farm Street, 7 December 1928). By 1885 Hopkins was becoming ever keener on music. In January that year, he told Bridges that he was composing a setting for two choirs of the first two verses, with pianoforte accompaniment, of 'The Battle of the Baltic', a war song by Thomas Campbell, popular author of the ballad 'Lord Ullin's Daughter' and 'Ye Mariners of England'. Its simple brag – 'Of Nelson and the North/ Sing the glorious day's renown,/ When to battle fierce came forth/ All the might of Denmark's crown' – is on a par with 'What shall I do for the land that bred me?', Hopkins's 'patriotic song for soldiers'. Hopkins described his work in enthusiastic terms recalling the reckless rush of words he had used to describe his freshman activities at Oxford:

Now talking of music I must tell you I have a great matter on hand. It is music to the Battle of the Baltic, the tune made long ago and now I am harmonising it. My first attempt in harmony was the Crocus. I got it sent to Sir Frederick Gore Ouseley [composer and Professor of Music at Oxford] a good time ago and he has not returned it. . . . This new thing will be intelligible, and in a few days I am going to send you the first two – or two first verses (I hold it is all the same). . . . There is a bold thing in it: in the second verse a long ground bass, a chime of fourteen notes, repeated ten times running, with the treble moving freely above it. It is to illustrate 'It was ten of April morn by the chime'. If . . . [probably Sir Hubert Parry, the composer and Bridges's friend] should approve it I am made, musically, and Sir Frederick may wallow and choke in his own Oozeley Gore. Then I have in the background Collins' Ode to Evening I mentioned to you before, which is a new departure and more like volcanic sunsets or sunrises in the musical hemisphere than anythin ye can conçave. (LI. 201–2)

Five weeks later Hopkins was ready to send Bridges the piano setting, but, full of admiration for his creation, announced that it was 'really meant for an orchestra – if I cd. orchestrate. But this indeed is to fly before I can walk. . . . The first verse surely . . . even on the piano sounds a success; but the ground bass in the second needs a body of easily distinguishable instruments to bring it out. My hope is that,. . . the whole wd. be quite intelligible with a choir (the bigger the better) and an orchestra. . . . There shd. be a great body of voices and the ground bass shd. be done by bells or something of the sort' (LI. 207–8).

Various settings were sent by Hopkins to professional musicians, some of them friends of Bridges, some Dublin acquaintances. His main musical adviser, a few of whose classes he may have attended, was Sir Robert Stewart, one of the most prominent conductors in Dublin, and holder of professorships at Trinity College and the Royal Irish Academy of Music. Almost without exception his compositions were returned by Stewart with criticism of elementary mistakes and of his arrogant attitude:

You will not like to be told, that . . . 4 crochet-rests, are not used, but one bar rest (semibreve) nor will you be pleased to hear that the Violin always plays from the [treble] clef which is often called the 'Violin clef' indeed. . . . Your viol. never plays from C clef on 4th line, but on the 3rd. A pause on 'DID' is absurd, and on 'AD-mired be' too . . . G sharp and E flat won't work together. . . . Is your music a duet for two tenors? or is it a 4 voice (SATB) piece ? . . . to accompany a tenor duet first, & then drop all accompt & end with a new, choral setting, is wanting in coherent plan. (L3. 427–8)

Once, in utter exasperation, Stewart asked: 'Can you play Pfte at all?'

Twentieth-century musical experts have not found originality or interest in Hopkins's song settings; comments include: 'musically without interest', 'all the most elementary work which would have been undertaken by a beginner in composition', 'very ordinary, and rather surprisingly showing no marked talent or even eccentricity' (L2. 169), and 'dull, standard Victorian parlour music' (professional musician to NW, 1990s). 'The Battle of the Baltic' setting has been judged as having 'many ideas, but Hopkins's inadequate knowledge of harmony prevented his making really effective use of them' (L2. 170). Nevertheless, Hopkins did sometimes write passionately and attractively about music: 'When I hear one of Chopin's fragmentary airs struggling and tossing on a surf of accompaniment what does it matter whether one or even half a dozen notes are left out of it?' he asked Bridges. 'Its being and meaning lies outside itself in the harmonies; *they* give the tonality, modality, feeling, and all' (L1. 214). And one wishes that Hopkins's Gregorian setting of Collins's 'Ode to Evening' still existed: 'Quickened by the heavenly beauty of that poem I groped in my soul's very viscera for the tune and thrummed the sweetest and most secret catgut of the mind. What came out was very strange and wild and (I thought) very good. . . . [It] was so delightful that it seems to me . . . as near a new world of musical enjoyment as in this old world we could hope to be' (L1. 199–200). Most people who have heard it performed think Hopkins's best extant music to be the touching setting of Canon Dixon's poem 'Fallen Rain'.

Hopkins's 1885 letters to Bridges are mainly concerned, however, with criticism of RB's poems and plays published around that time. His accounts are three-quarters full of fault-finding, and one quarter of praise for Bridges's mild reworkings of classical legend, in which the modern reader finds it difficult to be interested, and which lack the dynamic charge of Hopkins's poetry. Bridges's friend Samuel Butler said that had *Prometheus the Firegiver* been written by anyone else he would not have read it, while a *Spectator* reviewer had written of *Eros and Psyche*: 'it is the sort of thing that one may read with extreme pleasure and never desire to re-read' (Phillips, *Robert Bridges*, 124). Hopkins faintly praised *Eros and Psyche*, admiring 'the equable beauty of the work and the quaintness and freshness of the pictures', though 'Eros is little more than a winged Masher [fop, with an exaggerated manner]' (L1. 206), but he reserved his longest and most detailed judgements for the two plays *Nero* and *The Return of Ulysses*.

Nero was 'a closet play', not intended to be staged, and was really a long poem. Hopkins called it 'a great work . . . breathing a true dramatic life', although 'as an acting play I fancy there would be found defects in it'. It had 'plenty of story and action', but for a staged play there had to be not only 'the requisite stir of action but that action must be seen' (L1. 208). Hopkins found in it 'inimitable touches' and every soliloquy was 'beautiful to individuation', and he added: 'By the by the Irish, among whom I live, have no conception of this quality: their ambition is to say a thing as everybody says it, only louder' (LI. 210). (The second part of this judgement smacks of common English prejudice, though one wishes that Hopkins had enlarged on the lack of 'individuation'.)

Hopkins's comments on *The Return of Ulysses* tell us more about the critic than the dull play:

> The introduction in earnest of Athene gave me a distaste I could not recover from. . . . In earnest, not allegorically, you bring in a goddess among the characters: it revolts me. . . . Her speech is the worst in the play: being an unreality she must talk unreal. Believe me, the Greek gods are a totally unworkable material. . . . Even if we put aside the hideous and . . . unspeakable stories told of them . . . they are ignoble conceptions . . . not gentlemen or ladies, [but] cowards, loungers, without majesty, without awe, antiquity, foresight, character; old bucks, young bucks, and Biddy Buckskins. What did Athene do after leaving Ulysses? Lounged back to Olympus to afternoon nectar. (LI. 217)

This sample of Hopkins's puritanism was due partly to his priestly profession, and partly to Victorian inability, where morals were concerned, to sympathise with the reality of classical myths. 'I cannot take heathen gods in earnest; and want of earnest I take to be the deepest fault a work of art can have', he wrote to Patmore (L3. 360). It also accords with his patronising dismissal of modern Irish literature, with its unreal mythology. Another fault he found with Bridges's drama, however, is much more likely to find approval today: 'the archaism of the language. . . . I hold that by archaism a thing is sicklied o'er as by blight', and he added, perhaps recalling his own occasional lapses, 'some little flavours, but much spoils. . . . it destroys earnest' (LI. 218).

But Hopkins was, of course, quite unaware of the main reason why Bridges is unreadable today: 'his attempts to amalgamate classical and Renaissance forms were contemporary with the establishing of the taste for prose plays dealing with modern life and its difficulties' (Phillips, 120). Hopkins was similarly out of touch with modern drama, discussed with Bridges the possibility of producing a twelve-syllable or six-foot line which was not an Alexandrine, and sent him extracts from his own six-foot-line drama, *St Winefred's Well*, asking for his judgement: 'I have found that this metre is smooth, natural, and easy to work in broken dialogue [one six-foot line of verse broken into two speeches]. . . . In passionate passages I employ sprung rhythm in it with good effect' (LI. 203). In the first three months of 1885 Hopkins managed to revise for Bridges the seventy-line soliloquy of Caradoc after his killing of Winefred (see Chapter 6), and other, less dramatic passages. Bridges sent back much-needed encouragement; 'there is a point with me', replied Hopkins, 'in matters of any size when I must absolutely have encouragement as much as crops rain'. But he responded harshly to one casual remark of Bridges's: 'But how cd you think such a thing of me as that I shd in cold blood write 'fragments of a dramatic poem'? – I of all men in the world. To me a completed fragment, above all of a play, is the same unreality as a prepared impromptu' (LI. 218). His fragments were 'samples' to see 'if I cd be encouraged to go on'. But, despite RB's positive response, by the middle of May he found himself 'unable, with whatever encouragement, to go on with *Winefred* or anything else'.

Hopkins was most generous in advocating and encouraging the works of his friends. At Easter he had written to Patmore praising *Eros and Psyche* as 'full of beauty', and although suffering from his own 'coffin of dejection' and unable to create his own art, tried to spur Patmore on with his projected 'Marriage of the Blessed Virgin': 'You will never be younger; if not done soon it will never be done, to the end of eternity'. The same letter finishes with 'some hopes I might see you, for I think I may likely be in England this summer' (L3. 359–60). Patmore reciprocated by sending him the latest edition, the sixth, of *The Angel in the House*, which Hopkins found 'in the highest degree instructive . . . a book of morals and in a field not before treated and yet loudly crying to be treated' (L3. 362). If he had mixed feelings about its popularity – over ten thousand copies printed in England, and more than twice that number in America – he must have been pleased when Patmore told him: 'A very good critic assures me that your suggested corrections have had a very decided effect on the impression made by the whole poem' (L3. 363).

In June, Patmore's repeated invitation for Hopkins to visit him at Hastings became more insistent: 'What of course would be the greatest pleasure to me would be a visit, if possible, from you here. . . . I shall always regard my having made your acquaintance as an important event of my life, and there are few things I desire more than a renewal of opportunity of personal intercourse with you' (L3. 363–4). In August 1885 Hopkins at last visited Patmore at Hastings:

The Patmores were very kind. Mrs. Patmore is a very sweet lady. There are two Miss Patmores, daughters I suppose of Mr Patmore's first wife (he has had three), very nice, not handsome, one sadly lame since a child but a most gifted artist, a true genius: she draws butterflies, birds, dormice, vegetation, in a truly marvellous manner; also illuminates. By his present wife Mr Patmore has a very interesting and indeed alarming little boy 'Piffy' or Epiphanius (born on Twelfth-night), two and a half years old, of such a strange sensibility and imagination that it beats anything I ever saw or heard of. He treats flowers as animated things, animals as human, and cries – howls – if he thinks they are hurt or even hears of their being hurt: I witnessed some cases. I should not like it in a brother of mine. (L3. 172)

While at Hastings he also 'managed to see several old friends and to make new ones', the most notable being Purcell's biographer, W. H. Cummings, who showed Hopkins 'some of his Purcell treasures and others'; they agreed to correspond, although no letters between them are extant. Purcell had been Hopkins's favourite composer for a long time, and earlier that year Bridges had sent Hopkins some 'quotations from Purcell', to encourage his composition (LI. 219). At Hastings Patmore lent him poems by William Barnes, whom Hopkins found to be 'a perfect artist and of a most spontaneous inspiration; it is as if Dorset life and Dorset landscape had taken flesh and tongue in the man' (LI. 221). But there was one shadow over the Hastings visit: Patmore had shown Hopkins the manuscript of *Sponsa Dei*, a collection of notes that Patmore had written over ten years. Hopkins had objected to the parts dealing with the place of sexuality in religion, and he gave three examples of how religious meditation had become polluted by sexual incursion:

> (1) Molinos was condemned for saying . . . that during contemplation acts of unnatural vice might take place without the subject's fault, being due to the malice of the devil and he innocent; (2) Fr Gagliardi S.J. . . . found a congregation of nuns somewhere in Italy who imagined that such acts were acts of divine union; (3) such practices appear widely in the Brahmanic mystic literature, though naturally the admirers of the Vedas and their commentators have kept dark about it. (L3. 365)

Hopkins's reaction to *Sponsa Dei* so influenced Patmore that on Christmas Day 1887 he burnt every word. Hopkins did not retract his comments, even after learning of the destruction, and friends of Patmore's, including the influential critic Edmund Gosse, were incensed with him.

Hopkins was badly infected with the sexual puritanism common in parts of his age and religion, even though many of his poems and journals demonstrate his sensuous nature. Back in March one of his meditation notes had pondered on the event that led Pope Gregory the Great to send a mission to convert England: 'His meeting with the boys in the market place/ Angeli – natural endowments' (S. 259), and, on a retreat which he undertook immediately on returning to Ireland after his holiday in England, he was to make an attempt in a poem to come to terms with the conflict between his religion and his sensuous inclinations. It would be written in the form of Alexandrines, about which he had argued with Bridges in recent months.

On 21 August 1885 Hopkins left Dublin for Clongowes Wood College, in County Kildare.

*   *   *

The poem known as '(Carrion Comfort)' probably dates from just before 'To what serves Mortal Beauty?' and '(The Soldier)', both of which were written while Hopkins was on retreat at Clongowes from 21 to 31 August.

Hopkins did not use '(Carrion Comfort)' as a title, and it is misleading as a summary of the poem. It is a memorable phrase, but was assigned by Bridges for his own reasons in the 1918 First Edition and has no right to be the title. It implies that the poem has an identifiable unity which can be summarised, whereas the poem is a conflation of disparate elements into a sonnet form which confers a superficial unity at odds with the material.

'(Carrion Comfort)' posits the final stage of the poet's mental struggle, a looking back at his 'now done darkness' from his present position of assumed recovery. The octave attempts to re-enact the time of his worst despair (lines 1 to 4), and, now changing into biblical imagery, translate that despair into a metaphorical account of an anguished struggle between himself and some vast, all-powerful animal (lines 5 to 8); while the sestet, having changed imagery but still using biblical sources, identifies the struggle as between himself and God, and its purpose as part of the divine plan to purify him.

Although the poem's opening seems to have originated as the second part of an argument, the omission of the first part creates a fine dramatic shock. The first three words are particularly strong – 'I'll not' was a common emphatic complete sentence in Ireland and parts of the North of England. But there is a different kind of heightening in the rest of the first line, positive and negative forces alternating in a continuous antithesis – 'carrion' , 'comfort', 'Despair', 'feast'. The comparatively small vocabulary in the desolate sonnets shows their close relationship, and the difficulty of some of the repeated concepts, the poet being so puzzled by their complexity and unconstant nature that he works at them repeatedly without finding solutions. 'Comfort', for instance, looks simple, but the relationship of its concept to its realisation is explored in 'No worst, there is none' (line 3), 'My own heart' (5 and 6), and 'To his Watch' (8), as well as in '(Carrion Comfort)'. There is some kind of quest for 'comfort', but its object is chimerical, although a real, albeit partial and simplistic, comfort is gained in '(Ash-boughs)'.

Part of the difficulty of 'comfort' is that it occurs in two vocabularies in which Hopkins is fluent, the traditional religious one and the larger but vaguer secular one, which only partially overlap. The line from 'No worst', 'Comforter, where, where, is your comforting?', expresses one discrepancy, with the poet passing to the nearest spiritual equivalent of human comfort, 'Mary, mother'. In 'Not, I'll not, carrion comfort', the word means not just 'solace', but carries the older, religious sense, in which 'Comforter' is the Paraclete, of positive encouragement and incitement. The forcefulness behind 'Not, I'll not' is a self-willed attempted action of 'comforting' in this sense.

'Carrion' similarly conveys tones from religious culture in addition to its meaning of false-food; Hopkins's dramatic use of 'Despair' in line 1 establishes a context where the word 'carrion' can be spat out as a contemptuous insult, implying the 'fleshly' nature of man in the derogatory Pauline sense. It connects man with beasts by his sensual nature, and so sets up the opposition of true manliness in line 2, 'these last strands of man/ In me'. The religious connotation thus turns the word into a traditional Christian paradox, 'carrion' representing both flesh and non-flesh.

From the evidence of 'The Leaden Echo and the Golden Echo' (lines 13–16), written at Stonyhurst in 1882, 'Despair' was a hypnotic sound to Hopkins:

> So be beginning, be beginning to despair.
>
> . . . .
>
> Be beginning to despair, to despair,
> Despair, despair, despair, despair.

'Feast' was preferred to 'feed' presumably because the poet wanted concentrated self-indulgence, rather than merely sustenance. However, this first line pulls in opposite directions, dwelling too indulgently for its message on the sinful fruits; is the repeated 'not' sufficient to counteract the attractive 'comfort' and 'feast' which support the negative 'Despair', itself contradicting by its attractive sound the wretchedness it is supposed to indicate?

The pathetically indulgent aside '– slack they may be –' further weakens the poem's initial strong impulse. The implication is that a man by will and effort keeps the strands of his natural being twisted into the stiffness of life. If he slackens, he will collapse and die, although his body, like unwound rope-strands, will still be connected in his lifeless form. As 'feast' implies active participation in Despair, so 'untwist' describes a self-willed negative action of the protagonist, rather than passively allowing negative things to happen to him. It seems therefore to refer to suicide, which becomes more probable when we come to the cry 'I can no more', and 'choose not to be', with its echo of Hamlet's suicidal soliloquy. Despite the weak interpolation '– slack they may be –', line 2 continues the attack on weakness, changing its forces from the snappy petulance of the repeated 'Not' to a grander self-admiration – 'these last strands of man/ In me'.

Line 3 changes direction extraordinarily. The strong 'not', the defence against Despair, converges with positive 'can' in '*I can no more*'; and from that phrase emerges the positive attack of repeated 'can' – '*I can no more*. I can;/ Can' – used here with the strongly independent meaning 'to possess the power to act'. As a dramatic expression of final collapse of effort 'I can no more' is frequent in literature, but an origin outside Hopkins and his protagonist's situation is unnecessary: the poem's first version (folio 29 of the manuscript) has 'I can do none', and 'I can no more' is an obvious improvement, retaining its four monosyllables and despairing fall.

After the heavy collapse of '*I can no more*', the following positive 'I can' at the end of line 3 becomes muted; the tenor of the following line is away from action towards vague introspection, where words lose contact with the external world and express a return to self-occupied despair: 'Can something, hope, wish day come, not choose not to be'. This line lacks focus or anything positive. The previous assertiveness becomes merely an attempt to force a pre-scribed solution, without any real recuperation resulting. 'Something' suggests a catching at straws. 'Hope' is too imprecise to represent any real hope, and expresses only a wish for hope, perhaps prompted by Aquinas's prescription that hope is the opposite of despair. The progressive lengthening of the three expressions of imprecision, 'hope', 'wish day come', 'not choose not to be', enacts almost a departure into oblivion.

Poor Hopkins seems more than once to have similarly progressed from despair along the course prescribed by his religion only to be struck by the hollowness of a merely conceptual remedy. In this poem, both 'wish day come' and 'not choose not to be' are negative and passive, belying the verb 'can' on which they depend: day will come and existence will continue without any effort from a person in his normal state. The double negative shows what is happening here. The two 'not's ('not choose not to be') have lost the forceful-ness of the 'not's in lines 1 and 2. The suggestion is that Hopkins had actually been in Hamlet's position of seriously wondering whether to be or not to be. (We have already seen how the reality of friends' suicides had preyed on his mind earlier in 1885.)

In at least two respects line 4 prepares us for the abrupt change to the second quatrain of line 5. 'Wish day come' verifies the setting of darkness for the nightmare vision of 5–8, while the feeble ending of 'not choose not to be' makes more effective the dramatic explosion of line 5, 'But ah, but O thou terrible', and conveys the depressive pattern of subnormal torpor followed by supernormal violence.

These connections do not, however, outweigh the considerable incongruities of the second quatrain. In the first four lines Despair had been a personified inner impulse of the protagonist, an antagonist making a seductive, underhand suggestion of surrender; against this the protagonist attempted, apparently unsuccessfully, to rally his forces. The opposed forces are represented in speech by 'I' and 'thee' (similarly in the 1889 poem 'Justus tu es, Domine'). In lines 5–8, 'I' and 'thee' are again used to distinguish the sides of a struggle, this time with the subject and object reversed, 'Thou' and 'me', as though there has been a turn of argument in accord with sonnet convention. But not only does the new antagonist 'Thou' assume a quite different identity from Despair (the previous 'thee'), that of a fierce open-warfare assailant, but the whole scape has completely changed. The semi-conscious brooding of lines 1–4 has been replaced by a violent nightmare, and the dramatic quickening of pace in lines 5–8 denotes the quite different nature of this struggle. The personal confrontation which unifies the various aspects of the second quatrain's struggle is continually emphasised by the repetitions of 'me' (four times, and 'my' once) and 'thou' (twice, plus 'thy' and 'thee'), and the protagonist's tone of hurt questioning ('why *me*?') indicated by the continual emphasis on 'me' which is forced on any voice reading the poem aloud. The pictures of lines 5–8 are firmer than those of 1–4, and the lines more packed and staccato, with closely interlocking sounds; the tension is sustained for the whole quatrain (the outburst 'O' at the start of line 8, for instance, where tension would otherwise have slackened), and the powerful 'frantic' occurring straight after the caesura creates a similar emphasis to sustain that line's second half.

Hopkins often started sonnets with a layperson's observation, and then had to connect it to a priestly observation to finish the poem within a proper didactic framework. In this poem God does not appear in the first quatrain, and as Hopkins intended to use this sonnet to indicate a resolution of his mental trouble (as the last line suggests), he needed to introduce God. He saw the opportunity of combining in lines 5–8 his journal account of an incubus nightmare experienced as long ago as 1873, with biblical parallels which would suggest a simple, orthodox exegesis. Twelve years before '(Carrion Comfort)' he had recorded:

> I had a nightmare that night. I thought something or someone leapt onto me and held me quite fast: this I think woke me, so that after this I shall have had the use of reason. . . . I had lost all muscular stress elsewhere but not sensitive, feeling where each limb lay and thinking that I could recover myself if I could move my finger . . . the feeling is terrible: the body no longer swayed as a piece by the nervous and muscular instress seems to fall in and hang like a dead weight on the chest. I cried on the holy name and by degrees recovered myself. (J. 238)

It is perhaps a too simple process to then incorporate the biblical tradition of wrestling with a divine adversary, as Jacob, for instance, did, and further adding the lion image (as in Revelation 5.5, where God is 'the lion of the tribe of Judah'). A third tortuous biblical connection is then added, with the grain/chaff image of Matthew and Luke, where John the Baptist describes Christ in terms of a military hero, rather than the more usual New Testament meek saviour. But introducing traditional images after describing personal despair so powerfully breaks up the poem's continuity.

The outcome of the struggle in lines 5–8 is never in doubt. Whereas the victim is represented in the first sentence of this quatrain only by the single slight 'me', his adversary has numerous words with powerful sounds and meanings in support – 'thou terrible . . . thou rude . . . / Thy wring-earth right foot rock?' The victor of the struggle puts his foot on his defeated victim, lying in a heap, as a rude gesture of victory, in a traditional heroic way. (In his 1875 poem 'The Wreck of the Deutschland', stanza 2, Hopkins had similarly expressed his Lord's power over him in terms of a physical antagonist's superiority epitomised in a foot-image: 'heart that the sweep and the hurl of thee trod/ Hard down'.) The first lines of the second quatrain in this poem cleverly suggest multiple aspects of the struggle simultaneously. 'Wring-earth' shows God's potential power, and the puzzling implausibility of his deigning to 'rock' 'on me' (a much less violent and infinitely more selective process). 'Right' foot is used for its sound, creating the rocking of 'wring-earth right foot rock' by the return to the 'r' sound on alternate monosyllables. 'Scan' incorporates the idea of examining piercingly, which anticipates the severe judgemental process of the winnowing in lines 8–9. There is a judicious selection of divine attributes in these lines, so that the figure of God is never debased by being pictorially clear.

Although the protagonist is at the end of his tether in the first quatrain, and a scared victim at bay in the second, he is still able to summon forces to buttress his self-confidence. There is the forceful effect of 'Not, I'll not . . . not' in line 1, the memory of 'strength, stole joy, would laugh, cheer' in line 11, and the pride that comes with the Jacob-like realisation in line 14 that his wrestling adversary was no less than God. Conformity to the correct ideological stance destroys genuine continuity of direct expression in the poem. Answers to despair come from the Bible, not from reality. The optimism is literary and manufactured, and shows Hopkins's inability to face in this poem the kind of self-diagnosis he would undertake in his final three sonnets. In this poem there is not the sense of anguished verbal exploration that there was in 'No worst', 'To seem the stranger', and 'I wake and feel', with their fight against the sonnet form. Here the four sections of the sonnet are quite distinct, with artificial hinges betraying their discontinuity.

Hopkins attempts to start the vital connection between octave and sestet with 'fan' in line 7. But (except for 'lapped') the animal metaphors have been abruptly cut off and a different kind substituted. 'Fan' is here the technical term for 'to winnow away the chaff', in this context having an unusual violence, suiting 'in terms of tempest'. On retreat in January 1889, Hopkins wrote down his markedly precise picture of the biblical fanning, an Ignatian composition, turning metaphor into reality:

> *he* baptises with breath and fire, as wheat is winnowed in the wind and sun, and uses . . . a fan that thoroughly and forever parts the wheat from the chaff. For the fan is a sort of scoop, a shallow basket with a low back, sides sloping down from the back forwards, and no rim in front, like our dustpans, it is said. The grain is either scooped into this or thrown in by another, then tossed out against the wind, and this vehement action St John [i.e., the Baptist] compares to his own repeated 'dousing' or affusion. The separation it makes is very visible too: the grain lies heaped on one side, the chaff blows away the other, between them the winnower stands. (s. 267–8)

The precision with which he transfers biblical metaphor to his own senses, so that the fan appears before his eyes, explains Hopkins's apparent inability to distinguish between the two types of vision, the involuntary reality of the dreamt animal incubus, and the self-manufactured lesson-object, the fan.

To bring about a didactic outcome within the limits of a short verse form, Hopkins has to enlarge this nightmare experience quickly to represent the whole of his priestly career. He attempts this by introducing another from his past: 'me frantic to avoid thee and flee' resembles the account of his conversion in stanza 3 of 'The Wreck of the Deutschland': 'The frown of his face/ Before me, the hurtle of hell/ Behind, where, where was a, where was a place?' But the main attempt at unity is made by the question 'Why?' in line 5, repeated at the outset of the sestet in line 9, and the answering interpretation of the fanning in the rest of that line. This second 'why?' is a false echo, however. In line 5, 'why?' is hidden away, a bitter rhetorical question, whereas in line 9 'why?' is repeated *un*passionately, with the sense of present involvement with pain now gone. 'Why?' in line 5 was addressed to the 'thou terrible', while the 'answer' comes meekly in the voice of the former protagonist, whose calmness lacks authority.

The question 'why?' in line 9 originates a sound-drama, and an answer, represented by twin sounds, 'fly' and 'lie', 'fly' suggesting the mobile upwards flight from the fanning process, and 'lie', what is left after the chaff's outer husk, the *f*, has been discarded. Once the tempestuous process, signified by the reiterated tension of 'Why . . . might . . . fly . . . lie', is over, there is the wonder ('sheer') and peaceful clarity ('clear') of a completed visionary process. 'Sheer' Hopkins manipulated to suggest different things every time he used it – see 'The Windhover', 'The Loss of the Eurydice', 'No worst', and 'That Nature is a Heraclitean Fire'. In '(Carrion Comfort)', besides picturing the shining quality of the naked grain, Hopkins may have interwoven the adjectival meaning – 'acquitted (from guilt or crime)' – and the adverbial sense of 'bare'.

Line 9 tries to convey that the poet has effectively disposed of the mental despair of lines 1–4 and the physical turmoil and fright of lines 5–8. But I find the resolution too easy and verbal – are such complicated and powerful disturbances remedied by finding an appropriate scriptural text? There is naivety and superficiality in this quick application of emasculated metaphor to substantial troubles. Then in line 10 the emancipated protagonist, too different from his former fatigued and trampled persona to be a convincingly unifying narrator, quickly passes, by means of 'Nay in all', from one night's incident (lines 5–8) to its application to all the poet's priestly career. This rush to conclude every line of thought is less hectic than it had been in the sestets of 'The Starlight Night' and 'Spring', although based on the same prescription of completed Christian fable, rather than genuinely flowing literary shape, but there are other faults.

The protagonist in the sestet attempts to discount the experiences of the octave, with unaccountable lightness ('O whích one? is it eách one?') and without genuine explanation or reply.

The first discounting of the octave to emphasise the Christian remedy occurs in lines 10–11: 'Nay in all that toil, that coil, since (seems) I kissed the rod,/ Hand rather, my heart lo! lapped strength, stole joy, would laugh, cheer'. 'All that toil, that coil' recalls the weakly summarising ninth line of 'Spring', 'What is all this juice and all this joy?', which had seemed a clumsy standing back from the octave's subject matter, and had created a discordant second voice.

'Coil', from Hamlet's 'To be or not to be' soliloquy, was a commonplace Victorian expression of life's turmoil. And just as Hamlet quibbles on coil, a wound rope, which at death the soul 'shuffles off', so Hopkins refers back to the untwisting of 'these last strands of man/ In me' (lines 2–3). 'That toil, that coil' might, however, be considered facile as summary of the octave, and is modified by '(seems)' into imaginative description, as though the protagonist now is doubtful about those visions, but does not want to invalidate them. There are other attempts in lines 10–11 to lessen the octave's impact. 'Rod' which accords with God's harsh discipline in lines 5–8 is replaced by 'Hand rather', and yet, puzzlingly, remains in the poem. Another contradiction is Hopkins's adding in line 11, as though to provide more balance, a hidden supply of different happinesses, 'strength', 'joy', 'laugh', and 'cheer'.

'Cheer' in line 11 is intransitive, denoting an outburst of invigorating joy. But needing to consolidate the wrestling imagery of lines 5–7, by closing with his dramatic discovery, 'wrestling with (my God!) my God', Hopkins repeats 'cheer' in line 12, changing it into a transitive verb, and so making a false transition between lines 11 and 12; 'cheer' becomes no more than a verbal hinge connecting dissimilarities.

The meaning of 'Cheer whóm though?' and its logical place in the poem seem obscure. This transitive use of 'cheer' implies an object of congratulation, for which Hopkins gives alternatives of the two adversaries, God and the protagonist. But the first, intransitive, 'cheer' has no object, and is, alongside 'lapped strength' and 'stole joy', a product of the autonomous inspirational heart, rather than from the purposeful personal will which the transitive verb implies.

The self-congratulatory tone of the last line attempts a consolidatory confidence in accord with the sonnet form and requisite religious shape, but the lack of a continuous argumentative thread, after the powerful pictures and emotions of the octave, leaves the poem in pieces, a demonstration, rather, of the clash between Father Hopkins SJ, the priest, and Gerard Hopkins, the poet.

Chapter Eight

MORTAL BEAUTY

-+>-<+-

It was once well remarked that the priest knows better than anyone where 'Danger' is written up; and . . . he will keep off that part where the ice is thin between fun and sin.

Memoirs of Father Healy of Little Bray, 1895

But her long fair hair was girlish: and girlish, and touched with the wonder of mortal beauty, her face. . . . Heavenly God! cried Stephen's soul, in an outburst of profane joy.

Joyce, A Portrait of the Artist as a Young Man

Beauty [to the mind of Stephen's mother] . . . was often a synonym for licentious ways and probably for this reason she was relieved to find that the excesses of this new worship were supervised by a recognised saintly authority. . . .
He submitted himself to the perfumes of her body and strove to locate a spiritual principle in it: but he could not.

Sections XIX and XXII, Joyce, Stephen Hero

Spring and early summer of 1885 had probably been the most despondent time of Hopkins's life, when 'my spirits were so crushed that madness seemed to be making approaches' (L.I. 222). But most of August had been a holiday for him, spent in England. He had been with his family first at Oak Hill, Hampstead, and had then gone with them on holiday to the village of Easebourne, in a wooded and picturesque part of the South Downs in Sussex, before going the short journey to stay with the Patmores at Hastings. The end of the holiday saw Hopkins feeling 'buoyant'.

He arrived back at Stephen's Green in the early morning of Thursday 20 August, and the next day took the train into the flat lands of the County Kildare countryside, for his annual retreat at Clongowes Wood College, the prestigious boarding school run by the Jesuits in an Anglo-Irish mansion with extensive grounds.

The purpose of the annual retreat was to enable the Jesuit to examine his spiritual state, purge it, and renew himself. The retreatant, under the guidance of a director, undertook the Spiritual Exercises of St Ignatius, a methodical form of psychological drill. Jesuits, among the most disciplined in Christian religious orders, had been called 'men of the Exercises', and the distinctive character of the Society was said to be best demonstrated in the Exercises, where Ignatius's ideas and methods were at their clearest. For each of the sixteen years before this retreat Hopkins had studied and practised them. During the thirty-day Long Retreat of his Tertianship four years earlier, he had written sixteen pages of a rough draft of a commentary on them, and there are ninety further pages of detailed comment in his copy of the English translation.

It was on the second day of the eight-day retreat (the usual adaptation of the full four-week version) that Hopkins wrote the poem 'To what serves Mortal Beauty?'. Ignatius stressed the physical and mental separation necessary for the exercitant: 'Being thus set apart, not having his mind divided . . . but putting all his care and interest in one thing only, to wit, the serving of his Creator and the benefiting of his own soul, he comes to use his natural faculties more freely in diligently searching for that he so much desires' (The Twentieth Annotation). And if any activity (such as the writing of this poem) were performed outside the Exercises for that particular day it would nevertheless be intimately related to them: 'endeavour to preserve during each day the effect produced on the mind by the particular exercises of that day. For this purpose the reading should correspond with the subject of the meditations; and all reflections, however pious, should be avoided, if they be contrary to the affection sought to be produced in the soul'.

We can assume that the scrupulous Hopkins felt justified according to these severe standards in writing this poem. But does the poem conform? There are certain spaces in the Exercises where Ignatius invites the exercitant to interpose his own thoughts or choose examples relevant to his own case. It is there, where we detect Hopkins's self, that the interest of this poem as poetry and autobiographical document arises. The elements of this poem most plainly Hopkinsian are his choice of this particular subject, 'Mortal Beauty', for his meditation, and the extraordinary use of poetic language and form in which to express it.

Joseph Rickaby, a Jesuit contemporary of Hopkins's published a commentary stressing the proselytising, purposely *un*-literary character of the Exercises, which belonged, he stressed, 'to the class of books said to be written with the point of a sword rather than with a pen'. So although 'To what serves Mortal Beauty?' is a meditation ostensibly serving Ignatius's purpose, at the same time its form is calculatedly and blatantly artistic, risking downgrading the dogmatic message to secondary importance. At this stage of his life Hopkins had progressed so far beyond his novice puritanism over writing poetry that he could even do so during the most unequivocally regulated, professional part of his year, as long as the product was completely 'Ad Maiorem Dei Gloriam';

the poem is a form of officially sanctioned self-indulgence. The autobiographical relevance of this hardly needs underlining – Hopkins is using the
only competent means he has to advocate a vital enthusiasm of his which his
profession ignores or undervalues. One might say that the covertness is *because*
of that undervaluation; thus the poem shows the intense conflict between his
natural inclinations and the professional mould required of him.

A similar distinction between the ostensible and the hidden appears when
we consider the purpose of the poem, Hopkins's justification for writing it.
The main purpose of the Exercises was to overcome oneself and to regulate
one's life without being influenced by any 'inordinate attachment', an emphasis
reinforced by the 'Examen of the interior' on the first day of the Exercises,
which recommended 'the correction of a predominant fault'. It seems that
Hopkins selected his 'inordinate attachment' to human beauty as his 'predominant fault', and attempted to mortify his awareness of it, but, paradoxically,
also to justify it as a gift of God by cleverly using the example of Pope Gregory,
who was irreproachably influenced to send Augustine to convert England by
the angelic looks of the English slaves in Rome. Gregory's response was not
'Non Angli sed Angeli' – a corrupt version of the story – but (according to Bede,
Historia Ecclesiastica, bk 2, ch. 1) 'Bene . . . nam et angelicam habent faciem, et
tales angelorum in caelis decet esse coheredes' ('[the name of Angles] is
appropriate, for they have angelic faces, and it is right that they should
become joint heirs with the angels in heaven').

Hopkins felt himself over-responsive to human beauty; he had written to
Bridges: 'I think that no one can admire beauty of the body more than I do,
and it is of course a comfort to find beauty in a friend or a friend in beauty'
(LI. 95). But this kind of beauty, he continued, was 'dangerous'. As an over-
scrupulous Puseyite undergraduate at Oxford, he had noted in his diary of sins
the wrong sort of feelings when seeing Nash, a friend of his, naked, and even
when walking arm-in-arm with the handsome Baillie. He had irrevocably
given up painting when he joined the Jesuits because, he said, it dangerously
involved the senses; and as a student of painting he had enquired if it were
possible to paint the nude from printed illustrations, rather than have to face
the reality. But poetry had been allowed to creep back into his life, and there
Hopkins referred more frequently to human beauty than appeared usual in his
church, traditionally prudish over exaltation of bodily qualities. (In *A Portrait
of the Artist as a Young Man* the Jesuit-taught Stephen Dedalus prays to the
Virgin Mary whose beauty is symbolic and emblematic – 'like the morning
star' – but 'not like earthly beauty, dangerous to look upon'. When he has
discarded the Church's teachings the vision of the wading girl who replaces
the Virgin is 'touched with the wonder of mortal beauty'.) As human beauty
was natural it was God given, and so could not be evil; but the red-signal

word 'dangerous' had to be attached to it, as in both the poem and the letter to Bridges.

In his church, beauty was frequently confused with spirituality. Hopkins went on to say in his letter to Bridges: 'bodily beauty . . . is from the soul, in the sense, as we Aristotelian Catholics say, that the soul is the form of the body'. He seized opportunities of advocating the good of human physical beauty, and created others, in letters and poems. When commenting on Coventry Patmore's *The Angel in the House*, for instance, he determinedly opposed Patmore's insistent development of the concept of 'beautiful evil':

> It is certain that in nature outward beauty is the proof of inward beauty, outward good of inward good. Fineness, proportion, of feature comes from a moulding force which succeeds in asserting itself over the resistance of cumbersome or restraining matter; the bloom of health comes from the abundance of life, the great vitality within. . . . But why do we find beautiful evil? . . . nature is incapable of producing beautiful evil. The explanation is to be sought outside nature; it is old, simple, and the undeniable fact. It comes from wicked will, freedom of choice, abusing the beauty, the good of its nature. (L3. 306–7)

Bodily beauty appeared to be sanctioned by the church so long as it could be said to image the inner character. So it was with Christ, although here there was no scriptural authority, only a tradition (which seems to have been discarded in the twentieth century). As Hopkins put it in a sermon:

> There met in Jesus Christ all things that can make man lovely and loveable. In his body he was most beautiful . . . they tell us that he was moderately tall, well built and tender in frame, his features straight and beautiful, his hair inclining to auburn, parted in the midst, curling and clustering about the ears and neck as the leaves of a filbert, so they speak, upon the nut. . . . neither, his health being perfect, could a hair ever fall to the ground. (S. 35)

We can compare Hopkins's descriptions in poems of the physical beauty of Margaret Clitheroe ('The Christ-ed beauty of her mind/ Her mould of features mated well'), Winefred ('eyes . . . of immortal brightness'), the Bugler Boy ('freshyouth fretted in a bloomfall'), the Two Beautiful Young People ('bright forelock, cluster . . . of favoured make and mind'), and others whose looks mirrored their moral goodness.

Hopkins knew this was a weakness of his. Yet the 'Principle and Foundation' of the Exercises started: 'Man was created to praise . . . and serve God our Lord, and thereby to save his soul. All the other things on the face of the earth were created for man's sake, and to help him in the following out of the end for which he was created'. So human beauty was created to help man to praise and serve God, and therefore ways in which it could be used for this end *should* be found out. This is Hopkins's sanction for choosing this subject for the poem's meditation.

Nevertheless, the poem is not a calm, reasoned meditation, although its title and form suggest this was Hopkins's intention. He chose the sonnet form because it was second nature to him by now. Earlier that year Hopkins had sent Bridges observations about the six-foot line, the Alexandrine, which Bridges was using for *The Feast of Bacchus*, and he himself for *St Winefred's Well*. He felt that common pentameter enabled a poet to divide almost every line without thinking, and achieve variety effortlessly, whereas the six-foot Alexandrine's invariable division of each line into equal halves made it monotonous, unless one found some way of varying the measure (LI. 203). The choice of the Alexandrine and the graceful opening phrase show Hopkins's intention in this poem; but after establishing the measured language he felt the need to interrupt it with the surprising enjambement 'danc-/Ing', suggesting impulsiveness and danger.

The opening phrase is still more curious. Why did Hopkins prefer 'mortal' to 'human' or 'physical' or 'corporeal', or even 'outward', which are more direct meanings? The word is *just* adequate for his meaning in the sense 'of man', but this is only a transference from its primary meaning 'destined to die'. Hopkins had added a sadly fatalistic pre-judgemental qualification to 'beauty', a gratuitous moral sabotaging of its potential. His use of the word is connected with his religion and Ignatian exercises, in which 'body' was conventionally labelled 'corruptible' ('my soul imprisoned in this corruptible body'). The word conveys the standard attitude of a man thinking primarily of eternal things, to whom human beauty is on a secondary, much lower level. First-rate beauty belonged, according to that set of values, to Godly things of eternal value, while secondary beauty was merely of earthly things. So 'mortal' is at odds with Hopkins's immediate meaning, and with the pleasing sound of 'to what serves mortal beauty'.

Before he became a Jesuit, or even a Roman Catholic, Hopkins had looked on beauty as a forbidden indulgence, rather than as an earnest essential. On 6 November 1865 he had 'resolved to give up all beauty until I had His leave for it', acknowledging its low place in the Christian moral framework. But far from there being any sense of loathing (such as Joyce credits the Jesuit with in *A Portrait of the Artist*), whenever Hopkins mentions beauty in his poetry he cannot help being excited by it, in human or non-human nature. When he is looking at a natural scene, as in 'Spring' or 'The Starlight Night', as long as he attributes its appeal to God he feels free to convey directly his tingling responses – 'Since country is so tender/ To touch, her being so slender' ('Binsey

Poplars'). But with human beauty he has to exercise extreme care, danger continually flashing warnings between him and the face or body. In the undergraduate fragment *Floris in Italy*, Floris's disguised lover begs Sleep to 'Ply fold on fold across [Floris's] dangerous eyes', since 'on the face it is unsafe to look'. There is no sign of danger in the windhover's beauty until his qualities are metamorphosed into human ones, and then their effect is not only infinitely more beautiful, but also 'more dangerous'. Again, in 'The Leaden Echo and the Golden Echo', which poses less ascetically a similar question and provides a similar answer to this poem's, human beauty is 'dearly and dangerously sweet'.

In this poem 'beauty' is distorted and sabotaged between two powerful adjectives, 'dangerous' intensifying the moral suggestiveness of 'mortal'. But the poet then describes a passionate stirring – 'set danc-/Ing blood', which counteracts the moral straitjacket. This sets up doubts as to which side the poet is on: is he an involved partaker in beauty, or is he a committed moralist looking down on it? Or is he both – or neither? This ambiguity is carried further by the adjectival qualifiers 'O-seal-that-so' and 'flung prouder' being much stronger and preceding the tame concepts 'feature' and 'form'. 'Flung prouder' is emphatic and descriptive, 'form' being merely functional, while 'O-seal-that-so', a complete plot in miniature, has a powerfully dramatic immediacy, whereas 'feature' is flat and imprecise.

Other strange things happen at the start of the poem. The title has an archaic, rhetorical sound; Hopkins is using the obsolete 'serve to', with a conscious attempt at 'poetic' sound and archaism, contrary to his anti-archaic and anti-'poetic' principles; only three months before he wrote this poem he had written to Bridges : 'I hold that by archaism a thing is sicklied o'er as by blight . . . it destroys earnest: we do not speak that way' (LI. 218). Is this title an attempt at an Elizabethan highly wrought carved phrase, an *objet d'art* in sound? The repetition of this self-conscious title in the first words of the poem adds a degree of self-congratulation, which comes close to stopping the poem's progress beyond, and it is only after a personal 'aside' between dashes ('dangerous; does set danc-/Ing blood') that the productive flow of the poem starts. The title is a meditation point, paradoxically expressed in such an aesthetic manner that the narrative flow is halted and cannot continue until after the caesura in line 3; and there has been such a gap since the question that the argument's momentum has to be regained with the weak 'See: it does this'.

Even more awkwardnesses occur at the poem's start. The question mark which in the title immediately follows its question can only, in the body of the poem, follow these same words after a gap of two lines. By the time the question mark has been reached its question has been replaced in the reader's mind by much intervening, subordinate matter (from 'dangerous' to 'tread to'), which has included several distracting punctuation marks and breaks (two dashes, two caesural pauses, two ends of lines, a semi-colon, and a comma). Because of this break, a voice reading the poem could not satisfactorily alter its pitch to indicate the question mark. The separation of question from punctuation indicates that the shape of the poet's thought-flow is at odds with the syntactical form which he intends to contain it. Within the one 'sentence' there is a clash between a meditation question requiring a reasoned answer, and an unstructured cluster of personal musings about mortal beauty unrelated to that question.

The willed, calm control seen in the phrase 'to what serves mortal beauty' is never again in the poem counteracted as harshly as in the first three lines, but order is re-established when the patronising 'see: it does this' continues the broken-off meditation pattern. The asides from the argument in the rest of the poem are more likely to be either a personal hobbyhorse of Hopkins's (the patriotic reference in line 8), or over elaboration (the unnecessary 'a father' in line 7, and 'were all known' in line 10), or sentimentalities ('dear', 'sweet', 'home at heart'), rather than anarchic interventions, although in line 11 there are different rhythms each side of the caesural space (the conceptual, drawling 'World's loveliest – men's selves' is followed by the bursting self which 'flashes off frame and face', with the ['selves. Self'] making a deceptive connection).

In these and other ways 'To what serves Mortal Beauty?' articulates a struggle between attempts to control and disparage beauty and instinctive, almost involuntary, admiration of it.

* * *

The main imagery of the poem known as '(The Soldier)', the title given to it by Bridges, is military, and as Christ is directly compared to a soldier, it can be seen as a directly Ignatian poem, using the same metaphor as the Exercises. The structural similarity between the opening passages of 'To what serves Mortal Beauty?' and '(The Soldier)' is another indication of the shared Ignatian influence: the questions opening the poems, the elaboration, and the similar phrases introducing the answer ('Here it is' and 'See, it does this'). This poem probably forms the third stage of the Ignatian progression, common in retreats, from: (1) summary of the negative past, and desire to become positive ('Not, I'll not, carrion comfort, Despair'), to (2) correction of a predominant fault ('To what serves Mortal Beauty?'), to (3) advocacy of positive qualities. The three poems are also connected by the manuscript versions all appearing on one sheet of paper, and by the fact that they are all composed in Alexandrines, untypical of Hopkins except in this year.

The poem's first word, 'Yes', demonstrates the positive, pull yourself together mentality Hopkins is determined on as a remedy for slack, self occupied thinking. This is similar to 'Not, I'll not', with which he started the first of the three retreat poems, '(Carrion Comfort)'. Although composed during a retreat, there is no spiritual dimension until Christ's appearance in line 9. The octave shows the narrator not as an individual but representative of the old imperial society ('we áll'), conventionally responding to the heroic image of a soldier dressed in romantic red, as did Tennyson, Kipling, Newbolt, Chesterton, and Housman. Tennyson's 'The Charge of the Light Brigade' had been popular even in southern Ireland – one of Joyce's contemporaries at Clongowes Wood College recalled reciting it there about 1890 (Ellmann, *James Joyce*, 30). Patriotic and soldiering songs had been common at concerts at Stonyhurst College. In 1874 Hopkins had written an account of manoeuvres on Wimbledon Common, with a march past after, watched by 100,000 spectators: 'We did stand outside our gate and saw the march past and an unsheathing of swords by some cavalry, which is a stirring naked-steel lightning bit of business, I think' (J. 241–2). And later that year Hopkins had moved the (defeated) motion at the St Beuno's Debating Club that 'Eminence in arms is a better object of national ambition than eminence in commerce' (Thomas, *Hopkins the Jesuit*, 247).

The political and religious sentiments of this poem belong to its time, and it is difficult to sympathise with them. The poem also demonstrates how hard Hopkins found the task of trying to simplify his finicky, cloistered mind and fit it into a popular mould, even when he felt common sentiments. Comparison can be made with successfully popular stanzas from Housman's *A Shropshire Lad*:

> The street sounds to the soldiers' tread,
>   And out we troop to see:
> A single redcoat turns his head,
>   He turns and looks at me.
> . . . .
> What thoughts at heart have you and I
>   We cannot stop to tell;
> But dead or living, drunk or dry,
>   Soldier, I wish you well.

In Hopkins's poem Christ is an oddly narrowed and limited figure in the military context and in his novelettish sentimental reaction to the soldier ('he leans forth, needs his neck must fall on, kiss'). The poem relies on the narrator's role as representative onlooker, and yet Hopkins's typically strong and intimate feeling carries him too far in his picture of the Christ/ soldier relationship: Hopkins's sentiment looks crudely overdone when compared with Housman's restraint.

In line 9 comes the statement of the Ignatian analogy between a great temporal, military king and the spiritual king, Christ. In many of Hopkins's sermons there are references to this: 'Our Lord Jesus Christ . . . is our hero . . . . Soldiers make a hero of a great general. . . . But Christ, he is the hero . . . He is a warrior and conqueror' (s. 34). A sermon for October 1879 includes an extended metaphor of the battle between God and the Devil: 'The warfare the Apostle speaks of always goes on. Devils undying, their hatred undying . . . Nobility of this warfare . . . Choirs of angels, regiments with officers, ranks, discipline, subordination . . . Armour of God. . . . As we are soldiers earnestness means the same things, ready obedience to our Captain Christ' (s. 234). And then with 'He of all can reave a rope best', Hopkins gives Christ some sort of qualification for the job of general, experience of a simple but specialised manual task, the criterion accepted by the man-in-the-street. (Unfortunately 'reave' is a nautical term, not completely apt.)

This poem is not at first sight difficult to understand, even though difficult to sympathise with. But the thread of meaning is discontinuous, and the narrator does not seem to settle the conflict between the noble appearance of the military and the frail/foul reality; manliness in appearance and ideal is hoped to be indicative of the true worth. But the terms 'guess', 'mákesbelieve', and 'feigns' suggest self-deception, which is not counterbalanced by a statement of truth; the heart is guarantor, as so often in Hopkins's poems, but does not go beyond guessing and hoping, so the narrator says. Christ's entry into the poem does not solve the problem, but introduces fresh criteria for judging worth: 'some man do all that man can do'. Having been on earth ('served this soldiering through'), Christ well understands the human lot ('He of all can reave a rope best') and its limitations, and will judge worth not by heavenly ideals, but according to the reality of the human condition. Humans are deceived by outward appearance – if what they do goes by the name of 'good' it is overlooked that they are not, as they are in fact not, really good. Christ knows true worth better than anyone, but accepts that man's best is 'all that man can do'. Christ, unlike (it is implied) the perfect and unattainable standards of distant heaven, is sympathetic towards man's failings, so long as man does his best.

Once the plot is understood the poem seems to have a charm, even though the modern reader still finds it difficult to sympathise with all the soldiering imagery and sentiments of a distant age.

Chapter Nine

THE PORTRAIT

→>⤛⤛

hristmas 1885 had been a 'clouded' one for Hopkins. He felt he could not spend the holiday with his family at Hampstead, as he had visited them in summer, and he had exams to prepare for January. But in the following year he regretted not having taken time off, and when Christmas 1886 approached it was decided that he should spend it with the Cassidys of Monasterevin, one of the approved Catholic and upper-class families, some forty miles from Dublin, in County Kildare. Fr Delany had known the family since his brother Tom had been a curate there, some time ago.

Hopkins probably hailed a cab on the south side of St Stephen's Green to take him and his suitcase over on the far side of the city, near the Phoenix Park, to the Kingsbridge station, the terminus of the Great Southern and Western Railway, from which trains departed for the two cities of the South-West, Cork and Limerick. The light was fading as the train passed through Dublin suburbs to the rich, gently rolling pasturelands of the Pale, into the duller bogland countryside. Near Monasterevin, in the distance were the thickly planted woods and slopes of the Moore Abbey demesne.

The gas-lit Monasterevin station, tall and of grey stone, with a steeply slanting roof, resembled a compact gothic church; its upper storey formed the station platform, and at the bottom of steep steps were the booking office and entrance hall. The engine and front carriages of the train were stopped on the canal bridge beyond, and the line continued on to a long viaduct, the Metal Bridge, which carried the railway high over the river Barrow and its valley, the longest bridge on the line from Dublin to Cork. On approaching the first ever crossing of this viaduct, the engine driver reputedly said 'Now for Hell or Cork', and earned the name of Hellfire Jack. A Cassidy carriage was waiting for Hopkins, with Mr James Cassidy to greet him.

Immediately on leaving the station yard was a road beside the canal, on the opposite bank of which could be dimly seen a quay, and large sheds and warehouses with cranes and hoists were grouped around a yard, in which stood a grand three-storied house. In the great canal days of bad roads and no railways, when the quickest and most comfortable way to travel south-west from Dublin was in the heated and cushion-seated cabin of a fly-boat, drawn by two horses, with uniformed postillions armed with pistols and blunder-busses, this house had been a Grand Canal Company hotel. Now, although the passenger boats had long been discontinued, the agent who looked after cargo traffic lived there, in what was still known as the Bell-yard, from the days when a bell rang to tell the town of a boat's arrival.

The Cassidy carriage passed neat cottages built for British soldiers' families, and came to where a light and quaint bascule drawbridge (like that in Van Gogh's painting) continued the road over the canal, while a few yards away a heavy three-arched limestone aqueduct carried the canal high over the quiet and shallow River Barrow. The Barrow with its tributaries, and the Grand Canal with its branches, caused Monasterevin to be known as the Venice of Ireland; with the advent of the railway and its branch line, there were now no fewer than twenty-six bridges within a half-mile radius.

The carriage turned into the town's wide and straight Main Street, separated from the parallel river on its right side by gently sloping gardens and lawns. On the left of the street was a dignified terrace of three-storied Georgian houses, interconnected by a continuous internal corridor, built for Huguenot refugees from Catholic persecution on the Continent. Beyond, in a dominant yet detached position was the larger, wide and plain, but not inelegant, Monasterevin House, a typical early Georgian home for country gentry. It was seven o'clock in the evening. Mr Cassidy brought for introductions into the room where he had left him Hopkins's two lady-hosts, and they found him with his jacket off, by the fireside, sewing his waistcoat with needle and thread.

The life of Monasterevin was controlled by two interests – Cassidy's Distillery, a Catholic-owned business, and Moore Abbey, traditionally a Protestant grand house. Everyone in that town of just over a thousand people would be familiar with both, and have business with at least one. St Emhin, or Evin, a contemporary of St Patrick, had founded a monastery, Ros-glas, 'the green wood', in a perfect setting by the river Barrow, described as 'dumb' or silent, and the town derived its name from that – Mainistir-Emhin. In 1189, the first monastic settlement having disappeared, a new Cistercian monastery was established on its site, and became so important that, although just outside the English Pale, its abbot was entitled to a seat as a Baron in the Westminster Parliament. After the Reformation Rosglas Abbey became known as the Manor of Monasterevin, and passed through many Protestant hands, including those of Sir Robert Devereux, the Earl of Essex, Elizabeth's Lord Lieutenant in Ireland. In the 1880s the most ancient of the town's many bridges, the narrow, stone Pass or Ballagh Bridge, was still known by some as the Essex Bridge, from its having been crossed by the Earl's army in May 1599, in their march towards Munster. By the end of the seventeenth century, when Monasterevin had become one of the County Kildare's chief market towns, the Jacobean mansion built over the monastery's ruins had passed to the Earls of Drogheda, and had become known as Moore Abbey, after the family surname.

When Hopkins stayed at Monasterevin the now gothicised building enlarged by projecting wings was still known by that impossibly hybrid name, which proclaimed its (to Roman Catholics) heretical origins. In this monastic-style mansion and its extensive grounds were further blatant signs of its Protestant owners' romantic antiquarianism. A sculptured archway and parts of a rich gothic window from the Cistercian monastery had been incorporated into the neo-gothic mansion. A wide, winding path between ancient yews, another relic of the monastery, was known on the estate as the Monk's Walk, while Catholics called it the Dark Walk. Another path was known as the Friar's Walk; and a well had changed its name from St Evin's to Lord Henry Moore's. Remains from its Catholic past continued to be unearthed in the Moore Abbey demesne. When in 1846 improvements were carried out bones were found, and it was realised that the Earl of Drogheda's beautiful new sunken garden had been laid out over the Cistercian graveyard. Not surprisingly, there were tales of ghosts.

By that time, however, the whole town had been developed by the Earl and subsequent Marquises to form a rectilinear street plan, its two wide parallel streets connecting the canal with the main Dublin–Limerick road. Protestants and Catholics lived on friendly terms in the town. The old Protestant church which had formerly stood within the demesne of Moore Abbey was rebuilt on the Main Street as St John's, and on Drogheda Street, to the east, which had been laid out in the 1830s at the private expense of the Church of Ireland (despite its name, Anglican) parson, the Revd Charles Moore, Saints Peter and Paul, a large and brash new Catholic church, in the same ugly limestone as the Protestant church, was opened in 1847. The current Marquis of Drogheda had instructed his estate agent to plant and tend an avenue of alternate lime and horse-chestnut trees to the new church, to show his good will. A century and a half afterwards many of the trees still shade the path from the Catholic church to the Moore Abbey grounds.

The 1780s, when the Grand Canal opened and the Monasterevin Distillery had been founded by Mr John Cassidy, saw the beginning of the town's prosperity. With excellent canal and, later, rail transport, using the inexhaustible local turf as fuel, and water for brewing from the celebrated White Springs of Borraderra ('famed for its purity and sparkling appearance'), Cassidy's distilled 250,000 gallons of whiskey a year, and the main, ten-acre, premises on what had formerly been Abbey land had a hundred-yard frontage on the Dublin road. The thriving distillery was the liveliest feature of Monasterevin, and on working days made the Dublin Road end of the town a busy, noisy, and dusty contrast to the tranquillity and lazy dignity of the northern, Canal, end. The Dublin–Limerick road ran through the middle of the distillery buildings, and in the season was thronged with farmers and their carts, when the roadway would be strewn from end to end with corn, which attracted the town's stray fowls and ducks.

The distillery's proprietor, James Cassidy, grandson of John, owned property valued at over £150,000. In 1854, when he married, he had built Togher House, a mansion in the Italian style, in a plantation-bordered park, within sight of the Distillery, and had left Monasterevin House, his family home, in the hands of his sisters, Mary, the eldest, known as Miss Cassidy, and Eleanor, widow of Daniel O'Connell Wheble, who had been manager of the brewery section of the Cassidy business.

The Cassidys demonstrated the realistic working compromise frequently found in Ireland, but not so often acknowledged by nationalist historians, between the ruling classes and the native majority. John Cassidy had been a practising Catholic while also a member of the Vestry of the Protestant St John's church; though Irish, he was a magistrate, strictly loyal to British law. His obituary said that he 'ever proved himself attached to order and the law, and superior to the party influences of every description which surrounded him'.

His grandson James, imposing and always immaculately dressed, with a flower in his buttonhole and a little white dog at his heels, succeeded to the business in 1867, and spent the rest of his life in improving the distillery, and breeding racehorses. He was also a Justice of the Peace, notable for sticking to the letter of British law, and his name appears in a list of payments made by the British Government for unspecified services to the Crown. In 1862 his horse Sortie had won the Irish Derby, and in 1881 the same race had been won by his Master Ned. He shared this interest with the Third Marquis of Drogheda, a heavily whiskered man of about the same age, who had a racing establishment at Moore Abbey, and who, besides founding the Drogheda Memorial Hospital for sick jockeys, used to present each rider at the Punchestown races with a white saddle-cloth bearing a red number. The two men were the twin symbols of Monasterevin's prosperity and co-existing religions, and were often compared; the Marquis was not considered locally quite such a fine-looking man as Mr Cassidy.

By the 1880s the Cassidys had the comfortable rewards of being rich and dominant in every way within their little town. By fuelling the distillery with turf, Cassidys gave contracts to cutters of the local bogs, and through the credit notes issued at their corn-buyer's office controlled the income and production of the barley farmers in the surrounding area. The pressure of the local dependence on the distillery can be gauged from a curious document dated August 1873, now in a local public house. It is an elaborately illuminated address, couched in pompous terms of extreme deference, to 'James A. Cassidy Esq. J.P.', from 'the Tradesmen and Workmen employed in your extensive establishment', tendering 'our sincere and heartfelt congratulations on your restoration to health', and offering 'our sincere admiration of your generosity and proverbial kindness as an employer'. The obsequiousness and subservience of this document show the extreme contrast of this rural Irish locality with the essentially urban and dissentient English world that Hopkins pictured with such repulsion in his poem 'Tom's Garland', with its 'Loafers, Tramps, Cornerboys, Roughs, Socialists and other pests of society'.

Hopkins was for a short while removed from urban pollution, poverty, vices, dissent and liberalism, into a pastoral mode, able to pretend that his problems had gone away, although the winter countryside was not noticeably beautiful or dramatic, and was in fact often flat and featureless, like many boglands. He was completely free of teaching, examining, and other academic duties, with their various social and political pressures; there was space for him, physically and mentally. For once in Ireland he seemed to have escaped the pressure of politics, staying with loyalist Roman Catholics, in a town where the old hierarchical structures seemed securely in place.

His closest companions were the two comparatively elderly ladies, who, Hopkins wrote, made no secret of liking him. Their house had a private oratory, and Hopkins's only duty was to say Mass for the family. He also probably assisted at the busy Christmas celebrations in Saints Peter and Paul, where the Cassidys' presence was very noticeable. The Stations of the Cross had been given by Mrs E. M. Wheble in memory of her husband, and the two marble side-altars had been erected at the expense of the Cassidy family. At the foot of the statue of the Blessed Virgin was a diamond-shaped memorial plate inscribed with the names of deceased Cassidys.

Over Christmas the distillery was closed down, and the timeless restfulness of the surrounding countryside would have dominated the town to an unusual degree. From each house and cottage arose the pleasantly woody smoke of the turf fires. The spacious, unusually well-made streets, with their perfect camber, were no longer echoing with the clatter of Cassidy's horses and carts setting off to distribute St Patrick's Pale Ale, common porter, and six-year-old fat, creamy whiskey to nearby villages not served by railway or canal. Looking down from the Town Bridge or the Aqueduct Hopkins could now have heard the dumb Barrow, as well as seen its burlings. He spent Christmas and New Year at Monasterevin House, finding the people and their town very congenial.

And yet Hopkins could not escape Irish nationalist politics that easily. It must have been mentioned to him that the United Irishmen had been raised in nearby Kildare by Lord Edward Fitzgerald in 1797, and that in May the following year they had attacked and seized Monasterevin. It had been retaken by the local Yeomen infantry and cavalry, some of whom were employees of Cassidy's. It had been in the front sitting room of that very house, soon after the Battle of Monasterevin, that the Catholic curate of the parish, Fr Edward Prendergast, had been court-martialled by the British forces, followed at once by hanging from a tree on the other side of the Main Street, on the banks of the Barrow. The Cassidys had not owned the house at that time, but because of the family record of loyal administration of British law had been pointed at by republicans, who kept flourishing the memory of Prendergast's martyrdom. The town now has two memorials to him, a plaque and a prominent statue at a main crossroads, and in very recent history a statue of Miss Cassidy, next to one of Hopkins on the Main Street, became controversial for the same reason.

Besides the Cassidy sisters, Hopkins was introduced to relatives of Mrs. Wheble, Tristram, Ursula and Leo Wheble, children who lived nearby. In a letter to his mother, Hopkins described them and his feelings for them:

> They are half English, half Irish, and their nationality is thus divided: outwardly or in the body they are almost pure Paddy and Biddy, inwardly and in the mind mainly John Bull. The youngest boy Leo is a remarkably winning sweetmannered young fellow. (L3. 183)

Seeing a portrait of Ursula and Leo by an artist who had wanted to capture for posterity some of their youthful beauty before it vanished away, he seized the opportunity to write an elegy. In a poem written six years before in Liverpool, 'Spring and Fall: to a young child', Hopkins had put into verse his dismay at the inevitable fall of childish beauty and innocence into knowledge of mortality. But that had not been a true elegy, rather a lament.

The previous May, Mrs Waterhouse, Bridges's mother-in-law, whom Hopkins had met when he stayed with Bridges earlier that year, had written to him sympathising with his worries; he had told her of his troubles, with too much intimacy and detail. She had enclosed a gift of a book of hers. Unwilling and seldom able to spend money on gifts, Hopkins thought that this poem would make a suitable present in return, and started writing it 'in a commoner and smoother style than I mostly write in: I am sure I have gone far enough in oddities'. He wrote to Bridges:

> I am staying (till tomorrow morning, alas) with kind people at a nice place. I have had a bright light, and begun a poem in Gray's elegy metre, severe, no experiments. I am pleased with it and hope you will be and also Mrs Waterhouse, for I want her to see it. (LI. 248–9)

The poem's title, 'On the Portrait of Two Beautiful Young People', innocently anticipates the progression in the first line from 'admire' to 'sorrow': although the subjects are children, 'young people' is substituted, with the implication of inevitable growth from their present immature state. There is a formal distance in the phrase 'young people' which renders innocuous the potentially dangerous word 'beautiful'. The poet elegises on the heart's perception of time, the tyrant, who governs all natural beings, destroying them eventually.

The fine start, 'O I admire and sorrow', imitates the well-known beginning to Catullus's *Carmina* lxxxv, 'Odi et amo' ('I hate and love'). But whereas Catullus's speaker is a lover overpowered by opposing emotions, the emotions of Hopkins's speaker are carefully removed in force and immediacy. The narrator is distant from the young people because, although he knows them, he is contemplating only their representation in the portrait, and his emotions are withdrawn to a distance by 'admire' and 'sorrow'. Hopkins's use of the painting seems to have two purposes: one to prevent close confrontation between the onlooker and the children's beauty (compare the strained arguments of 'To what serves Mortal Beauty?'), and the other to facilitate the speaker's moral abstractions. He can contemplate the painting both physically and mentally, and express his heartfelt feelings in a more controlled and yet generalised way on the children's behalf. (The present whereabouts of the picture are unknown; the piece of decorative work sometimes reproduced in books is unlikely to be the original, as is claimed: it is neither a 'portrait', as the word is commonly understood, nor even an attempt to represent two specific people. It was over-enthusiastically spotted in the house of a distant Cassidy relative, and is now in the United States.)

Despite this difference from Catullus's opening, Hopkins is aiming at the same sharp dramatic effect by brutally locating opposing emotions in one subject. But those emotions, unlike love and hate, are not true antonyms. The complex word 'admire' involves approval as well as 'wonder' and 'looking at', whereas 'sorrow' is a term of simpler, more inward feeling. And the two words do not represent simultaneous feelings, despite 'and'; they are not consequent but subsequent emotions. The two words are accurate and suggestive: 'admiration' the conventional expansive reaction to art, wondering followed by enlargement of human awareness and sympathies, while 'sorrow' is opposed emotion entailing, in place of Art's concern for the outward object, a withdrawing inward of one's responses, a depressing realisation and awareness of human limitation. Fittingly the rising vowels of 'O I admire' are followed by the lowering to flat *o* in 'and sorrow'.

'Admire' and 'sorrow' are verbs with no predicate, the 'I' and its twin emotions being comprehensive in their world as the narrator looks on the picture, until the interpretive 'heart's-eye' takes over and analyses the emotions more precisely, in a process imitated by the build-up of lines 1–2. 'The heart', wrote Hopkins in a meditative note, 'is what rises towards good, shrinks from evil, recognises the good or the evil first by some eye of its own' (s. 257). The vague 'sorrow' takes root in changing to 'grieves', which presupposes 'for' or 'about' something definite; then the focus clears with 'discovering'; 'you' shows the moment of insight and acknowledgement, and the discovery itself, the uncovering of the hidden, is expressed in 'dark tramplers, tyrant years'. Evil has lurked for a long time unperceived, but the heart's eye has now seen through and discovered it.

'Dark' implies whole worlds of figurative uses, combined with equal propriety in this context: (*a*) hidden, imperceptible; (*b*) secretive, underhand; (*c*) sombre and gloomy, continuing the line of 'sorrow' and 'grieves'; (*d*) obscure in meaning, difficult to understand; (*e*) evil, Satanic; (*f*) ignorant of finer and moral things, without sympathy or enlightenment (appropriate epithet for 'tramplers'); (*g*) in the more specific imagistic sense of a progressive, mobile force which cannot be seen on the static and momentary surface of a painting, or in present moments of life in young people.

'Tramplers', contemptuous violators of rights (used recently to describe Mr Hyde in the Stevenson novel Hopkins much admired), also suggests tyrannous marchers onward, automatons who physically crush down, as of grapes, painfully extracting the juice of tears; and 'tyrant', the cruel omnipotent one who seizes sovereign power without legal or moral sanction, characterises age, which takes control of humans' lives without right or invitation, and then becomes unjust arbiter of their actions. The clash is between the children, with all their innocence, innate goodness, and natural unspoilt beauty, and the Devil. Hopkins joyed at children's original innocence: 'I liked the family', he wrote on visiting Ugbrooke Park in Devon, 'all the children spoke in a very frank and simple way which shewed innocence as well as good breeding' (J. 254). The Devil he characterised as:

> thrower of things off the track, upsetter, mischiefmaker, clashing one with another brought in the law of decay and consumption ['corruption'?] in inanimate nature, death in the vegetable and animal world, moral death and original sin in the world of man. (s. 199)

* * *

One of the several unfinished aspects of this poem is the role of the portrait. Although, like the Grecian Urn to Keats, the picture was to Hopkins the real-life motivating object of the poem (the portrait 'so much struck me that I began an elegy'), its symbolic function is not closely explored. The 'Ode on a Grecian Urn' ends by rejecting the real world in favour of the limited knowledge of ideal beauty presented by Art; but Hopkins is prevented by his priestly philosophical framework from thus wilfully indulging himself. He can not pretend that a temporary state is preferable to a permanent truth, and so is forced to take the opposite viewpoint to Keats's. But his emotional attachment to the temporary beauty of the portrait and its sitters will not allow him to express that opposition in words, although the logic of his argument demands it.

In his essay 'On Primitive and Sentimental Poetry' Schiller wrote that the elegiac longs for the ideal, and in this poem Hopkins conveys, while avoiding open expression, his longing for continuation of the golden days of youth. Like Gray's 'Elegy' Hopkins's is partly reverie, partly didactic, the pool of sadness in which the narrator uncovers his moral lesson sentimentally washing over and partly counteracting the impact of the harsh message. The message is the same as that of 'Spelt from Sibyl's Leaves', but this is a sentimental treatment whereas that was an austere one. The poet focused on the end of that poem and the end of the Judgement Day process simultaneously: the 'dapple-at-end' process had to be swiftly indicated and passed through on the horrifically inevitable march ordered by the sonnet form to the didactic conclusion.

Despite its subject matter of the tyrannically limiting nature of time, the form of 'On the Portrait' does not enforce an argument strictly contained within precise limits. Its length was elastic, an indefinite number of quatrains – Hopkins was always vague about how many: 'it should run to about twice the present length' (LI. 250). And so the narrator is able to dwell fondly on passing beauty, as well as indulging other undisciplined sentiments whenever they arise. Of course, this also makes inevitable the unfinished state of the poem, even the uncertainty as to how many stanzas it has in its finished state (there are four stanzas additional to those usually printed, which may or may not have been discarded by Hopkins).

Autobiographical considerations seem to surface continually in this poem. In Dublin, the place of tense work and introspection, Hopkins wrote the intensely packed and supremely finished sonnet 'Spelt from Sibyl's Leaves', while in Monasterevin, the relaxing and timeless place of country excursions, a gentle and rambling poetic effusion evolves and is never finished.

In 'Spelt from Sibyl's Leaves' subject matter from a St Beuno's poem, 'Pied Beauty', had been summarised by a one-word quotation, 'dapple', which dismissed abruptly ('dapple is at end') a vast collection of 'things' which had been vividly and lovingly elaborated and celebrated in that Welsh poem; and a similar referential process occurs in 'On the Portrait', where 'a juice rides rich through bluebells' takes us back to 'Spring':

> . . . blue; that blue is all in a rush
> With richness . . . .
> What is all this juice . . . ?

In 'On the Portrait' Hopkins has sufficient freedom of space and relaxation of pressure to complete a sight-and-sound portrait of the process he bewails, so that in keeping with the duality of 'admire and sorrow' there is, as though in an epitaph, both a celebration and a grieving in lines 3–4:

> A juice rides rich through bluebells, in vine leaves,
> And beauty's dearest veriest vein is tears.

The juice is not allowed to burgeon into joy, as it did in 'Spring', by remaining static; instead it 'rides', in the two senses of 'is contained within' and 'moves along on a journey'. This journey is along and through sound-locked syllables, by means of several patterned devices, including alliterating consonants ('rides rich', 'bluebells', 'in vine leaves'), and vowels which progress either intensively ('rides rich'), or downward ('in vine leaves'). (County Kildare, in which lies the town of Monasterevin, was, and still is, sometimes known as 'the bluebell county', and there were famous extensive bluebell woods in the lands of Moore Abbey, in which Hopkins must have walked.)

The contrasting 'vine' is not unEnglish as it may appear: a vine takes its place in the very English scene of Keats's 'To Autumn', and the word has commonly been used for the stem of any trailing or climbing plant. The word also justifies its place in the third line by purposeful phonic confusion with 'vein', the passage through which human blood 'rides', and which has an appropriate analogue in the 'veins' of leaves. By this confusion 'vine/ vein', made explicit by the metaphorical use of 'vein' in the following line, Hopkins conveys the consanguinity of humans and the plant world; and by his oblique expression of the relationship implies that the connection is delicate and hidden, and that more direct bluntness would be insensitive. Just as a liquid moving through the natural world bestows on plants their essential beauty, so the characteristic scape of human beauty, its life-blood, at its most precious and true, is liquid tears. The sentimental effect of this line has to do with its finely crafted rhythm and obsequious language – 'beauty', 'dear', 'true' (trans-formed into the antiquely noble 'veriest'). The sentiment after 'Beauty's' is intensified by the heavy emotional charge of the Herbertian 'dear' increased by the superlative, then climaxed in 'veriest'; the word's obsolescence underlines the inevitable destiny of physical beauty. From 'veriest' there is a swift monos-yllabic fall and a sweetly lingering death to the line in the diphthong 'tears'.

Such a death to one stanza makes the complacent congratulatory exclamation which begins the next a hollow contrast, which is what Hopkins intends with 'Happy the father, mother of these!' The insubstantial and superficial nature of that judgement is demonstrated by the halting of line 5's easy rotund flow by 'Too fast'; and the pedantic and at first sight unnecessarily clumsy qualifications of 'Not that, but thus far, all [= although]' imitate the coming to grips with a more subtle, qualified, but eventually more sober and accurate judgement on the parents, which is that, taking the reservations into account, they are still 'blest/ In one fair fall'.

The qualifications are all to do with Time. 'Happy the father, mother of these!' is a defective summary of the situation because, says the poet, it excludes the element of Time. 'Too fast', he protests, calling a halt at a particular moment in time – the moment of the portrait – so that from then onwards a double-perspective back into the past and forward into the future may be identified and expressed. We must not jump to a conclusion, because before one can judiciously summarise, account must be taken of the game of chance played by Time with people's lives between childhood and death. The later throws ('aftercast') of the dice involve all creatures in straining effort ('heft'), in merely hoping, rather than in certainty, about outcomes, taking risks by throwing the dice ('hazard'), and placing a stake upon a particular outcome ('interest'). 'Happy . . . of these' represents a wishful feeling of blessedness, rather than a true judgement; it is to be regretted, this domination of our post-childhood life by the whims of Time, but it is the condition of life.

It is only in the world of Art that Time's aftercast is ignored. And what is the relationship, he asks in the third stanza, between the young people and their painted representation? *Are* they like that? Comparing the portrait with the sitters in the flesh, the poet pictures the translation from life to art as a process in which physical features are transferred by minute and delicate touches of the artist's finger down beams (like those of a magic lantern) given out by the children's looks; when the beams strike the canvas they leave a permanent representation of the moment. Were it not for this painting the short period of youth, its 'hour' full of delight, would otherwise move swiftly away, be dissolved like dreams at daybreak, or like the momentary pattern of knots on a river's surface.

Although, as Hopkins said, the poem is 'an elegy in Gray's metre', the presence of Gray is hardly felt. The nearest that he comes is in lines 34–5 of 'Elegy Written in a Country Church-Yard': 'all that beauty . . . /Awaits alike th'inevitable hour', which is a similar expression of the elegiac commonplace in Hopkins's first stanza; and 'fleeted else' in Hopkins's line 11 recalls Gray's 'fleeting breath' (l. 42). A more interesting comparison is with Wordsworth's 'Ode: Intimations of Immortality from Recollections of Early Childhood', two lines from which Hopkins quoted in his journal for April 1871, and which he discussed in detail in a letter to Dixon only five weeks before he started writing 'On the Portrait':

> . . . in Wordsworth when he wrote that ode human nature got another of those shocks, and the tremble from it is spreading . . . I am, ever since I knew the ode, in that tremble . . . The ode itself seems to me better than anything else I know of Wordsworth's, so much as to equal or outweigh everything else he wrote: to me it appears so . . . Now the interest and importance of the matter were here of the highest, his insight was at its very deepest, and hence to my mind the extreme value of the poem. His poems rose, I hold, with the subject: the execution is so fine. The rhymes are so musically interlaced, the rhythms so happily succeed . . . the diction throughout is so charged and steeped in beauty and yearning . . . For my part I shd. think St. George and St. Thomas of Canterbury wore roses in heaven for England's sake on the day that ode, not without their intercession, was penned. (L2. 148)

A comparative reading of the two poems shows the clumsinesses, thin texture, and unfinished state of Hopkins's; and, as also happens when his Epithalamion on Everard's wedding is read after Wordsworth's 'Nutting', the sentiment of the Hopkins poem appears static and forced after the vigorous inspiration of Wordsworth's. And yet the extreme and exaggerated terms in which Hopkins praised Wordswoth's Ode show how deeply his own feelings had been engaged on the same subject. In both poems naturally unspoilt children, with supporting pastoral setting and decoration ('bluebells', 'vineleaves', 'burling Barrow brown', 'meadow', 'rose', 'flowers', 'pansy'), provide the occasion for the poet to question the 'fugitive' (Wordsworth, line 132) or 'fleeted' (Hopkins, line 11) passage of Time, and to attempt to provide some consolation on their destiny.

In Wordsworth's Ode and Hopkins's elegy, the poet in his dejection stands apart from the general rejoicing in youthful 'glory' and 'freshness': 'To me alone there came a thought of grief'. Both perceive the transient nature of the 'young delightful hour': 'The things which I have seen [as a child] I now can see no more', and 'beauty's dearest veriest vein is tears'. In the two poems youthful delight is seen as merely 'the glory and the freshness of a dream' which, with the daybreak of reality, will evaporate: Hopkins's 'that fleeted else like day-dissolvèd dreams' is similar to Wordsworth's 'At length the Man perceives it die away,/ And fade into the light of common day.'

Hopkins's sorrow, however, is occasioned by the sight of the children's beauty, and 'their delightful hour' means the hour which in the poet's eyes is delightful. The comparison between the mature poet's condition and that of the children is not made explicit; while in Wordsworth's Ode it is the poet's own youthful recollections of 'the hour/ Of splendour in the grass' which are directly compared with his present knowledge. However, Wordsworth does introduce into his poem an embodiment of that youthful hour, which may be compared with Hopkins's use of the painting. In stanza 7 of the Ode the poet asks his audience to look at the Child, as though they were in the auditorium of a private theatre, viewing a suddenly revealed live work of art:

> Behold the Child among his new-born blisses,
> A six years' Darling of a pigmy size!
> See, where 'mid work of his own hand he lies,
> Fretted by sallies of his mother's kisses,
> With light upon him from his father's eyes!

As in the Hopkins poem, the child is not himself so much as an actor on the stage of life, playing a part described to the audience by the poet in his role of tragic chorus. The cut-off nature of the stage underlines the blissfully innocent unawareness on the child's part of his role or its context in life:

> But it will not be long
> Ere this be thrown aside,
> And with new joy and pride
> The little Actor cons another part;
> Filling from time to time his 'Humorous stage'
> With all the Persons, down to palsied Age,
> That Life brings with her in her equipage;
> As if his whole vocation
> Were endless imitation.

In the Wordsworth poem, this idealised, representative Child is completely distinct from the persona of the Poet in his childhood, whereas in the Hopkins poem the distinction between the young people and their portrait becomes blurred after the fourth stanza, Hopkins being unable to manipulate all the elements of his poem as well as control them. In the address to the 'bright forelock' at the start of the fifth stanza it is unclear whether it is the actual hair or its painted representation which is being used as a synecdoche for the children. From then on the portrait is forgotten as the poet, having apparently shut his eyes, expands on the connected themes of corruption and moral choice.

Both poets lament, though selecting different imagery, the corruption that befalls childhood innocence, which both see as Heavenly. Hopkins continues his plant imagery with 'What worm was here, we cry,/ To have havoc-pocked so, see, the hung-heavenward boughs?'; while for Wordsworth: 'Heaven lies about us in our infancy!/ Shades of the prison-house begin to close/ Upon the growing Boy.' For Wordsworth also, the counterpart to the fragility of physical life is awareness of the spirit. The source and aim of life is 'God, who is our home' (line 65), and 'The Soul that rises with us' is 'our life's Star' (line 59). Hopkins uses the same image of a star as a direction guide to the fixed source and home of God: 'Where lies your landmark, seamark, or soul's star?/ There's none but truth can stead you. Christ is truth.'

The poems are remarkably dissimilar, however, in that to Wordsworth the Child's 'external semblance doth belie/ Thy Soul's immensity', whereas the brother's 'bright forelock' shows to Hopkins's eye his 'favoured make and mind'. Here the ideas of the poets diverge. In 'To what serves Mortal Beauty?' Hopkins had already attempted to justify his own strong response to physical beauty by theorising that external appearances expressed inward qualities, so that an onlooker could pick up what would otherwise remain hidden (in Plato's *Symposium* physical beauty leads to the divine, spiritual beauty). They had not only moral implication but even moral value. That poem, however, had ended on the unsatisfactorily weak note of '*merely* meet it'. In 'On the Portrait' Hopkins attempts to expatiate on that argument by saying that looks are the 'soul's own letters', the means of communicating between the soul and the onlooker. Hopkins is advocating the common argument against another Church tradition, that of St Paul, who opposed το γραμμα, the letter of the law, to its spirit (see, for example, 2 Corinthians 3.3). The portrait is a gratification of the wish expressed in 'To what serves?', 'the O-seal-that-so feature', which is here sealed in the painting, capturing on canvas the beauty which fleets in life.

* * *

After the fifth stanza the poet muses, and his arguments become less addressed to the young people and more solipsistic. The line of argument is increasingly suspended by examples and sidelong thoughts: 'maybe this sweet maid', and 'a warning . . . / . . . Good weighed'. 'Maybe this sweet maid' is, even then, a branch from a subsidiary branch of the argument, 'both for you and what sways with you'. The main argument of this sixth stanza is carried by only a small proportion of the total words – 'There's none but good can be good . . . None good but God' – and the kernel of meaning here is exaggeratedly lengthened by that fussy quibble on 'good'. By the end of this stanza the poem's line of argument has become obscured.

The seventh stanza, 'Man lives that list . . .', is interesting as biography rather than as part of the poem. Whereas the unity of Wordsworth's Ode was effectively sustained during changes of emphasis from recording personal emotional crises to pursuing metaphysical ideas, Hopkins appears to lose concentration and ride away from the track on hobbyhorses. In lines 25 to 28, for instance, he discourses on ethical *haecceitas*, each person's individual moral nature, in contrast to his more usual emphasis on the individual quality of a person's or a thing's physical being. The leaning in the will towards one moral side, 'all foredrawn to No or Yes', was created by Fate, and so when a man is called upon to make a moral decision, his mind has already been made up, to whatever is the original predestined inclination. 'Selfless self' is a paradox only in appearance, not in meaning, because the individualness of a person is not a matter for *his* choice, but for Fate's.

Hopkins comes closest here to expressing the fatalistic belief in the judgement process so graphically dramatised in 'Spelt from Sibyl's Leaves', 'black, white. Right, wrong'. Just as in that poem the world of physical beauty became of no account when the question of moral judgement arose, so in this poem the poet says that external beauty will always fall a prey to corruption. Even tree-boughs, hanging near heaven, are pitted by a worm's havoc. In 'Spelt from Sibyl's Leaves' the question of black or white is seen by the poet as a probable victory for black – 'a rack/ Where . . . thoúghts agáinst thoughts ín groans grínd'; and in 'On the Portrait', similarly, 'worst will [always prey on] the best'.

As often occurs in his Dublin letters and spiritual writings, Hopkins's inclination towards pessimism has closed down a comparatively open debating subject into a fatalistic corner. The only way he can think of to re-invigorate his subject and the cornered poet-figure is to switch to another line of thought. The abruptness of this change is made more obvious by Hopkins's brusque pseudo-dialogue: 'Enough', which is also used in a similar context in 'That Nature is a Heraclitean Fire' (line 16). But unlike the outcome of that poem here the poet cuts off his argument by protesting that his heart is being subjected to too much pain. The subject of the poem has now become the poet's emotions. The final two lines of that stanza, 'O but I bear my burning witness though/ Against the wild and wanton work of men', are like a parting shot over the shoulder, an affidavit that this poem is a genuine testimony although it has broken down into chaos. The poet signs himself off, although leaving his subject hanging, wet and unfinished.

* * *

Among several unfinalised and disturbing facets of this poem, perhaps the most curious is the battle for supremacy between the heart and mind of the speaker. Whereas a normal priestly progression might be from indulgence in emotional/ sensuous reaction to acknowledgement of the rational and moral metaphysical plan, in this poem there is a retrogression which – so far as the poem is concerned – reneges on the erstwhile conclusion reached at the end of stanza 5, 'Christ is truth'. After the failure in the sixth stanza ('There's none but good . . .') to implement the message of the climactic slogan 'Christ is truth', the poem reverts to a statement of the impossibility of moral choice – 'Man lives that list . . . all foredrawn to No or Yes'. This has more in common with the tragic fatalism of the classical world than with Christianity. The ambiguity between moral and physical corruption in the last two stanzas, however, is essentially Christian in origin, although the poet seems in the final two lines almost to contradict his earlier fatalism by his passionate condemnation of men's 'wild and wanton work'. The poet is plainly too emotionally involved with his subject and impulsive to bring the poem to a calm didactic conclusion.

Harold Bloom notes how in Wordsworth's Ode a child's growth is plainly outlined in three stages: the Child, or Natural Man, is followed by the Trapped, or Dejected, Man, and ends as the Mature Poet, who has accepted growth, which entails moving towards death. Testing these against Hopkins's poem, the narrator is in part the Mature Poet, and in part the Trapped or Dejected Man – two roles which are not played out in a logical order, but are muddled together, and in fact the poem finishes as it does, in an unsatisfactory non-conclusion, because the narrator's final complaint shows that he purposely remains Dejected Man.

Hopkins sometimes has difficulty in making a satisfactorily finished religious poem because there is too much emotional pressure on and attachment to the individual examples in his syllogisms, so that, when they are called on to enact their main function as merely representative fragments in the conclusion, they have too much weight for their minor role. In the St Beuno's poem 'Spring', for instance, the octave is too powerful to play merely a subordinate role to the moralistic sestet, and drowns the fable in 'juice and joy'.

* * *

There is little fresh observation in this poem; most of its themes have already been used by Hopkins several times over in previous poems. The heart as extraordinary and undisciplined perceiver had played parts in 'The Wreck of the Deutschland' (stanzas 18 and 29, for example), 'The Handsome Heart' (stanza 2), 'Spring and Fall' (lines 12–13), and 'Spelt from Sibyl's Leaves' (line 7). Beauty's innocence, vulnerability, and ignorance of mortality had been a theme in 'The Wreck of the Deutschland' (stanza 11), 'The Loss of the Eurydice' (lines 15–16), 'Binsey Poplars' (stanza 2), 'Andromeda' (stanza 1), 'Spring and Fall' (lines 12–15), 'The Leaden Echo and the Golden Echo', 'To what serves Mortal Beauty?', and 'St Winefred's Well'; and would be used again in 'That Nature is a Heraclitean Fire'. The poet had advocated the dedication of beauty to God in 'Spring', 'The Sea and the Skylark', 'The Bugler's First Communion', 'Morning, Midday, and Evening Sacrifice', 'The Leaden Echo and the Golden Echo', and 'St Winefred's Well'. God's beauty was described as changeless compared with mortal beauty in several poems, including 'Pied Beauty', 'As Kingfishers Catch Fire', and 'The Leaden Echo and the Golden Echo'. There is even a sense of the replaying of previously absorbed material in the background to the poem: the boy-bugler, in 'The Bugler's First Communion', had been 'born . . . of Irish/ Mother to an English sire (he/ Shares their best gifts surely . . .)', while the Wheble children are half English (in mind), half Irish (in body) (L3. 183). The bugler boy's looks, like the Wheble boy's, have a marked effect on the poet: 'freshyouth fretted in a bloomfall all portending/ That sweet's sweeter ending'. In the poet's eyes the bugler's 'drift' 'seems by a divine doom channelled', just as the beautiful young people would live to be fated by the 'list' in their will.

* * *

Hopkins added to and revised parts of the poem on and off for at least the next eighteen months, writing to Dixon on 30 July 1888 'I have done some more of my elegy and hope to finish it' (L2. 157), but the fact that he often reverted to old readings shows his lack of committed focus. Like his poem, his happiness at Monasterevin was not deeply engaged, merely a temporary relief, a 'change and holiday', though he came to regard Miss Mary Cassidy as 'one of the props and struts of my existence' (L1. 305). Monasterevin was never a true Arcadia for Hopkins, as North Wales had been, although he also spent the next two Christmases there, and one or two brief holidays at other times. After his death, two anecdotes illustrating the comparatively carefree nature of his vacations there were remembered in Monasterevin: how he had once seen a ploughman working in a field, and had jumped over the hedge to plough a drill himself. On another occasion, when walking on the roads south of the town he had been given a lift on a farm-worker's cart. After some time he asked the driver if they had nearly reached Monasterevin, to be given the reply 'We're not, then, but we'll be coming into Portarlington presently'. Hopkins had not asked the cart's direction, and they had been travelling further away from Monasterevin.

He came to regard the town's religious and political manifestations as typical of Ireland. The fact that Lord and Lady Drogheda were childless was due, as expected, Hopkins said, to 'the usual curse' on Catholic lands confiscated at the Reformation. At Christmas 1887 he assisted Fr Comerford, the parish priest of Monasterevin, in giving communion:

Many hundreds came to the rail, with the unfailing devotion of the Irish; whose religion hangs suspended over their politics as the blue sky over the earth, both in one landscape but immeasurably remote and without contact or interference. This phenomenon happens to be particularly marked at Monasterevan. (L3. 183)

By Christmas the year afterwards Monasterevin had become embroiled in nationalist politics, with Dr Comerford forbidding his parishioners to join the rent-boycotting campaign and refusing to take part in the activities of the Land League presided over by his own curates (L3. 190). In 1887 the poisoning of the local hounds threatened 'to put an end altogether to hunting in all that neighbourhood and with it to Punchestown races – what would mean on the whole the withdrawal of a great deal of money from the country. But that is how we live now', Hopkins wrote in pain to Dixon, 'and with fervour cut off our nose to revenge ourselves on our face' (L2. 153). His withdrawal into himself was – as shown in the Portrait poem – increasingly taking the form of self-consciousness about the ageing process, both external and internal. His 'heart and vitals' were, he said, 'all shaggy with the whitest hair' (L1. 250), and he wrote to Bridges in March 1887 'I am of late become much wrinkled round the eyes and generally haggard-looking' (L1. 253). In August that year he wrote: 'I was forty-three on the 28th of last month and already half a week has gone' (L1. 258). The Irish weather did not suit him ('nothing can be wretcheder than gloomy weather in Dublin', he told his mother, although Dublin's winter climate is usually milder than most of England's). In January 1887, there was little snow or lasting frost, but 'still I found the weather very trying, more than I ever did. Not that I took a cold, I never do to speak of in winter (I am too cold for it), but it exhausted me every morning and I felt as if kept on long it would kill me. One thing I am afraid it has done, ruined the good sight of my eyes and I shall have to get glasses. The focus is unchanged and objects at all distances as clear as ever, but they ache at any exertion. And any want of sleep makes havoc of them' (L3. 178). He duly bought a pair of spectacles for ten shillings, but a fortnight later was reassuring his mother 'there was nothing the matter with my eyes but general weakness' (L3. 179). Examinations always brought on eyestrain, even pain, and all the Dublin photographs of him show abnormally dark patches under his eyes.

Although he peppered Baillie with wild questions and conjectures about ancient Egyptian deities, and tried to keep up intellectual and political discussion by letters to Bridges, Dixon, and Patmore, he continued to lack in Ireland both sufficient mental stimulus of the sort he needed, and even 'a general stimulus to being, so dull and yet harassed is my life' (L3. 263). The only topic he seemed able to focus on at length in letters is the ever-present, frustrating, and insoluble one of Irish politics. He had no confidants in Ireland who thought and reacted as he did, and his English friends, although sympathetic and well wishing towards him, and generally of his English political persuasion, could not see the distant, newspaper-reported problems with the everyday urgency and proximity that made Irish politics so insufferable and yet inescapable to Hopkins.

He was still capable of the occasional enthusiasm for an intellectual pursuit (such as collecting Hiberno-English words for Joseph Wright's *English Dialect Dictionary*), or a short poem, but in general (he sadly admitted to Baillie), 'it is so doubtful, so very doubtful, that I shall be able to pursue any study except the needs of the day (and those not enough) at all. I have tried and failed so often and my strength serves me less' (L3. 275–6). He became increasingly conscious of projects started but probably never to be finished – a work on Homeric dialect, a book or at least a preliminary paper on the Dorian Measure.

It is noticeable that between the profoundly depressed poems of 1884–85 and the wonderful group of the last three sonnets of 1889, with their profound and controlled self-exploration, most of Hopkins's poems are escapes into more ideal worlds: the visual lyricism of the ploughman's looks and movements in 'Harry Ploughman', military idealism in 'What shall I do for the land that bred me?', praise for a saint's way of life in 'St Alphonsus Rodriguez', an attempt to shrug off the Doomsday pessimism of 'Spelt from Sibyl's Leaves' by finishing the Heraclitean Fire sonnet with Resurrection optimism, hoping to temper the elegiac sadness of 'On the Portrait' by admiration of corruptible human beauty and its portrayal in art, and epithalamic and Arcadian joys in the ode on Everard's wedding.

While still working on his elegy he was faced with the task of writing an epithalamion for his brother Everard's wedding. How would he cope with that opportunity?

Chapter Ten

THE EPITHALAMION

—>—<—

Despite its apparently haphazard variety of creative impulse, subject matter, and form, the poetry Hopkins wrote in the period 1884 to 1889 is closely rooted in his physical and mental circumstances. A major contrast in his life and state of mind at this time is between Dublin and escape-from-Dublin; and his poems echo this – usually their place of composition signals their kind of subject matter, form, and Hopkins's state of mind. For instance, 'On the Portrait of Two Beautiful Young People' belongs essentially to Monasterevin, a place of escape by virtue of its real-life subjects, its reference to the local countryside, and Hopkins's getting the happy inspiration for it only when on holiday there. 'Harry Ploughman' and 'Tom's Garland' were both composed within the happy three-week period in 1887 when Hopkins was at Dromore. 'What shall I do?', the recruiting song for soldiers, was composed in the Phoenix Park, which held many symbols of British imperial and military power; it is one of the few stretches of parkland within the boundaries of Dublin sufficiently spacious and self-contained for an individual to feel cut off from the city. Two further poems of a positive nature were also composed away from Dublin, '(The Soldier)' and 'To what serves Mortal Beauty?', at Clongowes, in the County Kildare countryside.

Generally, the more optimistic, outgoing, and expansively formed poems are composed on an escape-trip from Dublin, where his professional duties lay, with nagging doubts as to their value, reminders of his church's antagonism towards his native country, and the arduous examinations; the negative, self-absorbed, tightly formed poems ('No worst', 'To seem the stranger', '(Patience)', 'I wake and feel', 'My own heart', 'The times are nightfall', 'Justus quidem', 'The shepherd's brow', and 'To R. B.') are all Dublin compositions. ('St Alphonsus Rodriguez' is a Dublin poem provoked by an official occasion, and so does not fit this rough schema.) It is a rough schema, but it does seem to have some significance.

The outstanding exception is the Epithalamion, a lyrical scene of woods, river, foliage, and bathing, yet composed in the restricted atmosphere of a Dublin exam hall, the least likely workshop for any Hopkins poem of such luxuriance. The poem, as Bridges states on the manuscript, 'is in Gerard's most difficult manner', a style of exuberant pastoral imagery, which Hopkins usually employed when he was in the countryside.

In April 1888 Hopkins's brother Everard, sixteen years younger, was married to Amy Sichel. The following month Hopkins wrote to Bridges: 'I began an Epithalamion on my brother's wedding: it had some bright lines, but I could not get it done' (LI. 277). The poem was written on headed examination answer paper, probably while Hopkins was supervising an examination in the vast Great Hall of the Royal University building at Earlsfort Terrace, a short walk around the corner from the south side of St Stephen's Green.

The poem opens with a rejection of reality: this is to be a thought-created 'make believe' world, but not a fantastic one. The 'leafwhelmed' location is not precisely given – 'somewhere' – but it is English: 'Southern dean or Lancashire clough or Devon cleave' (the first version has 'Surrey dean'). The poem is for English people, who can conjure a typically English pastoral scene from their knowledge. In spite of this imprecision Hopkins was thinking of a specific locality: the schoolboys' bathing place in the river Hodder, near Stonyhurst College, in Lancashire, his memories of which could provoke the necessary emotions and poetry.

Hopkins had been at Stonyhurst from 1870 to 1873, when he studied at St Mary's Hall, and from 1882 to 1884, when he taught at the College. He had left Stonyhurst in February 1884 to take up his position in Dublin. There are several passages in his journals and letters from both those periods where he describes the Hodder and the boys' bathing place, known in the College as 'Paradise'. The environs of Stonyhurst are 'bare and bleak' (it is 'bleakish' again in 1882), but 'the rivers are beautiful' (LI. 26). There are several points of similarity between the Stonyhurst stretch of the Hodder and the Epithalamion bathing place. A local guidebook describes how in the two miles between the Lower Hodder Bridge and the Higher Hodder Bridge 'you will see this splendid river in its fullest flow and surrounded by luxuriant woods which clothe the heights on either bank'. Of the bathing place it says: 'the pools here are absolutely delightful – the river running over shelving rocks and forming small waterfalls which rush into the deep water' (Lawson, 16). After a short while there are two further natural swimming pools. The woods acting as enclosures, the succession of natural rock-enclosed pools, the waterfalls, and the boys at the hidden bathing place, are all similar to those in the poem.

The most telling similarity, however, is in Hopkins's use of the word 'fairyland'. It exists in three places in the Hopkins canon. The first is in a letter to his mother from Stonyhurst in June 1871: 'We bathe every day if we like now at a beautiful spot in the Hodder all between waterfalls and beneath a green meadow and down by the greenwood side O. If you stop swimming to look around you see fairyland pictures up and down the stream' (L3. 117). The second is in a letter of September 1882: 'the river Hodder with lovely fairyland views, especially at the bathingplace' (LI. 151). Over a period of eleven years 'fairyland' had been used to describe the spot. On the third occasion, in line 24 of the Epithalamion, it is used of a similar bathing place.

Another point of similarity is the river colour. In 1870 Hopkins wrote: 'Laus Deo — the river today and yesterday. Yesterday it was a sallow glassy gold . . . Today the river was wild, very full, glossy brown with mud'. In 1873 his journal records that the Hodder is 'where lit from within looking like pale gold, elsewhere velvety brown like ginger syrop'. In the poem it is 'a candy-coloured . . . a gluegold-brown/ Marbled river'. There are numerous similar close observations of the movement and shape of the falling water in the poem and these two passages (J. 200, 203). In the second passage Hopkins also uses the peculiar word 'raft' to describe the shape of a leafy mass as he does in line 25 of the poem.

There are other pieces of evidence, such as the proximity of both rivers at their bathing place to their moorland source. Line 4 of the poem gives 'Lancashire clough' as a guide to the hearer as he pictures the place. In the letter to Bridges quoted above Hopkins describes 'a clough with waterfalls'. This was Lambing Clough, through which the Hodder runs, and which Hopkins frequently mentions as a sight to show Stonyhurst visitors. In July 1873 he had taken his newly married brother Arthur and sister-in-law Rebecca to see the Clough (J. 234), the only event of the couple's three-day visit that he recorded, and he associated this spot with a new marriage of a close relative. His brother Cyril had stayed with Hopkins for three days the previous year, coincidentally three weeks before *his* marriage, and although there is no proof, Cyril was probably shown the same clough before his wedding day. And the connection between the bathing spot and his brothers' marriage must have remained with Hopkins when he hurriedly scribbled his Epithalamion on an answer book in the examination hall.

*   *   *

Hopkins described it as an epithalamion, but, strictly speaking, the poem has no title. Hopkins was a trained scholar and professor of Classics, and by describing his poem as an epithalamion was drawing attention to that poetic type, essentially classical in form and traditions, and binding himself to its edicts, the *Lex Operis*, which clearly distinguished its content and style from that of any other literary form.

The Greek word meant 'on [or "at"] the bridal chamber', and was used to signify a nuptial song in praise of the bride and bridegroom, and praying for their prosperity, but although Hopkins uses a Greek form of the word, his poem has less in common with Greek than with Latin epithalamia. Catullus, whose work Hopkins knew well enough to imitate in his translations of

Shakespeare songs published in the *Irish Monthly* (issues of November 1886 and February 1887), used as the basis for the most famous epithalamium of all, known as Poem 61, the traditional Roman marriage ceremony. Its form is that of a dramatic monologue. The conventional invocation to Hymen, the god of marriage, takes up a third of the poem, and is followed by an aside announcing the bride's arrival; the remainder of the poem is a series of addresses – to the bride, to the marriage bed, to the groom, and finally to the bridal pair.

Hopkins's poem starts with an invocation, but rather a vague one – not to Hymen, the god of marriage, but to the 'hearer'. There are some similarities here, though: invocations are usually addressed at the outset to some *outsider* to become an *insider*, a partaker of the joys on offer. Hymen in Catullus is asked to leave the lonely mountain and the haunted grove, to quit his customary haunts and join in a ceremony, while in Hopkins's poem 'a listless stranger' is 'beckoned by the noise' into active participation.

In Catullus, whose sexual proclivities are even plainer in other poems, the virgins at the ceremony are boys, who had the special prerogative of coarse licence on this occasion, and in the Hopkins epithalamion the celebrants are again virgin boys, expressing a certain amount of physical freedom ('riot of a rout', 'dare and with downdolfinry and bellbright bodies') though not overt sexual licence. Catullus, like Hopkins, delights in description of plants. Another feature of Catullus's poems which has a marginal place in Hopkins's epithalamion (where the 'boys from the town' escape to the country) is the contrast between town-bred dullness and effeminacy, on the one hand, and the healthy manners of the country on the other.

* * *

The most essential characteristics of the convention are: the poem, following classical models, praises the bride and groom, and joins in the jubilation of guests at the wedding. It revolves around the central wedding events: the religious ceremonies, the feasting, the ritual bedding, and the sexual consummation. The poet/speaker is physically present and plays a prominent role as master of ceremonies, invoking Hymen.

Edmund Spenser's 'Epithalamion' is generally considered the best Christian-age example, bearing comparison with Catullus's. That it has achieved this without discarding any classical conventions, and yet without provoking charges of blasphemy against Christian theology or of undue sexual licence, shows that a Christian-age epithalamion is not, *ipso facto*, doomed. Spenser's Christian humanism enabled him to use Christian as well as classical imagery, without apparently having difficulty in reconciling the two. A modern epithalamion was then possible, but how possible was it for Hopkins?

* * *

Two factors, I think, made the writing of an epithalamion an ill-starred venture for Hopkins. First, he would have trouble in overcoming personal scruples in writing within conventions closely associated with pagan ceremonial and sexual customs. And secondly, there would be difficulties for any Victorian classicist because of the difference between the nature of original Classical literature and nineteenth-century idealisations of it.

Hopkins's scruples about the place and purpose of art can be illustrated from the incident of Coventry Patmore's prose work, *Sponsa Dei*. Both Patmore and Hopkins, as Derek Patmore says, 'unlike Bridges . . . felt that they should dedicate their poetic powers to the glorification of God' (Derek Patmore, 192). And in Coventry Patmore's eyes: 'Gerard Hopkins was the only orthodox, and as far as I could see, saintly man in whom religion had absolutely no narrowing effect upon his general opinions and sympathies. A Catholic of the most scrupulous strictures, he could nevertheless see the holy Spirit in all goodness, truth and beauty' (D. Patmore, 189). Yet in spite of Patmore's sharing in Hopkins's dedication and admiring his wide sympathies, a difference in scruples and taste between them was a large part of the reason why Patmore destroyed the manuscript of his *Sponsa Dei*, the outcome of ten years' meditations and a work which, Patmore wrote to Bridges, 'could not but have made a greater effect than all I have ever written'. The whole tale is not known, but from the available evidence it is clear that it hinges on Hopkins's response to the work's subject matter. Edmund Gosse, who had read the manuscript, said:

> The subject of it was certainly audacious. It was not more or less than an interpretation of the love between the soul and God by an analogy of the love between a woman and a man: it was, indeed, a transcendental treatise on Divine desire seen through the veil of human desire. . . . Yet the scruple which destroyed it was simply deplorable; the burning of *Sponsa Dei* involved a distinct loss to literature. (D. Patmore, 195)

After reading the *Sponsa Dei* manuscript at Hastings in August 1885, Hopkins (according to Patmore) 'said with a grave look, "That's telling secrets"'. The theme of the work had already been explored in the three odes *Eros and Psyche*, *De Natura Deorum*, and *Psyche's Discontent*, which, Derek Patmore wrote, 'certainly dared to describe feelings and emotions that tore the veil away from subjects which Victorian Society considered both "unpleasant" and "unmentionable"'. Shane Leslie said that 'the flaming content of Patmore's *Unknown Eros* left Swinburne panting in his gilded brothel' (Patmore, 196).

Without documentary evidence, but plausibly enough, Derek Patmore writes: 'The austere spirit of Gerard Hopkins recoiled before the passionate heat of such passages as this from the Ode *Eros and Psyche*':

> O, heavenly Lover true,
> Is this thy mouth upon my forehead press'd?
> Are these thine arms about my bosom link'd?
> Where join two hearts, for juncture more distinct?
> By thee and by my maiden zone caress'd
> . . . .
> Kiss me again, and clasp me round the heart,
> Till fill'd with thee am I,
> As the cocoon is with the butterfly!

And Derek Patmore comments that:

> to such a man there was something disturbing and almost shocking about the pagan delight with which Patmore exalted the human body. The difference between them was that whilst Hopkins considered his religious vocation more important than his poetical genius, Coventry Patmore, like Hopkins's other friend, Robert Bridges, felt that his poetic mission transcended all religious scruples. 'The poet', he says, 'alone has the power of so saying the truth, "which it is not lawful to utter"'. (Patmore, 197–8)

I see no good reason for reconstructing the *Sponsa Dei* episode in terms other than Derek Patmore's.

It is difficult to see how a poet with such strong personal scruples and involved in such a typical late-Victorian dilemma could become, as an epithalamist should, a wholehearted participant in the series of wedding actions and liberal emotions. How could Hopkins hope to relinquish personal control to the sensual indulgence of the epithalamion, passing when it wanted into sexual explicitness, and, without any sense of deviation, into conventional bawdiness? The patron god of epithalamia, as I have said, is Hymen, and the same Greek word represented the virginal membrane.

Nor would the kind of Victorian classical education that Hopkins had undergone, with its repression of sexuality and neutered vocabulary, have encouraged him to sympathise with certain important conventional epithalamic emotions. 'Anthos', the Greek for flower, was also bawdy for the female sexual parts, but does not appear as such in the standard *Greek-English Lexicon* of Dean Liddell and Robert Scott, Master of Balliol when Hopkins was there. The Christian Fathers, wrote Frederic Raphael, 'of whom our pedagogues were the pusillanimous descendants, built their systems on the theology of the Greeks, but (like Plato) they took a shocked view of the Gods . . . . Genial Aphrodite, Sin Herself in Christian eyes, was particularly purged' (Raphael, 928).

Hopkins might in some matters of religious and moral and political scruples be accused of a narrowly Victorian Manicheism, with some passage such as the following as evidence:

> Could I speak too severely of [Greek mythology]? First it is as history untrue. What is untrue history? Nothing and worse than nothing. And that history religion? Still worse. I cannot enter on this consideration without being brought face to face with the great fact of heathenism. . . . For myself literally words fail me to express the loathing and horror with which I think of it and of man setting up the work of his own hands, of that hand within the mind the imagination, for God Almighty who made heaven and earth. Still he might set up beings perfect in their kind. But the Greek gods are rakes, and unnatural rakes. . . . Are the Greek gods majestic, awe inspiring, as Homer that great Greek genius represents them? They are not. The Indian gods are imposing, the Greek are not. Indeed they are not brave, not self controlled, they have no manners, they are not gentlemen and ladies. They clout one another's ears and blubber and bellow. You will say this is Homer's fun, like the miracle-plays of Christendom. Then where is his earnest about them? At their best they remind me of some company of beaux and fashionable world at Bath in its palmy days or Tunbridge Wells or what not. Zeus is like the major in *Pendennis* handsomer and better preserved sitting on Olympus as behind a club-window and watching Danae and other pretty seamstresses cross the street – not to go farther. You will think this is very Philistine and vulgar and be pained. But I am pained. (L2. 146–7)

*   *   *

That passage, with its head-on clash between the classical and Christian worlds, casts severe doubts on Hopkins's ability to sympathise with epithalamic conventions. The potential struggle would be as great as that of the Christian authorities who had to allegorise the epithalamic *Song of Solomon* into unsympathetic Christian contexts before its inclusion in the Bible.

Two possible ways of writing a modern, Christian-era, epithalamion would be either to pretend a non-Christian ethos and write within neo-classical conventions, as Spenser did in the main, or, as a Christian, to use the pastoral as an allegory and employ the tradition of Christian natural science. And Hopkins himself continues the same letter to Dixon on Greek mythology by suggesting that it could be put to allegorical use in modern literature:

But I grant that the Greek mythology is very susceptible of fine treatment, allegorical treatment for instance, and so treated gives rise to the most beautiful results. No wonder: the moral evil is got rid of and the pure art, morally neutral and artistically so rich, remains and can be even turned to moral uses. (L2. 147)

The main difficulty was that of the two different but coincident plots, describing events and yet having their application, their real significance, present on another plane at the same time. In spite of some effort to get the poem within this tradition, by inventing hearers and characters, Hopkins is fundamentally at a fatal distance from the actual wedding, both by the allegory, and by his puritanical separation of the poet from the partaker. There is a subsequent damaging lack of dramatic power. I shall try to pinpoint some of the difficulties.

Bound by his own priestly profession, as well as by his scruples, Hopkins considers himself forced to make the marriage a Christian one, although epithalamic conventions are intimately bound up with pagan rites. His consciousness of the classical world as basically pagan, and therefore morally repulsive, cannot but severely undermine the poem. As a result he substitutes 'hearer' for the traditional 'Hymen', in the first line, and so makes the important initial invocation almost meaningless. Hymen's role would be immediately obvious, while the 'hearer' is shadowy, and instead of providing a framework for the ensuing poem provides a puzzling irrelevancy. Then there is a gap between 'hear' and what is heard – the shout in line 8: Hopkins seems to forget what the hearer has to hear while he is concentrating on the scenery and losing himself in it. As happens in several of his poems, Hopkins's trust, similar to that of Ruskin's when he put a passage of Wordsworth's *The Excursion* on the title-page of each volume of *Modern Painters*, that the beauty of the natural world in telling its own story leads automatically to a God-involved conclusion, betrays him. The landscape descriptions in the poem have no force of plot behind them, in spite of the many verbs of action. They remain a picturesque romantic vision of Arcadia.

The 'virgin scene' of Wordsworth's 'Nutting' can be compared, with its protagonist's journey 'toward some far-distant wood', its 'fairy water-breaks', bower and water freshness; a pre-Fall idyll in Wordsworth, pre-marriage in Hopkins. Wordsworth's poem describes an actual experience in its entirety, while Hopkins is working something out and does not know how it will end. Hopkins's is a scene of nature notes, but without imaginative power given to the protagonist to carry the plot through and out of that scene, whereas Wordsworth's poem is based on a plot, with the natural scene forming part of that plot.

The traditional dramatic character of Hopkins's narrator is never established, while the hearer is unidentified and vague. Everard and Amy are not mentioned or even implied until the application is started. The bather is again a rootless person without a definite role.

The poem does not seem to be leading towards any praise of the bride and groom, but of the marriage state in general. There is no sense of this particular marriage, nor events of the wedding day. The occasion is not at hand, as it should be, and Hopkins seems to have little sense of urgency or involvement. He is instead trying to be a priest in a poem, and justifying the Christian marriage state, working out arguments unnecessary and irrelevant to the bridal couple.

Other reasons prevented Hopkins from wholehearted participation in the poem. In epithalamia the ceremony and the poem cannot be separated, but Gerard has no possibility of taking part in the wedding itself; an identification between the reality and art becomes even less possible when the ceremony is held in another country, across the water, and according to Christian rites unacceptable to him or his Church. Then Everard is the brother that Hopkins knew least – sixteen years' difference between them, with next to no contact.

As well as having these disadvantages, Hopkins was writing a poem of joy in Dublin, where he could not write joyous poems. This was a special occasion, with a set time limit – set by the day of the wedding. Here was his opportunity to give Everard a personal wedding gift. The time was presented to him when his over-scrupulous conscience could not be upset by writing a poem: invigilation over an examination for (probably) three hours, with normal work forbidden. Because he is in museless Dublin and within doors (the Great Hall in Earlsfort Terrace was without views, its windows being too high to see out of), there is no alternative to using the poetic store in his memory of Stonyhurst images and the visits of Cyril and Arthur Hopkins about the times of *their* weddings. So basically it is a poem of past impressions pasted together. Apart from these difficulties, as soon as this limited period was up he would have the dreaded exam papers to mark. The poem was fated not to be completed.

As an epithalamion it is unsuccessful, and can only be appreciated as a pastoral scene. Even then, the wonderful descriptions of the wood-bower, trees, and river water are interrupted, once the stranger starts stripping to bathe, by unfortunate poeticisings of banal referends: 'down he dings', 'his bleached both and woolwoven wear', 'careless these in coloured wisp'. It is not just a matter of the stranger miraculously enabled to take his trousers off before his boots.

But 'Hark, hearer' is a reminder that Hopkins wanted his poetry recited aloud, not read silently, and this poem can be transformed by an uninhibited declamation into an unrivalled scene. When heard, the glories of his pastoral journals, the imagery and observations of which are frequently echoed in this poem, are transformed into another dimension by the poetic rhetoric and rhythms, sound manipulation, and other devices. There is remarkable magic in the river description: 'where a candycoloured, where a gluegold-brown/ Marbled river, boisterously beautiful, between/ Roots and rocks is danced and dandled, all in froth and waterblowballs, down'; and also in the wood:

> . . . silk-beech, scrolled ash, packed sycamore, wild wychelm, hornbeam
>   fretty overstood
> By. Rafts and rafts of flake leaves light, dealt so, painted on the air,
> Hang as still as hawk or hawkmoth, as the stars or as the angels there,
> Like the thing that never knew the earth, never off roots
> Rose.

This transformation has another dimension, though, joy turning to poignancy if we picture the poet in his workshop of an exam hall, knowing that in a few hours he would have to mark those dreaded and unending scripts.

*   *   *

As relief from yet another tragic episode in Hopkins's Dublin life, one can turn to a little-known modern dialogue, written by Philip Dacey with humour and knowledge of Hopkins, 'Gerard Manley Hopkins meets Walt Whitman in Heaven'. It has been decreed that the two poets spend eternity in their heaven, a 'swimming hole', surrounded by naked young men, a scene much like the one in the epithalamion.'Whitman' comments:

> You're the first pagan Jesuit
> I've ever met. My pleasure.
> No wonder that poem never saw
> Completion. To turn material like that
> Into a wedding gift would require
> A miracle. You're not St Hopkins
> Are you, yet? Unless a couple
> Of the swimming boys wed.

Dacey gives here an alternative, hidden reason for the poem's unfinished state – the inability of Hopkins's nature to empathise with a conventionally heterosexual marriage. It is sometimes thought that when Hopkins said that, in spite of Whitman being 'a very great scoundrel', he 'always knew in my heart Walt Whitman's mind to be more like my own than any other man's living' (LI. 155), he was referring to their shared homosexuality. Whether that is so or not, Dacey's recognition of their probable joint exultation in an idealised male bathing scene is perceptive, particularly as Hopkins would never give a more precise explanation of the affinity he perceived. It certainly gives another plausible, if furtive, reason for the dichotomy readers commonly feel between Hopkins's exultation and the poem's lame tailing off.

Chapter Eleven

TOM, DICK, AND HARRY

-->-<+-

Then in comes both Tom and Dick
With their pitchforks and their rakes
'The Merry Haymakers', ballad, 1695

Tom, Dick, and Harry were three fine men;
But we'll ne'er look on their likes again.
Traditional ballad

In December 1886 Hopkins had at last finished 'Spelt from Sibyl's Leaves' and sent it to Bridges, and at the New Year, staying with Miss Cassidy at Monasterevin, had begun his poem in Gray's elegy metre. On 17 February he wrote to Bridges that 'Tomorrow morning I shall have been three years in Ireland, three hard wearying wasting wasted years.' During that time he had 'done God's will . . . and many many examination papers.' He had become increasingly conscious that he should be advancing his subject by writing learned papers or longer studies, but 'I see that I cannot get on, that I shall be even less able hereafter than now'. He should, he thought, have been able to 'throw myself cheerfully into my day's work', but he could not: he was 'in a prostration'. He needed only one thing – 'a working health, a working strength' (LI. 250–1).

But his letters are seldom without lighter moments and his kaleidoscopic mind quickly moves on to another subject. He had perceptively realised some time ago that the Victorian age was the great age of the novel, and that the modern novel was equivalent in its 'abundance of genius' to Elizabethan drama. Constantly he tried to rouse Bridges's interest in his favourites – Stevenson, Hardy, and Blackmore – and in February 1887 reported that having read through *Wives and Daughters* by Mrs Gaskell he could say 'if that is not a good book I do not know what a good book is' (LI. 251).

His summer holidays that year were, as usual, 'broken' by the mountains of examination scripts: 'all July no doubt will be littered with papers and I am afraid more than July' (L3. 181). But in September he had been on holiday at Loyola House, Dromore, County Down, eighty-six miles from Dublin, on the Belfast road. It had once belonged to Bishop Percy (celebrated for his *Reliques of Ancient English Poetry*), and now housed a community of about thirty Jesuits, most of whom were novices. The house was sufficiently far away from Dublin and its daily duties, constant political talk, and Irish news, for Hopkins to feel able to relax and open his mind to new subjects. He read a novel which happened to be in his bedroom, *Christie Johnstone*, by Charles Reade. It contained 'some nonsense but more sense; enough wit, too much rollick; a somewhat slipshod brilliancy; an overboisterous manliness; but a true mastery of the proper gifts of a romancer . . . It would be worth while reading all that Charles Reade has written' (LI. 261–2).

In a letter soon after he enthused to Bridges over wordpainting in modern novels: 'It is in modern novels that wordpainting most abounds and now the fashion is to be so very subtle and advanced as to despise wordpainting'. Wordpainting was 'in the verbal arts, the great success of our day. . . . Wordpainting is in our age a real mastery and the second rate men of this age often beat at it the first rate of past ages' (LI. 267). But over the same period that he had been reading and praising modern novels he had been creating his own wordpainting – in verse, the most intensive wordpainting he ever composed. In September 1887, he was 'in pretty good spirits', had been touching up some old sonnets ('No worst' and '[Carrion Comfort]'), and within a few days at Dromore had 'done the whole of one, I hope, very good one and most of another'. Both poems show that Hopkins's mind was – temporarily – free from the strains of Irish politics (he had reported to his mother back in March that 'Ireland is outwardly pretty quiet, except where evictions are attempted'). The second one was ten lines of 'Tom's Garland', and the completed one was 'a direct picture of a ploughman, without afterthought'.

'Harry Ploughman' puzzles most readers because the violence of its individual parts causes the poem to disintegrate into separate details; it is unique in Hopkins's work for its lack of the conventional unities of moral/ lesson and narrative plot. The poem can only make sense if it is looked at (or, preferably, listened to) as a wordpainting, as Hopkins demanded: 'I want Harry Ploughman to be a vivid figure before the mind's eye; if he is not that the sonnet fails' (LI. 265).

Following John Ruskin's lead, Hopkins's early journals had developed nature descriptions beyond the static and visual qualities of painting, such as colour, into the more tense and active drama of light-and-shade contrast, together with texture and movements, etched by unique vocabulary. Then in Wales these new-found principles had burst into and transformed Hopkins's poetry, key words being 'pied' and 'dappled', and 'Pied Beauty' the poem expressing his new aesthetic. Mobile and complexly visual qualities of items in the natural scene are perceived by the extraordinarily aware poet in their most significant and characteristic parts and movements – he 'catches' them and describes these inscapes in his new wordpainting vocabulary.

The emphasis is more on the act of seeing than on the objects seen. Artistic rather than argumentative unity is the artist's goal: shape, texture, and movement are more important than precise meaning. By the time he was composing 'Harry Ploughman', Hopkins felt that his word-hoard used to inscape nature, his store of vocabulary treasured for its suggestive power and reverberations, could be transferred by poetic metaphor to anything he wished. And so, although the whole poem describes the ploughman, there is a key tension between the octave's infusion with cloudscape and the sestet's with liquid.

For example, 'broth', which had been used in his journal long ago in a description of a whirlpool, is now used to describe the hair, the frothy, cloudlike down on Harry's arm (the hairs do not appear to be rooted in or to rise vertically from the arm, but seem to form a separate thick covering parallel to the arm). Similarly, 'rope', which Hopkins had used for clouds and waterfalls, could suit Harry's thighs. 'Curded' and 'barrowy', which had both appeared in an early cloudscape of Hopkins's ('Clouds showing beautiful and rare curves like curds, comparable to barrows, arranged of course in parallels' [J. 66]) now described muscled limbs: 'each limb's barrowy brawn, his thew/ That onewhere curded'.

In the octave Harry is painted in 'curves, circles, and lines', and soft textures are attributed to 'hard, solid muscles and limbs'. But then in the sestet, the photograph-like stalling of vigorous movement is largely conveyed by 'compressed imagery of wind and liquids':

> Harry's waist is *liquid*; the plough *wallows* (as if in a liquid). His muscles (*thew/ That onewhere curded, onewhere sucked or sank – / Soared or sank*) have the pattern and texture of clouds (which are often *curded* or *curdled*); in places they are sucked in like 'the great limbs of the waterfall in which the water is packed' which are '*tretted* like open sponge . . . where the yeast has supped the texture in big and little holes' (J. 177). Harry's *curls* are *windlaced*, as lightning in the Journal *laces* the clouds, and this implies not only that the wind is swirling *through* the curls but that it has somehow laced them *together*. The *furls* (furrows) 'rhyme' the *curls*; they *curl* over in a curved or semi-circular movement like water shooting out (*with-a-fountain's shining-shot*) from a fountain and dropping back to earth. And the furrows shine, as Hopkins had observed in his Journal: 'On the left, brow of the near hill glistening with very bright newly turned sods' (J. 133). (Milroy, 173–4)

In order to avoid lengthy modifying phrases, which would divide simultaneous actions into several successive parts, in 'Harry Ploughman' Hopkins substituted compressing and compounding devices for normal syntax. As Milroy shows (219–20), 'with-a-fountain's shining-shot' is invented to describe 'the *furls* (furrows) along which Harry's feet (*broad in bluff hide*) race with the plough are *shot with the shining of a fountain*'; by this means 'the quick movements, the texture, sheen and shape of the furrows' are inscaped, all these many instantaneous effects are 'perceived . . . in a unity'. The syntactic distinction between subject, verb, and object, which disunifies a unified action, is thus overridden. And what Hopkins perceived as a 'desperate deed', interrupting the word 'windlaced', so that it became 'wind-lilylocks-laced' is justified, as Milroy says, by comparing 'See his lilylocks windlaced' ('laced by the wind'), thus destroying 'the unity of this small inscape, which suggests the perceived inseparability of the wind and the locks. . . . Objects and motion are all one'.

Two further devices which are intended to add to the power of the picture are firstly, what Milroy calls (225) the 'eternal truth' usage of the present tense throughout the poem, suggesting, as in a painting, that the description is of something permanent and timeless. Not so indisputably successful is the vowel elision of 'S cheek crimsons', where Hopkins is too pedantically attempting to incorporate the force of common speech.

* * *

The total lack of ethical concerns in 'Harry Ploughman' is in the interest of artistic, wordpainterly qualities. I should add that Hopkins's guilt at not providing a non-artistic unifying device was the probable cause of his slapping on the unfortunate military squad imagery of 'one crew, fall to;/ Stand at stress', 'finds his, as at a rollcall, rank', and 'sinew-service'. 'Stand at stress' (based on the army squad's traditional shouted order 'Stand at ease!') takes us into the jingoistic, vicariously military world of Hopkins's recruiting song for soldiers, 'What shall I do?'.

* * *

It is commonly charged that Harry is not a human being but a painting, and it is true that Hopkins's inscape-vocabulary has limits. It can successfully be applied to nature, but, except in certain situations of mental stress (such as in the desolate sonnets), does not comprehend human beings. And so when his poetry deals with humans, the total effect can seem forced and artificial, even when the language is strongly individual. The effect on many readers is incomprehensibility, even after several readings. Hopkins lacked large areas of human experience (he has been characterised as 'a man of the cloister'), and the vocabulary to deal with them. Even though it has several technical similarities with 'Harry Ploughman', its companion-piece, 'Tom's Garland' is an example of a theme for which his narrow genius was unsuited.

* * *

By Christmas 1887 Hopkins had finished writing 'Tom's Garland', the second of his two Dromore sonnets. The degree of removal from thoughts of Ireland afforded to Hopkins by Bishop Percy's house at Dromore, perhaps associated with the largeness of the grounds and its English layout and memory of Percy's part in English literary culture, is shown in both poems by their English subject matter and focus: it is as though Hopkins, body and mind, had never left England. Regarding their style they are unique and yet closely related. However, the ploughman poem displays freedoms and self-indulgence – in unusual choice of imagery, its 'burden-lines' and the possible use of a chorus to recite them, its 'very heavily loaded sprung-rhythm', its breezy lack of guard; 'Tom's Garland', on the other hand, heavily contrasts with its constantly puzzling ellipses, its unreal characters, and the doubts it casts over Hopkins's political knowledge and anachronistic philosophy, his right and competence to pronounce so confidently and in such caricature terms on such matters.

I know of only one person who was able to understand this poem without using Hopkins's 'crib', and whether one agrees with the principle or not it has, I think, to accompany the poem. Hopkins himself was aware of the problem and issues, and concluded (writing on 'Harry Ploughman') that 'it would be an immense advance . . . to distinguish the subject, verb, object, and in general to express the construction to the eye'. But it would not do for his poems: it would seem 'a confession of unintelligibility'. On the other hand, 'my meaning surely *ought* to appear of itself'. He concluded, reluctantly, that he would have to 'prefix short prose *arguments* to some of my pieces', even though they would expose him to 'carping'. Most poems 'should be at once intelligible; but every-thing need not and cannot be.' If it were possible to 'express a sub[t]le and recondite thought on a subtle and recondite subject in a subtle and recondite way and with great felicity and perfection', then something would have to be sacrificed, and that would probably be immediate intelligibility. It did not seem to him sufficient objection if the argument were longer than the poem (LI. 265–6).

Dixon was bewildered by 'Tom's Garland' and wrote to Bridges asking his help; but Bridges was no more capable of understanding it and asked Hopkins to explain. On 10 February 1888 Hopkins wrote back: 'I laughed outright and often, but very sardonically, to think you and the Canon could not construe my last sonnet; that he had to write to you for a crib'. It was plain that he had reached the limit in obscurity if neither of his poet-friends could understand the poem. Nevertheless, he persisted, if it were read out dramatically the qualities which appeared strange when it was read silently would seem coherent and effective. Reluctantly he provided the crib.

'The well ordered human society [or 'commonwealth'] is like one man; a body with many members and each its function; some higher, some lower, but all honourable', Hopkins wrote. The king or queen represents the head, 'who has no superior but God and from heaven receives his or her authority'. At the lowest limit of society is the labourer, representing the foot of the body politic, wearing boots which are 'garlanded' with hobnails, symbolising his relationship with the ground; for 'it is navvies . . . who . . . mainly trench, tunnel, blast, and in other ways disfigure, "mammock" the earth and, on a small scale, singly, and superficially stamp it with their footprints'. The navvy's place is the lowest in the commonwealth, but 'this place still shares the common honour, and if it wants one advantage, glory of public fame, makes up for it by another, ease of mind, absence of care'.

Then Hopkins described the scene of the poem: 'at evening, when they are giving over work and one after another pile their picks, with which they earn their living, and swing off home, knocking sparks out of mother earth', not now with picks but with the striking of their boots. Their working day over, they 'take all easy', and 'so to supper and bed'. There follows what Hopkins calls 'a violent but effective hyperbaton or suspension' (the bracketed part in lines 5 to 8), 'in which the action of the mind mimics that of the labourer – surveys his lot, low but free from care; then by a sudden strong act throws it over the shoulder or tosses it away as a light matter'. The character of Hopkins then enters the poem, 'indignant with the fools of Radical Levellers'. But then a further thought strikes him: 'this is all very well for those who are in, however low in, the Commonwealth and share in any way the Common weal; but that the curse of our times is that many do not share it, that they are outcasts from it and have neither security nor splendour; that they share care with the high and obscurity with the low, but wealth or comfort with neither'. Then in the final couplet comes the narrator's conclusion: 'this state of things, I say, is the origin of Loafers, Tramps, Cornerboys, Roughs, Socialists and other pests of society' (LI. 272–4).

* * *

Hopkins's social thinking had not undergone much change since 1865, the year when he had copied into his commonplace book (Bodleian MS. Eng.poet.e.190, fol. 54) Ford Madox Brown's sonnet 'Work', written as an appendage to and description of his famous painting, also called 'Work'. Brown and Hopkins were taking part in the nineteenth-century debate on Work and Labour, Carlyle being the well-worn common source of both sonnets' advocacy of work as a panacea. The Carlyle factor is made explicit on the right of the painting, where there is a portrait of the sage, together with one of F. D. Maurice, another prominent participator in the Work debate. When the painting 'Work' and 'Tom's Garland' are compared, it can be seen that Hopkins found the seed of his poem in Brown's painting.

For two years in the 1850s Ford Madox Brown had lived and worked in Hampstead, while Hopkins was also living there. He became something of a local artist, painting landscapes of places well known to Hopkins: 'An English Autumn Afternoon', for instance, gives a good idea of Hampstead as it was when Hopkins first lived there. His most detailed picture of the Hampstead locale was the arched oil painting, 'Work', now in the City Art Gallery, Manchester. The background to 'Work' was painted in summer 1852 on a spot by a raised group of houses, now called 'The Mount', on the west side of Heath Street, a few minutes' walk from Oak Hill, where the Hopkins family lived. The view is still recognisable today, not far from the Heath. It is likely that the eight-year-old Gerard Hopkins, newly arrived in Hampstead, would have watched what must have been a prominent village spectacle during that summer, when, Brown wrote in his diary, he was 'painting there all day for two months', working away next to 'extensive excavations, connected with the supply of water, [which] were going on in the neighbourhood'. Brown noted the encouragement offered him by local small boys. 'Work' was completed in 1862, and was then retouched for its first public exhibition in Piccadilly, London, in 1865, the year that Hopkins, in London for the university vacations, copied the sonnet.

*   *   *

Hopkins would have had a copy of the exhibition catalogue in which Brown gave a long account of the painting. These are extracts:

Seeing and studying daily as I did the British excavator, or <u>navvy</u>, as he designated himself, in the full swing of his activity (with his manly and picturesque costume) . . . it appeared to me that he was at least as worthy of the powers of an English painter as the fisherman of the Adriatic, the peasant of the Campagna, or the Neapolitan lazzarone. Gradually this idea developed itself into that of <u>Work</u> as it now exists, with the British excavator for a central group, as the outward and visible type of <u>Work</u>. Here are presented the young navvy in the pride of manly health and beauty; the strong fully-developed navvy who does his work and loves his beer; the selfish old bachelor navvy, stout of limb, and perhaps a trifle tough in those regions where compassion is said to reside; the navvy of strong animal nature, who, but that he was when young <u>taught</u> to work at useful work, might even now be working at the <u>useless crank</u>. Then Paddy with his larry and his pipe in his mouth. The young navvy who occupies the place of hero in this group, and in the picture, stands on what is termed a landing-stage, a platform placed half-way down the trench; two men from beneath shovel the earth up to him as he shovels it on to the pile outside. Next in value of significance to these is the ragged wretch who has never been <u>taught</u> to <u>work</u>; with his restless, gleaming eyes he doubts and despairs of every one . . .

. . . In the very opposite scale from the man who can't work, at the furthest corner of the picture, are two men who appear as having nothing to do. These are the brain-workers [Carlyle and Maurice], who, seeming to be idle, work, and are the cause of well-ordained work and happiness in others – sages, such as in ancient Greece published their opinions in the market square. (Clayre, 316–19)

The similarities between this account of the painting 'Work' and Hopkins's poem are remarkable. The choice of an almost Stakhanovite navvy as the central example of a workman, and the use of the word 'navvy' occur in both 'Tom's Garland' and Brown's prose account; the artistic and symbolic function of Brown's navvy (who is blatantly British, like Hopkins's), 'as the outward and visible type of <u>Work</u>' is precisely the same as Hopkins's. Hopkins in fact uses, in the 'crib' letter he wrote to Bridges, the similar phrase 'visible badge' when he is explaining the outward symbols by which he conveys his inner meanings. Brown's prose description of his navvy closely resembles the navvy in 'Tom's Garland': 'Here are presented the young navvy in the pride of manly health and beauty; the strong fully-developed navvy who does his work and loves his beer.' Brown's workman is 'in the full swing of his activity', and Hopkins finds also (in line 8 of the poem) the word 'swings' to be particularly appropriate to his navvy's physical and mental attitude. ('Pile' – in line 2 of the poem – also occurs in both descriptions of the work activity.) The way in which Brown's prose explanation introduces a companion navvy is noticeable: 'Then Paddy with his larry . . .'. This resembles the phrase in Hopkins's second line, 'then Tom's fallowbootfellow', in that in both instances the peculiar use of 'then' signifies the change of focus in the onlooker's eye from one object to the next.

Other basic similarities include the use in both 'Tom's Garland' and Brown's prose account of the contrast between the two poles in the working world – the navvy, as representative of manual labour, and the brain-worker. The symbolic navvies in both are workers who 'mammock the earth' (in Hopkins's 'crib') or 'shovel the earth' (Brown); they are of strong animal nature but compensatorily defective in subtler qualities: 'treads through, prickproof, thick/ Thousands of thorns, thoughts' ('Tom's Garland', lines 7–8), and 'selfish . . . perhaps a trifle tough in those regions where compassion is said to reside' (Brown).

The heroic (albeit defective) working navvies in both are contrasted with the workless, who are characterised similarly by Brown and Hopkins: 'the ragged wretch who has never been <u>taught</u> to <u>work</u>; with his restless, gleaming eyes he doubts and despairs of every one'. Later in the account Brown calls this wretch 'the Pariah' (that is, socially outcast dog). This can be compared with Hopkins's foreboding of the 'Undenizened' in the closing couplet of his poem: 'This, by Despair, bred Hangdog dull; by Rage,/ Manwolf, worse; and their packs infest the age'. 'Hangdog' and 'Pariah' are similarly capitalised.

* * *

The overall similarity is more remarkable when we compare the painting 'Work' and the poem 'Tom's Garland'. Both works attempt to combine detailed observant description in a realistic scene with far-reaching symbols, in order to convey with personal feeling a complex social message. Both artists are unable to express straightforwardly all their aims; nor can they combine successfully widely differing types of material within the limits of their art forms; and therefore, realising the gap between aim and effect, are forced to attach extra-artistic guides, or 'cribs'.

Hopkins's curious repetition of 'Tom' (seven times in lines 1 to 6) has often been noted, but not satisfactorily explained. It gives a ghostly effect, as though the narrative voice of the poem's opening were that of a man at a window commenting on what is happening outside, while he himself is immobile except for his mind, with some undefined barrier set between the active life he describes and the passive one he lives. There are certain similarities with the narrative voice in other poems Hopkins wrote in the 1880s, such as 'Spring and Fall' and 'On the Portrait of Two Beautiful Young People'. But in this dramatic posture in 'Tom's Garland' he resembles even more both the voice of Brown's catalogue commentary on his painting (see particularly the passage starting 'Here are presented . . .'), and also the role Brown gives to the Carlyle and Maurice figures in the painting. These two figures, who appear as a single unit, play the role of intermediary between the onlooker of the picture and what is taking place within it, turning the picture into a lesson. The Maurice figure looks at the action in the painting, and the Carlyle figure looks at the audience, plainly aware of them; but both heads stem from what is in effect the same physical body, so closely together are they standing – Brown's original intention was to have only one figure. Both have contradictory dual roles, as fictional characters in the painting and participants in its 'plot', and also as real-life people. Like some flirtatious nude in a Renaissance picture, the Carlyle figure invites the looker-on to admire, enter the painting, and join in, the picture being thus transformed into a moral lesson, a weapon.

It is not just the Victorian theme of honest labour that is being affirmed, but that theme as seen through Carlyle's vision. The sandwich-boards of the men on the right of the painting prescribe votes for 'Bobus', who in Chapter 4 of the Proem to *Past and Present* is a 'Sausage-maker on the great scale', an example of the Victorian bourgeois capitalist. Both Brown and Hopkins are plainly advocating Carlyle's creed in *Past and Present*:

> There is a perennial nobleness, and even sacredness, in Work. Were he never so benighted, forgetful of his high calling, there is always hope in a man that actually and earnestly works: in Idleness alone is there perpetual despair . . . . Consider how, even in the meanest sorts of Labour, the whole soul of a man is composed into a kind of real harmony, the instant he sets himself to work! Doubt, Desire, Sorrow, Remorse, Indignation, Despair itself, all these like helldogs lie beleaguering the soul of the poor dayworker, as of every man: but he bends himself with free valour against his task, and all these are stilled . . . . The man is now a man.

The relationship between Hopkins and Carlyle comes out plainly in this passage, not just in shared thoughts and philosophy, but also in the verbal echoes (and emphatic noun capitalisation) in the second coda of the Hopkins poem: 'This, by Despair, bred Hangdog dull'.

Hopkins's poem and Brown's painting also share shortcomings which originate in Carlyle, particularly their unreal picture of the rewards of physical work, showing the limitations of their own social contacts and experience. Such ignorance of the human effects of the Industrial Revolution became less understandable as the nineteenth century wore on, with the documentary evidence heaping up. Brown's support of Carlyle's doctrines was not total, but Hopkins suggests no such modification of his agreement with Carlyle. The comparatively unmitigated narrowness of Hopkins's dogma is also evident in the way that in the closing couplet of 'Tom's Garland' the narrator's vehement response to the results of unemployment seems to express emotional and sensuous repulsion from the human victims themselves, rather than rejection of, and disgust at, their plight.

In Brown's painting various printed pieces of political and social propaganda are introduced, from the sandwich-boards in the election procession winding up the Heath Street hill on the right, to the advertising bills pasted on the wall on the left; and more subtly, numerous characters, alone or in a group, represent social types and attitudes, adorned with appropriate symbols. Hopkins's poem also contains a variety of representative types in the Work debate, with their own symbols. Some are straightforward characters in the scene – Tom and Dick; then there are unindividualised groups representing specific qualities, as the Hangdogs and Manwolves (lines 19 and 20): participants in starring roles, and participants in crowds. But also, as in the painting, there are various means of commenting and types of commentator. After the initial ghostly commentator who describes pictorially the scene and Tom's nature from behind his barrier, a quite different commentator emerges in line 9, whose tone and rhythm of speech are completely novel to the poem – 'Little Í reck ho! lacklevel in, if all had bread'; this conveys the exaggerated rhetoric and staginess of an opiniated character who reacts, rather than a narrator who looks and sees. And in line 10, 'What! Country is honour enough in all us' confirms this character as a Conservative club armchair blusterer, quite unable to control his emotions, let alone guide a reader to a balanced opinion.

Again, a distinctly different character's voice puts over the last nine lines, dealing with the unemployed, and starting with 'But nő way sped' in line 12; it is that of a worried and socially concerned commentator, who is finally unable to control his emotions. But those emotions are not bluffly dismissive, like those of the Conservative blusterer: rather are they vehemently pointed. There are then at least these three quite different but definite narrative voices, and perhaps others half hidden (what is the dramatic source of the parenthesis about Tom's mind in lines 5–8, for instance?).

*　*　*

Both Brown and Hopkins were trying to squash within a precisely limited art form unsuitable material, which was both expansive and recalcitrant. Brown tries to force an extraordinary and impossible amount of meaning into every painted figure, by means of typification and symbolism, but it is not clear from the sole evidence of the painting what his symbols represent. Compared with those of the more dogmatic Middle Ages, symbols and types had not only less currency in the nineteenth century but also less validity. Some form of verbalisation, with its potentially much greater powers of expressing complexity and fluidity seems more likely to represent adequately the nineteenth-century experience than the unalterably single image of visual art. Brown wanted to express argument, the process of moving from one position to another, the natural medium for which is the sentence containing not just a subject but also its predicate, in a form which also demonstrates the connecting process. Above all, the canvas is too full of undifferentiated items of interest for the mind of the onlooker to feel comfortably aware of what the artist intends it to do. The unity of Brown's prose explanation is at odds with the reactions of the onlooker to the painting itself.

That Hopkins was aware of a similar possible disparity between amount of material and capacity of the chosen art form is evident from his tacking on to the conventional sonnet length the two-part coda of lines 15–20. This can be justified in one way by arguing that the extraneous part of the sonnet is taken up with the unemployed, those left over from the main, working, body of the commonwealth; the form of 'Tom's Garland' demonstrates that the third group, of unattached people, are 'undenizened' and 'beyond bound'. What is not so apt, however, is Hopkins's attempt to put over arguments at the same time as making the particles of that argument alive to the mind's eye. And so, apart from the inappropriately symbolic word in line 1, 'garlanded', the first eight lines become a lovingly fashioned portrait of an actual scene. After this comes the speaker of 'Commonweal . . . in all us', which is harmfully different in nature, being a combination of implied character sketch and dogmatic opinion. Then, uneasily, the reactionary, simplistic speaker changes style without warning, into the symbolic language of head and foot (in lines 10–12), the connection with the foot-garland of line 1 being awkwardly made, and leaving the reader bewildered as to what precisely are the continuous lines of communication in the poem. The poet wants to make the argument, but temperamentally and artistically he prefers to put a lot of effort into avoiding precisely those grammatical parts which would best convey the argument. In the interest of thick texture, for example, he composes 'But nő way sped' in line 12, which is incomprehensible as argument, unless by some other means the reader fills in the missing parts of speech; and to do that would, ironically, destroy, as Hopkins said, the very poetical quality at which he was aiming.

Like Brown also, Hopkins is not able to combine symbols with realism. His 'crib' letter shows how comparatively simplistic are the poem's symbols; but the poem makes them and their purpose obscure. They become meaningless shorthand. Again, like Brown's, Hopkins's symbols are not just simple things inefficiently made obscure, but also are suspiciously outdated as to their validity. Both Brown and Hopkins are attempting an argument they were incapable of putting over in their chosen art form, and on a subject in which they were insufficiently learned.

*   *   *

One noticeable difference needs to be commented on, however. Although Hopkins wrote 'Tom's Garland' while he was living in Ireland, he emphasises by their names the Englishness of Tom and Dick. This is despite the fact that Brown had realistically introduced elements of Irish immigrant labour into 'Work'. It is unlikely that there would be any English navvies in Ireland, even less likely in the small town of Dromore, where the poem was written. It is remarkable how before he came to Ireland a large part of Hopkins's poetry refers to a specific place, Welsh, Scottish, or English, according to where he was living ('Penmaen Pool', 'The Silver Jubilee', 'In the Valley of the Elwy', 'The Loss of the Eurydice', 'Binsey Poplars' and 'Duns Scotus's Oxford', 'Inversnaid', and 'Ribblesdale', for example); whereas in Ireland, apart from the reference 'I am in Ireland now' in 'To seem the stranger', the description of the river Barrow in 'On the Portrait of Two Beautiful Young People', and the odd borrowing of a dialect word ('disremember' in 'Spelt from Sibyl's Leaves'), Hopkins avoids reference to the country. The avoidance in 'Tom's Garland' glares.

It is instructive to compare his well-known, much earlier (2 August 1871) letter to Bridges:

> I am afraid some great revolution is not far off. Horrible to say, in a manner I am a Communist [but in an 1874 letter he says: 'I have little reason to be red: it was the red Commune that murdered five of our Fathers lately' (LI. 29)]. Their ideal bating some things is nobler than that professed by any secular statesman I know of . . . Besides it is just. – I do not mean the means of getting to it are. But it is a dreadful thing for the greatest and most necessary part of a very rich nation to live a hard life without dignity, knowledge, comforts, delight, or hopes in the midst of plenty – which plenty they make. . . . What has the old civilisation done for them? . . . They got none of the spoils, they came in for nothing but harm from it . . . . England has grown hugely wealthy but this wealth has not reached the working classes [cf. 'gold go garlanded/ With, perilous, O nó']; I expect it has made their condition worse. (LI. 27–8)

'Tom's Garland' shows Hopkins apparently ignorant of contemporary radical social theories, of the constant flow of documentary evidence of poor working-class conditions, and even of the new Toryisms of the Primrose League and the Young England movement, besides the more generalised social writing of the established sages, such as Ruskin. In the 1880s, society as a whole was becoming interested in learning of the conditions of the 'submerged' classes. The Roman Catholic church was particularly concerned with the state of the poor because its proportion of working-class adherents to middle and upper classes was much larger than that of other churches in Britain, and church-going, being obligatory, was far commoner among the Catholic working class than among working-class Protestants. Catholic attitudes ranged from that of a writer in the *Dublin Review* who declared that 'inequality was a law more universal than gravity, that true Christians who suffered would always remember that Christ suffered far more, and that the hope of immortality was the one sure protection against revolutionary violence' (Vaughan, 335–51), to the calculated sympathy of Cardinal Manning:

> The public feeling of the country is not and never will be with either Anglicanism or Dissent. It is not irreligious, the leaders of the Labour Unions are religious men; but its Unionism and public action is outside of all religion. It therefore

is ready to listen and even to be led by a Catholic, if only he has their confidence [Manning himself helped settle disputes in London docks]; and that confidence is created by what we *are* chiefly, and by what we *do* in sympathy with the people. (Purcell, 2. 637)

Hopkins's ideal of a commonwealth is shown primarily in his sermons. One note, 'De Regno Christi' (s. 165–6), connects Hopkins's ideas of the social contract which should exist between a king and his subjects and the relationship between God and men: 'God first entered into relations . . . with men in Adam and a commonweal arose – with its sovereign and one subject . . . This commonweal may be looked on as not only a polity of sovereign and subject but also in the light of property, where God is the landlord, man the tenant. . . . Life will be a lease, with its terms; breaches of the divine law will be encroachment on the landlord's or on a fellow tenant's right'. When to Hopkins's willingness to jump into the deeply complex and distressing social debates of the 1880s, armed only with a superficial knowledge of Carlyle and, as his letter implies, outdated orthodoxies from Plato, St Paul, and Hobbes, combined with strong, fastidiously conservative reactions against social levelling and disorder, are added the implications of this priestly moral dictate, I find the resulting picture frightening, in what can be inferred of Hopkins's attitude towards both the English working classes and the struggles of tenants in Ireland.

Chapter Twelve

SOLDIERING

->-<-

M ost visitors to Saint Beuno's, the college in North Wales where
Hopkins had spent three years in the 1870s studying theology, consider
its most prominent architectural features not 'a sort of farmyard and medley of
ricks and roofs and dovecots', as Hopkins characterised it, but a squat, defiant
tower at its north-west corner, with a parapet of arrow-slits, and, as kitchen
entrance, an archway protected by a huge, but theatrically flimsy wooden
portcullis. St Beuno's is situated near Offa's Dyke, in traditional Anglo-
Welsh border-raid countryside, and its architect, Joseph Hansom, probably
intended a quasi-belligerent joke. But from its foundation by a former soldier,
St Ignatius Loyola, the Society of Jesus had extensively used military symbolism
and ideals, with a General in command of his Company, and 'soldiers' a common
description of its professional religious fathers and brothers. The Society was
an army of soldiers fighting a never-ending war against the forces of Satan.

From its early history of exile, persecution, and suspicion the Society had
been conscious of enemies. Seated at supper every night Hopkins heard a
reading from the 'Menology', a history of the Society's early struggles against
persecution. From 1848, the year of European revolutions, the English Province
had constantly received violent news of Jesuits exiled or killed, sometimes
welcoming refugees into their communities. Hopkins had met exiled Spanish
Jesuits, and dramatised their experiences in a letter to his mother; Mrs Hopkins
had also received a bloodthirsty account of the Russian church persecuting a
Catholic sect in Poland:

> Cossacks are sent into the village, the peasantry are driven by the knout to the
> Church, when they refuse they are scourged to blood, then put into the
> hospital till their wounds are healed sufficiently for them to be flogged again.
> Some have died under the lash. . . . In one village the people being brought to
> the altar and refusing to communicate, their mouths were forced open with
> the sword and the Precious Blood poured down. (L3. 133)

Hopkins had been educated in militarist sentiments. His classical training
at Highgate School, where he drew up remarkably fine plans of the battle of
Naupactus, from Thucydides' description, and at Balliol College, Oxford, had
consisted partly of delving into primitive societies to whom war was a natural
state, and whose literature was largely concerned with heroic warfare. Warfare

was associated with glory and admirable self-sacrifice, rather than with pity and reaction against the arbitrariness of violence and the illiberality of militarism.

During his annual retreat at Clongowes Wood College in August 1885 Hopkins had written the poem known as '(The Soldier)', with military imagery and Christ compared to a soldier. And he often referred in his sermons to the Ignatian analogy between Christ, the spiritual king, and a great temporal king: 'Our Lord Jesus Christ . . . is our hero . . . of whom it is written he went forth conquering and to conquer.' The whole of a scrap of sermon in 1879 had been an extended metaphor of the battle between God and the Devil: 'Nobility of this warfare . . . Choirs of angels, regiments with officers, ranks, discipline, subordination . . . Armour of God . . . As we are soldiers earnestness means the same things, ready obedience to our Captain Christ' (s. 234).

In a changing world the army seemed to many Victorians one of the main guardians of the national ethos, helping to preserve manly and gentlemanly qualities. Its hierarchic structure and traditionally clear-cut values appealed to Hopkins, particularly its attachment to heart-stirring qualities of uniforms and trumpets, close male comradeship, courage and loyalty, and military displays. It was in the year that Hardy's *Far from the Madding Crowd* had first pictured the naive Bathsheba Everdene impressed by Sergeant Troy's flashing-sword display that Hopkins had been thrilled by the 'stirring naked-steel lightning' of some cavalry's unsheathing of swords (J. 242).

The vast British Empire depended on its army; imperial and military ideals went together, and Hopkins's naively jingoistic reactions to both were automatic, rather than thoughtful. But the late 1870s and early 1880s had been humiliating for the British army. The troops entering Zululand in 1879 marched no more quickly than Julius Caesar's legions. The price for that war had been high:

> 1,430 Europeans . . . and nearly one thousand Natal Kaffirs had been killed; 1,385 British soldiers had been invalided home; moreover the war had cost the British £5,230,323. In view of the fact that one side had fought with assegais and knobkerries and the other with breach-loading rifles and modern field pieces these losses reflected little credit upon the victors. (Judd, 108)

In April 1880 Gladstone had inflicted a crushing electoral defeat on Disraeli, having campaigned against Disraeli's imperial adventures in the Transvaal, Zululand, and Afghanistan; Gladstone's Liberal administration was strongly against excessive military expenditure, and many regiments sailed for home. But the new administration did not stop British military humiliations, nor the general public dissatisfaction with military policy and planning back home.

Hopkins's military thrills were entirely vicarious, like those of many other literary glorifiers of the Thin Red Line, who would help to create the idealistic innocence with which British officers would sign for Kitchener's training camps in 1914. Like Tennyson's hero in *Maud*, who had cleansed himself of the filthy commercial world by going off to fight in the Crimea, Hopkins saw a clear moral opposition between the clean military ethos and the sordidness of the civilian industrial world.

Hopkins trusted that the army had the power to reassert truer values than had been shown by the newly enlarged democracy, which had put Gladstone back in power. Gladstone had earned Hopkins's bitter moral censure for his attacks on Vaticanism in the mid-1870s, when Hopkins had attacked his policies in a St Beuno's debate. To Hopkins, as to vast numbers of British (including Balliol students, who defaced a wall in their Garden Quadrangle with a slogan still visible a hundred years later), Gladstone had been responsible for one of the most humiliating disasters in military history:

> Do you know and realise what happened at Majuba Hill? 500 British troops after 8 hours' firing, on the Dutch reaching the top, ran without offering hand to hand resistance before, it is said, 80 men. Such a thing was never heard in history. The disgrace in itself is unspeakable. Still it might have been slurred over by pushing on the campaign. But Gladstone was equal to himself and the occasion. He professed that the Queen's honour was by this dishonour vindicated . . . and stamped the memory of Majuba in the minds of all African colonists for ever. (L3. 293)

Hopkins wrote this account in May 1888: the battle had taken place over seven years earlier, in February 1881, yet was still preying on his mind. His strong emotions had falsified the numbers: there had been about 350 British riflemen and about 200 Boers.

Victorian armies often found it difficult to prove their known superiority over their opponents, and the Boer War was an obvious example. Although the Afrikaners looked like tramps, their patched clothes provided excellent camouflage, while the efficient-looking British troops were clothed in bright red jackets, ideal targets for sharpshooters, as well as stiflingly hot on the veldt. The stirring symbol of Hopkins's poem provoked fervour back home, but helped to bring about defeat in the field. This was the last battle in which red coats were worn by British soldiers, although Hopkins either did not know or ignored this fact.

During his five years in Ireland Hopkins was mentally preoccupied with politics more than at any other period of his life, yet more conscious of his inability to take part. His frustration frequently burst out in letters to Bridges, Patmore, and Baillie, particularly, but also occasionally when he wrote to his mother. At the College he was daily confronted with the issue of Irish Home Rule, and placed in an anomalous position – Roman Catholic yet imperialistically pro-British. Nearly all his colleagues and students favoured Home Rule, the only differences between them based on the questions 'by what means?' and 'how soon?'. Hopkins's attitude towards Home Rule has puzzled commentators, and is a complex one. Once it had taken a settled form it was briefly this: England had done great wrong to Ireland in the past, but had long ceased doing it by the 1880s. Now the Irish are an ungovernable race, with no principles of civil allegiance or obedience, but the English attitude towards Ireland is also at fault: the English know and care little about Ireland. The Irish cause is not just, and was always accompanied by crime, but is irresistible and inevitable; the only practical solution is for Ireland to be granted Home Rule, so that further bloodshed may be spared.

So it appeared that Hopkins's head had reluctantly got the better of his heart over Irish politics. And yet he still remained passionately opposed in all ways to the one English politician who could bring about Home Rule, Gladstone, and to all republicans and republican activity. Although an entry in his private spiritual diary shows that he was conscious of his immoderate responses to Gladstone, the G.O.M. was still his bête noire. He 'ought to be beheaded on Tower Hill', Hopkins agreed with Baillie's sentiment in a letter, and he deserved to be known as, not the affectionate Grand Old Man, but the Grand Old Mischief-Maker.

Gladstone seemed to Hopkins to epitomise the wavering and breaking-up qualities of English liberalism, preventing the ideal well-ordered human society. The English race 'gapes on while Gladstone negotiates his surrenders of the Empire', Hopkins wrote of the Prime Minister in 1885 (LI. 210). The great aim of 'Empires before God', he told Patmore, should be 'to be Catholic and draw nations into their Catholicism' (L3. 367) (he had already outlined his ideal society in 'Tom's Garland').

*   *   *

Hopkins's summer holidays in 1887 had been notably unsuccessful. As so often before he had not had a proper rest and was unable to do holiday tasks which should have provided genuine recreation. On his return from London and Haslemere to Dublin in September he had the perennial task of setting new examination papers, as though there had been no break in his mournful routine: '[I] scarcely feel any better for my holiday unhappily', he told Baillie. He also had an attack of eczema, 'a fashionable complaint − to use a consideration which is like the flower upon the nettle'; the college had to buy a special medical soap for his exclusive use. 'For this and other reasons', he wrote to Baillie, 'I could wish I were in the Highlands' (L3. 288), and he recalled his too hurried visit in September 1881, when he had been temporary curate at Glasgow, to Inversnaid, on Loch Lomond, which had made a deep and lasting impression, and where the 'pensive or solemn beauty' of the place had resulted in 'Inversnaid', his only Scottish poem.

His next year's summer holidays were again much needed. At the end of May 1888 he had written to Bridges in a 'sour unspiritual tone' (as he described it), regretting his lack of success in a paper on Sophocles refused by the *Classical Review*, and in failing to complete in time the Epithalamion written for his brother Everard's wedding in April. By the end of June he was working on examination papers all day, and was as usual dragged down in spirits. He wrote to his mother: 'It is great, very great drudgery. I can not of course say it is wholly useless, but I believe that most of it is and that I bear a burden which crushes me and does little to help any good end' (L3. 184–5). His examining, 'the first end I labour for', he saw 'little good in'. Regarding his other university duties, mainly his teaching, 'unless things are to change, I labour for what is worth little'. And 'in doing this almost fruitless work I use up all opportunity of doing any other'. Everything in this letter of 5 July was negative. A major connection with English information and opinion for Hopkins had been *The Times*, and now the college had stopped taking it, a sign of distancing from mainland Britain unthinkable in any Jesuit institution in England. And the weather had been so wet and cold that after leaving off his winter clothing for less than a week he had put it back on. Even staying with his friends the O'Hagans, on the idyllic promontory of Howth, was marred by the bleak situation of their villa residence at Baily, on the edge of Dublin Bay, and by the fact that Aubrey de Vere, the poet and Newman's appointee as Professor of English Literature in the old Catholic University, whom Hopkins had been invited to meet, had been called away suddenly. This disappointed Hopkins, 'till it was mentioned that [de Vere] did not think Dryden a poet'; at that 'I thought and perhaps said, I have not missed much' (L1. 280). Hopkins was unable to write the letter he owed his father, and was too jaded to make any plans for a holiday.

However, he eventually remembered the previous summer's wish for a holiday in the Scottish Highlands, and when his six weeks of examinations were over, at the beginning of August he and Robert Curtis travelled to Scotland. At the Glasgow International Exhibition Hopkins heard an organ recital ending with a chorus by Handel, probably his third favourite composer after Purcell and Weber: 'it was as if a mighty besom swept away so much dust and chaff' (L1. 281). To Hopkins's mind Handel's music asserted a much-needed, cleansing sanity. From Glasgow they probably caught the train which travelled along the north bank of the Firth of Clyde to Helensburgh, and then veered north-east until it met the west bank of Loch Lomond just beyond Ben Lomond, and only a short distance from Inversnaid, on the opposite bank.

Their holiday headquarters was Fort William, capital of the West Highlands, close to the historical battle sites of 1431, 1635, 1688, and the Glencoe massacre of 1692, and centre for walking and climbing excursions among the Ben Nevis range of mountains, the lochs and glens, and the Leanachan, Killiechanate, and Nevis forests. Although they climbed up the Pass of Glencoe, about fifteen miles away, and to the summit of Ben Nevis (only about three miles from Fort William) 'on the most brilliant days', and visited Lochaber, where they were 'happily pestered with no sentiment' (LI. 278), all was not well, in spite of the magnificent scenery. 'The vein urged by any country sight or feeling of freedom or leisure', as a few years ago he had described the proper holiday response which he used to enjoy, was now clogged. In spite of his tourist excursions, or even 'because of them I cannot sleep (which is the very mischief)'; they had no boating or bathing – the suitable nearby spot, on the eastern shore of Loch Linnhe, was too close to the high road for modesty. Several other reasons for the failure of this holiday were offered to Bridges, ranging from the dearth of interesting people to talk to, to the dullness of Curtis, who read until he dozed *Uniplanar Kinematics of Solids and Fluids*, a book in which Hopkins had no interest.

Because of Curtis's self-absorption Hopkins also took to reading, for a shilling bought *The Old Curiosity Shop* and the American R. H. Dana's *Two Years Before the Mast*, and entered their fictional worlds much more completely than he had done his live Highland surroundings. He enjoyed resisting the pathos of Little Nell's death, keeping 'a thoroughly dry eye and unwavering waistcoat', but was more fascinated by Dana's true narrative, its seamanship 'bristling with technicality . . . which I most carefully go over and even enjoy but cannot understand: there are other things though, as a flogging, which is terrible and instructive and it happened – ah, that is the charm and the main point'. The most stirring and strongly expressed emotion aroused in Hopkins on this holiday was this naive and strange-looking reaction to a description of intentionally cruel and violent action in a moral, disciplinarian cause.

Hopkins had been given leave to prolong his holiday but, characteristically, did not find it 'very convenient' to do so, and, besides, 'I scarcely care . . . I am feeling very old and looking very wrinkled and altogether . . .' (LI. 279). Here he broke off his letter to Bridges, depressed at his own cynicism. Nevertheless, two days later he was on the train for Whitby, on the North Yorkshire coast, a favourite holiday spot of the Hopkins family, with whom he spent a further week.

But back at Stephen's Green in the first week of September he was trying to set an MA examination paper, 'in a distress of mind difficult both to understand and to explain'. He was near the end of his tether, he told Bridges:

It seems to me I can not always last like this: in mind or body or both I shall give way – and all I really need is a certain degree of relief and change; but I do not think that what I need I shall get in time to save me.

Then negative thoughts mingled with recalled pictures of melodramatic violence and pathos; he continued his letter:

This reminds me of a shocking thing that has just happened to a young man well known to some of our community. He put his eyes out. He was a medical student and probably understood how to proceed, which was nevertheless barbarously done with a stick and some wire. The eyes were found among nettles in a field. After the deed he made his way to a cottage and said 'I am blind: please let me rest for an hour'.

Hopkins had often been fascinated by gruesome detail, but he then realised he needed to fit it into some line of thought in his letter; however no easy continuity came to him, pen poised over his desk in the fading light, in the upstairs room overlooking Lord Iveagh's formal park of empty walks among dark trees and shrubs. His letter wandered on:

He will not say what was the reason, and this and other circumstances wear the look of sanity; but it is said he was lately subject to delusions. I mention the case because it is extraordinary: suicide is common. (LI. 282)

Some three years earlier, a letter of his had described details of friends' suicides, which he had come to regard as symptomatic of the tragic anxiety of the individual male in modern life, but he did not expound on suicide in this letter. Instead he briefly related the case of another medical student, four years before, a 'manly and winning' Englishman, 'the sweetest mannered boy', who 'went astray', 'made a mess of it', and left for Australia.

The topic of medical students led him to observe 'there are as many doctors as patients in Dublin, a'most'. He needed to tell Bridges of his latest poetic venture, and this suggested the opportunity: he had often thought that by his age a man should be his own doctor, able to prescribe remedies for himself, and his letter continued: 'Feeling the need of something I spent the afternoon in the Phoenix Park, which is large, beautiful, and lonely. It did me good, but my eyes are very very sore'. The park, of nearly two thousand acres, granted to the Dublin people by a lord lieutenant in the mid-eighteenth century, had deep woods and glens with many deer, and ornamental walks, dells, and drives, with the graceful outline of the distant Dublin and Wicklow mountains on its southern side. It was also noted for its military monuments –

the vast Wellington obelisk, over two hundred feet high, its four sides richly adorned with bronze bas-reliefs, depicting the Iron Duke's victories, and the more recent monument to Palmerston's Lord Lieutenant, Lord Carlisle, and the bronze equestrian statue of Lord Gough. There were other reminders of bloodshed: the Vice-Regal Lodge, the summer residence of the British Lord Lieutenant, in sight of which Lord Frederick Cavendish and Mr Burke had been assassinated only six years previously by a gang of Invincibles, and the Fifteen Acres (now in fact comprising about two hundred), Dublin's traditional duelling ground, where Daniel O'Connell had once killed a man, and where now the troops of the Dublin garrison were frequently reviewed, providing extensive military spectacles for admiring crowds. The headquarters and principal barracks of the Royal Irish Constabulary, traditionally considered by republicans to be mere tools of British military-law enforcement, were also situated near the park entrance, where recruits and cadets were drilled and trained to use arms.

Here in the park, amid formalised English parkland and signs of British heroes and military presence, Hopkins 'had a great light':

> I had in my mind the first verse of a patriotic song for soldiers, the words I mean: heaven knows it is needed . . . I hope you may approve what I have done, for it is worth doing and yet is a task of great delicacy and hazard to write a patriotic song that shall breathe true feeling without spoon or brag. (LI. 283)

The song 'What shall I do for the land that bred me?' eventually stretched to four verses. Hopkins's exhaustion, depression, feelings of uselessness, and his wandering attention had combined to make him latch on to an emotional pick-me-up, brought on by the military images of Phoenix Park: this call to the English nation's men of military age to rouse their patriotic spirit and enlist in the army. Patriotic feeling as antidote to lack of energy and focus – Hopkins needed such a remedy, but this particular one could not work in his own case, despite the 'I', 'me', and 'we' of the song's narrator. There are several elements of the song which shed ironic light on Hopkins's own situation: not least, at a time when he is becoming more and more dissatisfied at the uselessness of his service in Christ's army, he shouts out that he is strongly desirous of enlisting in the British, secular, army. It is 'a patriotic song for soldiers', not for civilians, but at least two lines of it ('Call me England's fame's fond lover,/ Her fame to keep, her fame to recover') are plainly personal, and the caricatured idealistic sentiments of the remainder could only have been written by one who shared those feelings. Hopkins could never have actively participated in military service, of course, with his slight build and shortness (he would almost certainly have been recruited at Balliol College for an 1860s

Volunteer force if he had been eligible – some of his Oxford friends had been pestered to join up in 1863). The sentiments of the song are doubly unreal because of their crude picturing of military life and its rewards – bluster, not imagination, apparently the source.

And yet Hopkins's temporary putting aside of his life's profession for this indulgence, this replacement of black-coated, intellectually trained, Jesuits by red-coated common soldiers, living by the flag, sword, and rifle, as guardians of the nation's moral heritage, has another side. In spite of its lack of conviction and reprehensibly crude sentiments and poetic craft ('man on'/ 'cannon' must be the worst rhyme Hopkins ever penned), this poem's sentiments, for once, are truly representative of a large section of contemporary public opinion in England (though, of course, not in Ireland). Brought up, like all Europeans, on sentiments of passionate national and warlike pride, the English of the 1880s were increasingly uneasy at the military and naval state of the nation. In the first issue of *Punch* for 1888, the main cartoon, 'Birds of Ill Omen', had expressed unease at the widespread European pessimism about increasing military build-up and the possibility of war. A newly published official report on torpedo-boat trials held the previous May had given a dismal picture of collisions, running aground, exploding furnaces, difficulty in steering, leaking main valves, and dead and injured crew, and *Punch* had expressed the demoralised nation's sentiments in a satirical poem 'The Trials and Triumphs of a Torpedo-Boat'. In the same issue a cartoon of two guardsmen sitting on one horse derided the fact that one guards' regiment had 1,200 men but only 820 horses. At the beginning of February, on the eve of the new Parliamentary session, *Punch* expressed disillusion about Britain's current military state, particularly the (Conservative) government's parsimony over military spending. There was a vivid dramatic sketch, 'Taken at a Disadvantage', or 'What it might come to any day, if affairs should happen to be left in the hands of an "Unintelligence Department"' (the Intelligence Department was the forerunner of MI6). An Admiralty official reading *The Times* finds 'War declared by France last night', 'Gibraltar invested by a French fleet', 'Fifteen ironclads and fifty torpedo-boats [i.e., modern equipment not available to the outdated British Navy] assembled at Brest', 'The command of the Channel threatened!' Eventually the tourist vessels of the Ryde Steamboat Company try to blockade the French Fleet, 'pending the six months or so it may take the "Department" to get things a little more organised and in hand to meet the immediate necessities consequent on a sudden outbreak of war.'

It was not just the French who were potential enemies: the Russian bear lurked in several *Punch* items, and the major cartoon of 18 February 1888 was of Bismarck, in a Prussian helmet, with a sword and spurs, hypocritically speaking of peace while increasing the German army by 700,000 men and its expenditure by £14 million. In May that year 'Macaulay Junior' contributed 'The Next Armada', with familiar targets of general unpreparedness for defence, red tape, lack of modern rifles, ships, and horses, wrong-sized ammunition for the artillery, dangerously out of control 'exploding guns' on the ironclads; the Plymouth and Portsmouth dockyards having been captured, defenceless, the British fleet surrendered after quarter of an hour, two million foreign troops had landed, the Bank of England had been seized, and the country held to ransom. Such alarmist predictions and expansive logic were on a par with Hopkins's large emotions based on small experience.

For most of 1888 serious and passionate criticism of the military and the government's defence policy had been the most prominent feature of *Punch*, the same old targets being attacked in several different ways by many contributors. This contrasted oddly with *Punch*'s perennial social targets of the Royal Academy, upstart tradesmen aping the aristocracy, empty-headed guards officers, chinoiserie, society mothers seeking husbands for their daughters, and aesthetic costumes and mannerisms. Like Hopkins, *Punch* found Gladstone's 'G.O.M.' sobriquet inappropriate: a leader of the Opposition who pledged support for the Government's military policy should rather be called 'A Mild Old Muff'. (Gladstone had just been defeated at the 1888 General Election, having lost his majority over the issue of Irish Home Rule.) One cartoon pictured the contrast between a delicately effeminate guards officer and a brawny, active clergyman, implying some sympathy with the rhetorical stance Hopkins adopts in his patriotic song.

But enthusiasms such as that expressed in 'What shall I do?' could not last long with Hopkins. The reality of his everyday life and position, and his inability to take active part in any important debate, must have returned to him the same day that he wrote the song. In September 1888 Hopkins wrote his third soldiering piece, 'In honour of St Alphonsus Rodriguez'. Again military imagery is employed: 'Glory', 'a flame off exploit', 'fell strokes', 'scarred flesh', 'scored shield', 'trumpet . . . that field', 'fighter', 'forge the day', 'sword we wield', 'heroic breast', 'outward-steeled', 'fiercest fray'. But those images occur only in the first eight lines, and Hopkins uses them to make the contrast between blatant, obviously worthy deeds, with their swift recognition and rewards, and those unspectacular, more subtle deeds which achieve merit and fame only after time has elapsed and by gradual unremarked increment.

Hopkins plainly discovered sympathetic parallels between himself and Alphonsus Rodriguez. Like Hopkins, but unlike many early Jesuits, Alphonsus came from a middle-class mercantile family, and at the age of forty-four (Hopkins's age when he wrote the poem) had joined the Society of Jesus as a lay brother. He had a gentle personality (in contrast with one's impressions of the early militant Jesuits), and was employed in a job of humdrum drudgery, that of hall porter, dying after a long period of mental and physical anguish.

Hopkins wrote the poem so that it would be sent to Majorca in time for the celebrations of Alphonsus's canonisation. The canonisation must have seemed like some heavenly sign to Hopkins that personal drudgery and endless inner suffering could achieve official sanction and recognition, both on earth and in heaven. After years during which the more plainly meritorious kinds of religious service within the Society, like martyrdom, preaching, and top administrative jobs, had eluded him, he now appeared to be in a wearying, unsatisfying, and unending period in Dublin; he badly needed appreciation and reward. The result is a poem which deals with Hopkins's struggle within the mind; the theme is close to that of the 1885 sonnets, but has had to be objectified, because the poem was 'written to order' for a specific occasion, and was to be sent to Majorca. In ironic opposition to the immediate and outward, conventional military display advocated in 'What shall I do for the land that bred me?', this poem praises invisible, silent, and gradual qualities. Hopkins's sympathy with Alphonsus must have been more personal than this poem's comparatively distant feeling for the saint's 'war within', 'unseen brand', and persecution by evil spirits (LI. 293) reveals, but the speaker will not allow himself to proceed more intimately. The biographer has to wait for more private occasions.

On the other side of the sheet of notepaper on which early drafts of this poem are written is a note about examination papers from a colleague. Examination marking was perhaps the most obvious symbol of the nature of his work in Dublin, and the pain of his life there, the equivalent of Alphonsus's drudgery. Hopkins had been marking scripts in Stephen's Green and, with the note in his pocket, had taken a tram over to Phoenix Park, so that he could walk there and rest his eyes. Earlier that summer he had complained to his mother about exam drudgery, but after writing this poem there is no sign in the letters or notes or poems that Hopkins wrote in the remaining nine months of his life that he felt any reward for the years and years that had gone by of 'world without event'.

Chapter Thirteen

THAT NATURE IS A HERACLITEAN FIRE

→>-<←

In 1887 and 1888 Hopkins spent time and energy attempting to promote the works of his three English poet friends, Bridges, Dixon, and Patmore, so that after his death it was remembered in Dublin that 'he was always talking about their poetry'. He would ask his friends to send him parcels of their books, and distribute them to the occasional acquaintance among the more eminent professors at Trinity College, such as Edward Dowden and Robert Yelverton Tyrrell, whom he met at academic or social functions, or to the few local literati he knew, such as Katharine Tynan. Occasionally Hopkins tried to persuade Dublin journals to let him write reviews of his friends' works, but nothing ever came of these attempts. He continued to offer criticism to the authors in letters. Hopkins's loyalty to his poet friends was seen as a narrowly English nationalist gesture, and created another barrier between him and his Dublin surroundings. In England at this time Patmore was fairly well known, although not recognised among the first rank, Dixon unknown, and Bridges would not become famous until the new century. In southern Ireland, acquaintance with the works, and even the names, of these three essentially English poets was less likely, because of less widespread literacy and reading habits, but mainly through the recent rise of Irish nationalist culture.

An Irish Jesuit in daily contact with Hopkins was Father Matthew Russell, who had edited the *Irish Monthly* for over twenty years. This journal became a rallying point in 1880s Dublin for younger artists of all sorts who had no salon of their own, apart from the exclusive parties given by eminent people like Justice Fitzgibbon, Professor Dowden, and Sir Samuel Ferguson. Practically everyone in Dublin who was writing, said Katharine Tynan, came to Russell sooner or later. He was 'the reconciler', publishing and bringing together Anglo-Irish along with native Irish, Protestant along with Catholic. One day, Russell tried to coax Hopkins out of his seclusion in order to meet his protégée Tynan. But Russell had some difficulty in getting Hopkins to cross Stephen's Green and into John Yeats's studio at number 7. He was quite proud of bringing Hopkins and Tynan together for, said Tynan later, 'Father Hopkins could not always be trusted to make friends'.

Tynan was in her early twenties when she and Hopkins first met. Three descriptions of her at this time: 'wonderful rose-and-white Irish complexion with very fine brown hair with natural curls' (Pamela Hinkson's idea of her mother), but W. B. Yeats described her as 'a very plain woman', while Hopkins found her 'a simple brightlooking Biddy with glossy, very pretty red hair'. About twice a week she sat for her portrait on a dais in John Yeats's studio amid a hospitable atmosphere of friends and their friends. These sittings, she said, were 'easily and naturally' transformed to 'symposia of art and literature of one kind or another'. Later she recalled this first meeting with Hopkins: 'He brought an air of Oxford with him. He was not unlike Lionel Johnson, being small and childish looking, yet like a child-sage, nervous too and very sensitive'. (In portraits of Johnson, 'poet and aesthete', he appears a babyish, languid figure.) This is very similar to Yeats's impressions. Hopkins had 'a small ivory-pale face', said Tynan. In fact Hopkins's face was long and large in proportion to his small body; he was only about five feet two inches tall. Tynan took Hopkins to be about twenty, while a friend of hers thought he was only about fifteen.

At this meeting Hopkins 'complained that Father Russell would not shave regularly', and argued with John Yeats about 'finish or non-finish' in painting, Hopkins disagreeing with Yeats's impressionistic lines. Hopkins eventually saw the completed portrait of Tynan in the Royal Hibernian Exhibition, and conceded that it was 'a faithful likeness and a pleasing picture', but added 'I do not agree with his slight method of execution in that work or in others'. (The portrait has such indistinct lines that it is difficult to reproduce.)

John Yeats, said Tynan, was 'tremendously receptive and interested in all who came'. He was 'greatly delighted' with Hopkins's visit, and later 'lamented that Gerard Hopkins, with all his gifts for Art and Literature, should have become a priest'. Tynan reported this to Hopkins, who replied: 'You wouldn't give only the dull ones to Almighty God, would you?' At this meeting also, Hopkins was presented by John Yeats with a copy of his son's *Mosada*, the dramatic poem previously printed in the *Dublin University Review*, and now reprinted privately, with his father's pen-and-ink sketch portrait of the son as frontispiece. John Yeats gave him the booklet, said Hopkins, 'with some emphasis of manner', which 'for a young man's pamphlet was something too much'. 'Happily', Hopkins added, 'I was not required then to praise what presumably I had not then read'.

By chance though, Hopkins already knew of W. B. Yeats as a young poet who had written some striking verses, and who had been 'perhaps unduly praised by the late Sir Samuel Ferguson'. Hopkins seldom read more than a fraction of what his commentators say he did, and had seen only a small amount of Ferguson's; he found him to be 'a poet as the Irish are . . . full of feeling, high thoughts, flow of verse, point, often fine imagery, and other virtues, but the essential and only lasting thing left out – what I call *inscape*, that is species or individually-distinctive beauty of style'.

Yeats was not tarred by Hopkins with the same brush as Ferguson, although there is a certain implied community in their Irishness. Hopkins had read another of Yeats's poems, 'The Two Titans', Yeats's first published Irish poem, subtitled by him 'a Political Poem'. It was the framework of a vision, with a grey-haired youth, perhaps partly Yeats, representing Ireland, and a sibyl England. The poem is historically interesting to Yeats scholars because for the first time Yeats identifies himself closely with Ireland, even to the point of representing his country by a young man instead of by the traditional Cathleen ni Houlihan; and it also foreshadows *The Wanderings of Oisin*, which Yeats began in late 1886. Hopkins critics have assumed he was referring to *Mosada* in the following remarks, but they obviously relate to 'The Two Titans':

> It was a strained and unworkable allegory about a young man and a sphinx on a rock in the sea (how did they get there? what did they eat? and so on: people think such criticisms very prosaic; but commonsense is never out of place anywhere, neither on Parnassus . . . nor on the Mount where our Lord preached).

In spite of this, Hopkins found that he could praise 'fine lines and vivid imagery' in the poem. The letter in which he wrote this criticism of 'The Two Titans' was addressed to Coventry Patmore, and in his reply Patmore agreed: 'You have Coleridge's authority for requiring good-sense in every kind of poetry' (L3. 375).

Often in 1887 and 1888 letters occurs the pathetic and ultimately ironic juxtaposition of other authors' finished, published work with Hopkins's own never published or completed projects: his work on Greek metre from the Dorian measure to metre in general, a book on 'Statistics and Free Will', another on Aeschylus's *Choephoroi*, and yet another on Sophocles (both set authors at Balliol in the 1860s). He had planned also to write on Greek negatives, and on Patmore's long poem *The Angel in the House*. The diversity of these projects suggests unreality and lack of focus. Since Hopkins's undergraduate days many academic subjects had become more sophisticated, specialised, and thorough, relying less on the inspired brilliance which had served in 1860s Oxford; Hopkins had not kept up to date with any specific study, let alone with such a wide range as this list of enthusiasms suggests.

Often when discussing an enthusiasm in a letter Hopkins would start confidently: 'I have been reading the Choephoroi carefully and believe I have restored the text and sense almost completely in the corrupted choral odes', but then continuing in the realms of vague possibility: 'Perhaps I might get a paper on it into the *Classical Review* or *Hermathena*', and the discussion would end in hopelessness: 'but when will that book or any book of mine be?' (L1. 255). This cadence became frequent in 1888. There is a similarity with some retreat notes, where the opening voice is full of spirit, but becomes disconnected, and finishes in despondency. He allowed knowledge of previous failure to influence a current project against being tested in reality. Another bad omen occurring in 1887 and 1888 is for his account of an enthusiasm to demonstrate unreality by changing terms and losing definition: 'I have written a good deal of my book on the Dorian measure or on rhythm in general. Indeed it is on almost everything elementary and is much of it physics and metaphysics. It is full of new words' (LI. 254).

Tennyson and many other modern poets had closely followed developments in linguistics and philology, but Hopkins was out of touch with recent scholarship in these and other subjects. Yet his Balliol arrogance had not deserted him, and, impetuously, he wrote to the eminent Cambridge scholar Professor W. W. Skeat (they had both been pupils at Highgate School). Skeat was leader of the new school of philology which had arisen around 1880, and Hopkins challenged some entries in his ground-breaking *Etymological Dictionary*, which had been published from 1879 to 1882. Most of Hopkins's suggestions concern words which he had dwelt on during his undergraduate days, such as 'scope'. Skeat's answer, dismissing Hopkins's theories, came from a different world. For instance, denying Hopkins's suggested derivation of 'keeve', Skeat replied in the new technical language that he took it 'to answer to an A.S. *cêfe, variant of cyfe, which is merely Lat. cupa with mutation, just as our coop is Lat. cupa without mutation'; and Skeat sounded a warning note when he described the work of a Scottish amateur philologist who had wasted part of his life in constructing a dictionary 'full of elaborate & ridiculous etymologies' as 'all valueless', because 'he did not know his business' (L3. 431).

But Hopkins did take part in one modern linguistic project, collecting Irishisms for Joseph Wright's vast, innovative *English Dialect Dictionary*. The name 'Hopkins, Rev. G.M. (Ir.)' appears along with those of six other collectors of Irish words, and numerous names of English, Welsh, and Scots contributors. He asked students and colleagues at 85 St Stephen's Green to help him, and one of them, George O'Neill, imperceptively recalled in 1919, when he was a Jesuit Professor of English at University College:

> Dublin was not too happy a situation for studying the *nuances* of provincialism, and certain humoristic youths, getting wind of what was wanted, added further complications. They plied the too trustful collector with idioms and vocables, often highly-coloured, entirely of their own invention or interpretation. A few wonderful things were forwarded to Dr. Wright, but he seems to have been on his guard; the initials 'G. M. H.' do not occur very often in the Dictionary, and then not (so far as I have remarked) in connection with any very notable specimen of Irishism. ('Gerard Hopkins', *Essays on Poetry*, 124–5)

From today's perspective, when Hiberno-English is a specialised study, the inclusion of 'Irishisms' in an 'English Dialect' dictionary seems patronising and unprofessional. All the Irish people Hopkins had met in his years in Ireland would know more than he could collect, and he was both unsystematic and inspirational in the words he sent to Dr Wright. But the 89 entries that appeared (several years after Hopkins's death) in the E. D. D. with '(G. M. H.)' after them are interesting for what they show about their contributor (see White, 'G. M. Hopkins's Contributions'. Meant to be illustrations of how a word or expression was used, some are stories in their own right, and illustrate Hopkins's ear for dialogue and anecdote, making one regret the limitations professionally imposed on his writing. Despite the occasional patronising tone, there is a sense of humour not often found in the E.D.D. Hopkins's contributions fall under nine of the thirty-two possible counties – Antrim, Dublin, Galway, King's County (modern County Offaly), Kildare, Limerick, Louth, Meath, and Tipperary – probably all parts of the country he knew:

'If you are going out will you carry us with you?' said by schoolboys to their master. That is the wagonette we carried to Powerscourt. [Powerscourt gardens and waterfall in County Wicklow were, and still are, a famous place for day-excursions from Dublin.]

Begorra, bedad, begonnies. If your bees are as big as ponies and your hives no bigger than ours are, how do your bees get into your bee-hives? – Begob, that's their own affair.

Here comes Paddy from Cork with his coat buttoned behind.

Then my master shall call at you? He should have his meat tender. His meat should be tender.

Craw-thumper: Lit. one who thumps, heavily beats, the craw, the breast, in saying the *confiteor* or other prayers.

A few quotations were taken from observations a long time ago in Hopkins's journal, such as the entry for 'Bang'. In May 1874 he had recorded 'Piece of Irish from Br. Gartlan – 'That bangs Bannagher [a town in King's County] and Bannagher bangs the devil" (J. 243). And in a letter to Bridges, Hopkins had written:

I must tell you a humorous touch of Irish Malvolio or Bully Bottom, so distinctively Irish that I cannot rank it: it amuses me in bed. A Tipperary lad, one of our people, lately from his noviceship, was at the wicket and another bowling to him. He thought that there was no one within hearing, but from behind the wicket he was overheard after a good stroke to cry out 'Arrah, sweet myself!' (LI.197) [The youth was William Gleeson, from Nenagh in Co. Tipperary, who became a Jesuit, still remembered in the Irish community as late as the 1980s.]

Hopkins's interest in philology at Oxford in the 1860s had continued throughout his adult life, even though he was not fluent in modern developments, and the appearance of his name printed in the *English Dialect Dictionary* as one among a vast list of late-Victorian amateur philologists (Thomas Hardy's name is also there) brings home the fact that in some ways Hopkins was quintessentially of his age.

* * *

As far as his own poetry was concerned, by the end of 1886 there was an insurmountable national barrier: although Matthew Russell had asked him to contribute to the *Irish Monthly*, Hopkins had submitted to Russell only two impersonal translations of Shakespeare's songs into Latin, none of the many English poems lying about in manuscript. This was Hopkins's circumspect way of expressing his none-too-high opinion of Russell's and his contributors' standards, as well as a safeguard against letting slip his personal feelings about himself and Ireland. However there was the occasional letter to an Irish friend expressing his reactions to the nationalist bias of contemporary writing. He wrote to Dr Michael Cox, a fellow examiner of the Royal University:

> Irish writers on their own history are naturally led to dwell on what in history is most honourable to Ireland: every patriotic spirit would feel itself so led. They are also led to dwell on what in history is most dishonourable to England: this also is natural, and there is plenty of room for doing it. Still it is the way with passion to exceed. . . . It is desirable that Irish writers on Irish history should be on their guard especially on this matter, and, failing that, it is left for Englishmen like myself to do what we can . . . to point out untruths and overstatements and understatements due to passion and correct them. The devil is not so black, the saying is, as he is painted.

It is unlikely that a patriotic Irishman would have responded positively to such an innocent lecture from an Englishman. He had come to feel, the letter continued, 'not only with sorrow but with the deepest indignation and bitterness' that Irish writers sometimes wilfully suppressed circumstances favourable to

England in its conflicts with Ireland, and he cited one writer who 'cared only for the food of his hatred against England'. In a later letter to Dr Cox, Hopkins similarly responded to an Irish problem, her want of commercial prosperity, by saying that 'so far as there is blame Irishmen must be in great part to blame for that' (HRB 3 [1972], 6–9).

*　*　*

Hopkins had become a very private poet, at an opposite pole to the Russell/Tynan/Yeats chatty causerie-coterie, not just because he was English but because the public personality displays, blowing one's own trumpet with presentation copies, and general politicking triteness of Dublin artistic life were alien to his nature.

As with the Epithalamion, the poem 'That Nature is a Heraclitean Fire and of the comfort of the Resurrection' owes its inception to a welcome break in Hopkins's almost continuous examination schedule. Summer 1888 seemed to consist of continuous rain, and one 'windy bright day' after rain, Hopkins was marking his papers, suffering from eyestrain, when 'I put work aside and went out for the day, and conceived a sonnet'. That was on 26 July. He was still writing the sonnet in mid-August, when he wrote from a holiday in Scotland:

> I will now go to bed, the more so as I am going to preach tomorrow and put plainly to a Highland congregation of MacDonalds, MacIntoshes, MacKillops, and the rest what I am putting not at all so plainly to the rest of the world, or rather to [Bridges] and Canon Dixon, in a sonnet in sprung rhythm with two codas. (LI. 279)

The twenty-four-lined sonnet has three codas and a burden-line, and was eventually sent to Bridges some time before 25 September. It is often compared to 'Spelt from Sibyl's Leaves': the narrators of both poems see in the natural scene before them portents of a pre-Christian cosmological fable, consisting of a pessimistic vision of the future of the earth and mankind. But there are major differences between the poems. 'Spelt from Sibyl's Leaves' has a unified vision, while the title of the Heraclitean Fire poem shows that its argument will be in two parts: a thesis put forward and illustrated, followed by its rejection and replacement by a conventional Christian panacea message.

Because of the title's argumentative form, most commentaries treat the poem as though its structural pattern resembles that of an Ignatian meditation; even when a commentator allows that the pattern is not precisely Ignatian, a common conclusion is that it is nevertheless Christian: 'Instead of a colloquy with God, as prescribed by Ignatius, Hopkins continues the reflection and

⊷ 175 ⊶

shows the effect of Christ's election on the meditator's psyche (line 6), his experience of general mortality (lines 18–20, second coda) and what he can hope for in the life hereafter (third coda and burden line)' (Walliser, 167).

Commentary emphasising the teaching of the piece but ignoring its poetry relegates Hopkins to the ranks of orthodox, even sectarian, religious preachers. The distinctiveness of Hopkins's poetry is less due to common understandings of Roman Catholic doctrines than to his departures from conventional metaphysics formulated before he entered the Society of Jesus. At Oxford, in Michaelmas 1866, Hopkins had studied under Jowett pre-Socratic philosophy, and had written about the opposition between the sixth-century BC Eleatic philosophers (especially Parmenides) and Heraclitus, 'whose teaching about flux is the reaction against the supremacy of principles established by reason', and which substitutes for Parmenides' idea of the universe as a single, unchanging whole 'the sole unity of variety, the certainty of change' (Brown, 176–7).

Heraclitus did not play a significant part in Hopkins's Jesuit studies or teaching, but he is mentioned by Hopkins in a letter of 1881 as a writer who selects 'striking' examples (L2. 61). Probably Hopkins's interest had been reawakened by the first authoritative text published in England, Bywater's 1877 edition (all previous editions had been German). Heraclitus's text survives in about 120 incisive fragments; the longest, Fragment 1, gives an immediate clue to his affinity with Hopkins: 'My own method is to distinguish each thing according to its nature, and to specify how it behaves' (Wheelwright, 19).

This recognition of the significance of, and desire to describe external behaviour are in direct opposition to the intellectualising tradition of modern Western religion, and share common ground with the natural descriptions and observations in Hopkins's journals and poems, and with his ideas of 'inscape'. Heraclitus's cynical observation in the same fragment on the dullness of people around him must also have struck a chord with Hopkins: 'Other men [apart from me] . . . are as forgetful and heedless in their waking moments of what is going on around and within them as they are during sleep' (Wheelwright, 19); similarly Hopkins realised 'how sadly beauty of inscape was unknown and buried away from simple people and yet how near at hand it was if they had eyes to see it' (J. 221), and many of his St Beuno's poems either urge people to pay more attention ('Look at the stars! look, look up at the skies!'), or criticise men for having lost the ability to react to their God-made surroundings ('We . . ./ Have lost that cheer and charm of earth's past prime'). Imperceptiveness about Nature he later allied to almost wilful ignorance of God's presence, though his order and church would not have recognised Hopkins's terms and method of connecting the physical world with moral argument.

As far as can be seen from the few surviving fragments of Heraclitus's work, Hopkins makes use of some central ideas, but also shows partiality for his characteristic temperament, contrasting him with the workaday minds of prescribed authors on his training courses. The fragments most relevant to the poem are 20, which restates the ancient theme of unceasing change, and 29 to 32, dealing with the image of fire:

20. Everything flows and nothing abides; everything gives way and nothing stays fixed.
29. This universe . . . has not been made by any god or man, but it always has been, is, and will be – an ever-living fire . . .
30. [The phases of fire are] craving and satiety.
31. It [fire] throws apart and then brings together again; it advances and retires.
32. The transformations of fire are: first, sea; and of sea, half becomes earth, and half the lightning-flash. (Wheelwright, 29 and 37)

Concerning the common question whether Heraclitean fire is physical or symbolic, denoting permanent change, Hopkins takes the commonsensical line that it is actual and symbolic, physical and metaphysical. The Heraclitean observations which appealed to Hopkins were the dynamic nature of the visible universe (lines 1 to 9 of this poem), and pessimism about mankind's role and destiny (lines 10 to 16): 'Although this Logos is eternally valid, yet men are unable to understand it – not only before hearing it, but even after they have heard it' (fragment 1, Wheelwright 19). Also precisely relevant to Hopkins and his Ruskinian observation, as exemplified in 'Pied Beauty', that opposites create special harmony ('swift, slow; sweet, sour; adazzle, dim'), is the Heraclitean precept: 'Opposition brings concord. Out of discord comes the fairest harmony' (fragment 98, Wheelwright 90).

Increasingly conscious in Dublin of changes in his appearance and health, and declining confidence about future self-fulfilment in intellectual ventures or everyday pedagogic duties, Hopkins did not find in his religion's conventions acknowledgement of the reality or subtleties of his usual mental state. Unable to keep up with developments in modern psychology because of the rigid intellectual schemata he had vowed to uphold, he had to fall back on ancient authorities when he needed to formulate and express feelings that did not fit available Catholic structures. When he had portrayed in 'Spelt from Sibyl's Leaves' the replacement of his guilt-free indulgence in Nature's joys by guilt and moral puritanism, his vision of Judgement Day had originated in the writings of the pre-Christian pagan Sibyl (although she had been deemed orthodox by later Christians). Similarly, when Hopkins wished to explore his paradoxical reactions to a windy, bright day after rain, he found that the most relevant philosophical basis was the work of Heraclitus the Obscure, who had flourished five hundred years before Christ.

Heraclitus and Hopkins see in Nature change and fire. For Hopkins the fire represents spectacle, continuous movement, and changing form and substance, and the poem's natural description includes many fiery images: 'glitter', 'dazzling white', 'lights and shadow', 'bright', 'fuelèd', 'bonfire burns', 'spark', 'firedint', 'dark' (as the negation of man's 'spark'), 'shone', 'star', 'black' (as another negation of fire's light), 'shone/ A beacon, an eternal beam', 'wildfire', 'ash', 'flash', and, of course, 'diamond', the unburnable but permanently glittering substance.

In the first nine lines Hopkins draws on many natural observations previously recorded in his journals and poems. On 25 October 1870, for instance, he had described sky features in the countryside near Stonyhurst: 'herds of towering pillow clouds, one great stack . . . knoppled all over in fine snowy tufts' (J. 201), and the fragment of poetry 'The furl of fresh-leaved dogrose' pictures the sun as 'forth-and-flaunting'. As in the poem, in his Stonyhurst journal Hopkins had used 'march' to describe cloud movement: 'great bars or rafters of cloud all the morning . . . marching across the sky in regular rank' (J. 208), and 'tackle', as of a sailing-ship's rigging, had denoted a natural feature in his Swiss journal of 1868 (J. 176). As in the nature poems written in Wales, not just the *sights* of Nature are described in this poem but the motions; features are personalised and the subjects of active verbs – clouds 'flaunt', 'chevy', and 'throng', an elm 'arches', the wind 'ropes, wrestles, beats earth bare'. The writer/onlooker plainly is enjoying the scene, and there is apparently nothing ominously negative in line 9's climax and summary: 'Million-fuelèd, nature's bonfire burns on'.

In 'Spelt from Sibyl's Leaves' there is a gradual but continuous focus change from Nature to Man, which takes place over five lines up to line 9, where Nature's aesthetic qualities are finally nullified into black and white, and replaced by human ethical concerns, but in this poem the change in lines 9–10 is startlingly abrupt, in spite of Hopkins's attempt to connect Nature and Man by describing Man as Nature's 'bonniest, dearest to her'. The poem's subject has changed from Nature to Man. Nature continually and beautifully changes and constantly renews, while Man is for once only and does not last unless he is redeemed; such redemption will make him both permanent and fiery (like a diamond). The tone has, also without premonition, changed from triumphal to tragic – 'all is in an enormous dark/ Drowned', 'O pity and indignation!', 'death blots black out'. Then the emphasis again changes, from a impersonal narrator to one with individualised emotions – 'grief's gasping, joyless days, dejection'; and new shipwreck imagery is added, with 'my foundering deck' and the answering 'beacon'.

Some readers find unsatisfactory the abrupt 'Enough! the Resurrection'. A pious concept is suddenly thrust into the train of thought, and is said by the narrative voice to counteract the negative fate of man ('death blots black out') and the resulting despair. At this point man and nature are united (at last) as 'trash' and 'ash'. Dogma has been impersonally introduced without the elaborate and close engagement that there was in the description of nature. A new special voice has come in which lacks any attempt at reasoning. The enthusiastic last four lines carry a special charge, but depend on the reader's thoughtless acceptance of the unexplained sudden switch to another way of thought. It has been said that the argument of the poem has not been continued and resolved. Moreover, in Hopkins's writings after this poem there were no convincing signs that his deep problems had been solved.

Chapter Fourteen

RETREAT AT RAHAN, NEW YEAR 1889

+>-<+

On 24 December 1888, Hopkins started out from St Stephen's Green to spend the Christmas holiday at Monasterevin, where he had been unusually happy on previous occasions. Having recently suffered from sleeplessness, which he attributed to the unseasonably mild weather, he looked forward 'to the country for more chance of sleeping'. 'Man', he wrote to his mother, 'like vegetation needs cold and a close season once a year' (L3. 191).

Miss Mary Cassidy's welcoming house was on the first of Monasterevin's wide, straight, militaristic streets, which gave the town, so the Irish said, an English feeling. Recently the hot-headed curates of St Peter and St Paul's had given support to the pockets of Land League agitation in the surrounding countryside, but their parish priest, Dr Comerford, had, according to Hopkins, 'the unusual courage . . . to forbid boycotting'. Monasterevin had traditionally housed and supplied British troops, and now the Cassidy ethos, firmly pro-British yet Roman Catholic – a combination essential for Hopkins's peace of mind, but rarely encountered by him in Ireland – dominated the town.

Monasterevin House was free over Christmas from the noise of dray and cart convoys and distant canal traffic. Hopkins was able to relax in the comfortable, privileged female domesticity of Miss Mary and other ladies, with children sometimes about, and waiting servants; he was the welcome, looked-up-to male guest, and moreover a priest, to be made a fuss of, his every need catered for. In return he said Mass in the house's small private oratory, and chatted authoritatively and wittily, reviving his Balliol manner, here openly welcomed, at table and in the sitting room. He strolled in the large gardens and orchard, and walked along the banks of the Barrow, in the grounds of Moore Abbey, where there were kingfishers, or across the bascule bridge, where the canal crossed the river, and along the road to the steep incline of the Earl of Essex's narrow bridge.

There were visits to the church on the Earl of Drogheda's street, or along the winding wooded drive to the nearby Togher House, the grand home of Mr Robert Cassidy. Sometimes he walked in the extensive woods of larch, ash, oak, and box (from which clay-pipe moulds were fashioned) on the Moore Abbey estate, where in May there had been acres of bluebell carpets. But 'unhappily', as he informed his mother, he had to make his yearly retreat at St Stanislaus College, Rahan, Tullamore: 'unhappily' because it was 'a severe tax on my short holidays'. Ignatius had recommended that a Jesuit on retreat should seclude himself 'from all friends and acquaintances and from all earthly solicitude . . . by moving from the house in which he dwelt, and taking another house or room, that there he may abide in all possible privacy'. The annual retreat should have taken place back in the summer, but Hopkins could find no time for it then, preoccupied with vast numbers and several sets of examination papers, the marking of which each year he found difficult and dispiriting.

So, early on New Year's day 1889, Hopkins had to board the train for the hour's journey over the long railway viaduct through flat country to Tullamore. Although Tullamore was the principal town of King's County (now County Offaly), it was in a remote part of Ireland. British law did not recognise the right of the Society of Jesus to exist, and Jesuit institutions purposely shunned publicity and set up in obscure country parts to avoid legal challenges. Rahan, a trap-ride from Tullamore railway station, was the estate of Miss Maria O'Brien, a pious heiress who later became a nun in the nearby community of Killina. She had leased part of it to the Society in 1814, as their second foundation in Ireland. It became known to the Jesuits, though not to local people, by her name for it, Tullabeg (*more* = great, *beg* = little), and for most of its existence had housed a secondary school, St Stanislaus College, the rector of which, from 1870 until his transference in 1882 to be President of University College Dublin, had been Fr William Delany, Hopkins's superior. It had now changed function, and had recently opened as the novitiate of the Irish Province.

The college was situated in bleak, typically midlands bog country. No walks into the surrounding countryside were possible except on narrow and featureless roads which crossed flat stretches of nothingness, relieved only by desolate black clumps on the horizon. There were few trees, and vicious east winds howled across the landscape; the drive was lined with tall, skeletal beeches, on the tops of some of which were black lumps of ancient crows' nests, and there were formal yews at the boundary wall dividing the college grounds from farm buildings. Elsewhere were occasional gloomy conifers, from which came coarse crow sounds. The college buildings were severe, barrack-like blocks, with bleakly classical high ceilings; not a glimmer of gothic, as little decoration or human warmth as possible – only low Doric pillars and plain steps for the front door; a later belfry tower with minimal, pattern-book carvings stood on the edge of a group of buildings next to the public church. A private chapel, bedrooms, and refectory made up one block. Regulation walks were either silent patrols along paths of the gloomy retreat conifers, boundaried by occasional holy statues of standard pattern as turning point, or to the cemetery of St Carthage (patron saint of Waterford, birthplace of the first rector), with its gravestones of priests, such as 'P. Joannes Cunningham SJ' and 'P. Patritius Clavin SJ', who had died before their time, aged 41 and 38 respectively. In winter (a Jesuit said to me) it was a suitable place for 'a composition on Hell'.

An account written for Tullabeg's 150th anniversary suggests other factors hostile to Hopkins, relating its history largely in terms of priests and pupils who had actively contributed to 'Ireland's shaking off the shackles of the [British] penal laws'. Two students in the 1830s, for instance, Williams and Smyth, had joined the Young Irelanders, Smyth assisting in a prison escape and later becoming a nationalist Member of Parliament. In the 1840s Fr Alexander Kyan had been nephew to Esmonde Kyan, 'one of the gallant men of '98, who gave his life for Ireland on the scaffold for his part in the rising in Wexford'. An 1850s pupil Alfred Aylward was praised for having joined the Fenian Brotherhood, assisting in the famous Manchester prison-van escape, being mentioned in dispatches as 'causing harm to British interests in South Africa', acting as a secret service agent for the Russian government, and having fought against Britain in Riel's rebellion in Canada. A later Tullabeg Jesuit, Fr Tom Murphy, was 'proud of one thing only: he was a collateral descendant of Fr John Murphy, the patriot Wexford priest of 1798'. In the second half of 1888 the town of Tullamore had been the subject of Parliamentary and newspaper discussion over the allegation by Hopkins's *bête-noire* O'Brien in *United Ireland* and repeated at a special inquest that the death of the republican John Mandeville in July 1888 had been because of ill treatment the previous year in Tullamore gaol, where he had been imprisoned with O'Brien. Hopkins mentioned Mandeville and O'Brien in a bitter attack on the outcome of the Parnell commission, in a letter of 1 March 1889 (L3. 193–4).

It is unlikely that the unmistakably English Hopkins would have met with any welcome other than distant politeness during his six-day retreat at Tullabeg. Sympathy with and close knowledge of the English ethos, limited to areas of the Irish middle class who had professional and administrative ties, such as Hopkins's friends the Cassidys and the legal family, the O'Hagans of Howth, would be notably lacking in rural areas such as King's County.

* * *

His first extended retreat task on 1 January was to meditate on the First Principle and Foundation of the Spiritual Exercises. The text of Ignatius's *Principium sive Fundamentum* started: 'Man was created to praise, reverence and serve God Our Lord, and by so doing to save his soul. And the other things on the face of the earth were created for man's sake and to help him in the carrying out of the end for which he was created.' It was a voice from another age, and its anachronistic message could be accepted only by people who had wilfully ignored the revelations and implications of *The Origin of Species* and *The Descent of Man*.

On another retreat, that of August 1880, when he was still stationed in England, the first sentence of Hopkins's notes had divided Creation into 'the world without' and 'ourselves the world within'. Acknowledging that whereas most people would focus on the former, he had found that 'the latter takes on [my] mind more hold', and he seized the opportunity he had created to think and write about his own individuality, in a passage which is itself the most distinctive of all Hopkins's religious-occasional prose writings, and the prime demonstration of his solipsism:

> I find myself both as man and as myself something most determined and distinctive, at pitch, more distinctive and higher pitched than anything else I see . . . more important to myself than anything I see. And when I ask where does all this throng and stack of being, so rich, so distinctive, so important, come from / nothing I see can answer me. . . .
>
> When I consider my selfbeing, my consciousness and feeling of myself, of I and me above and in all things, which is more distinctive than the smell of ale or alum, more distinctive than the smell of walnutleaf or camphor, and is incommunicable by any means to another man (as when I was a child I used to ask myself: What must it be to be someone else?). Nothing else in nature comes near this unspeakable stress of pitch, distinctiveness, and selving, this selfbeing of my own. (s. 123)

But those celebratory words had been written in England, in the comparatively calm past, before Hopkins's profoundly depressing time in Ireland. Here at Tullabeg, again he immediately sets about building an argumentative structure to enable him to explore his own case, the world within; but now he focuses on the overriding mental preoccupation of all his five years in Ireland, the insoluble moral quandary in which he has been unwillingly placed: 'All moral good, all man's being good lies in two things – in being right, being in the right, and in doing right . . . Neither of these will do by itself. Doing good but on the wrong side, promoting a bad cause, is rather doing wrong. . . . Nor plainly is it enough to be on the right side and not promote it' (s. 261).

Men are constituted, Hopkins goes on, to follow one of these two principles and neglect the other. 'The Irish think it enough to be Catholics or on the right side'. As their Catholic cause is the right one, 'they think . . . that all that they and their leaders do to advance the right side is and must be right.' The English, on the other hand, think 'he can't be wrong whose life is in the right': they lead more unselfish, upright lives than the Irish, but have the wrong or no religious principle. The English follow a reasonable philosophy in their way of life, but the Irish have religion. Thus the two nations are deeply at odds with each other. (Hopkins's analysis of the Irish-English conflict is in terms which neither side would recognise.)

The ideal solution for Hopkins would be 'Our King back, Oh, upon English souls!' ('The Wreck of the Deutschland', stanza 35) – the re-conversion of England, its return to the true faith. But in the meantime Hopkins is in Ireland, on the right, Catholic, side, but forced, by his teaching post at University College, to partly help an evil cause, Irish nationalism:

> But how is it with me? I was a Christian from birth or baptism, later I was converted to the Catholic faith, and am enlisted 20 years in the Society of Jesus. I am now 44. I do not waver in my allegiance, I never have since my conversion to the Church. The question is how I advance the side I serve on. This may be inwardly or outwardly. Outwardly I often think I am employed to do what is of little or no use. Something else which I can conceive myself doing might indeed be more useful, but still it is an advantage for there to be a course of higher studies for Catholics in Ireland and that that should be partly in Jesuit hands; and my work and my salary keep that up. Meantime the Catholic Church in Ireland and the Irish Province in it and our College in that are greatly given over to a partly ['immoral' crossed out] unlawful cause, promoted by partly unlawful means, and against my will my pains, laborious and distasteful, like prisoners made to serve the enemies' gunners, go to help on this cause. (s. 261–2)

Hopkins's summary of his life's moral progress is in simplistic military terms, consistent with the soldiering imagery of the Society of Jesus: 'enlisted', 'allegiance', 'advance the side I serve on', 'prisoners made to serve the enemies' gunners'. But the attractively black-or-white moral judgements of actions and the subsequent rewards for following the right, which professional religious life had seemed to promise the self-dissatisfied Oxford undergraduate of the 1860s, were not apparent in 1880s Ireland. Naively, and in the self-effacing way he has been taught, he lays part of the blame on himself; but he is puzzled by the complex and paradoxical nature of events which shape his life. The simple question 'how I advance the side I serve on' cannot be simply answered. Common sense and observation tell him that, although taking part in the great new Jesuit enterprise, the university education of Irish Catholics, he does little good at University College, and can imagine being more useful in another job. He is made to help a cause which his conscience tells him is wrong. Besides providing a national Catholic higher education, his college was also a source of intellectual sustenance and encouragement to potential revolutionaries, and would furnish leaders for the Easter Rebellion of 1916 against British rule. He is servant of an immoral cause – disobedience to the English law of the land, by which Ireland is legally bound. Significantly he deletes his first judgement, 'immoral', which involves criticising the morals of his superiors, to whom he owes unquestioning obedience, and changes it to the safer, more objectively true 'unlawful'.

His criticism is nevertheless of his Church, his Jesuit Province, and of his immediate community – he has been forced into local disloyalty by a greater loyalty. Summarising the moral state of his active life he continues:

> I do not feel then that outwardly I do much good . . . and this is a mournful life to lead. In thought I can of course divide the good from the evil and live for the one, not the other: this justifies me but it does not alter the facts. (s. 262)

It seemed to him that he could lead this life well enough if only he had 'bodily energy and cheerful spirits', but these God would not give him. That evening, he was continuing the same train of thought when

> I began to enter on that course of loathing and hopelessness which I have so often felt before, which made me fear madness and led me to give up the practice of meditation except, as now, in retreat and here it is again.

The purpose of meditation was to extricate a man from his negative states and empower him to start mentally afresh; but the official Ignatian process had seldom worked for Hopkins. It had been formulated to enable worker-priests to break off everyday activities and restore initial principles by disciplined mental efforts, but not with Hopkins's nervous scrupulosity. Introspection and regurgitated, undigested emotions, as letters and poems written in Dublin show, already formed an overstrong part of his everyday life, and an even more focused mental concentration could only exacerbate his problems and confirm their inescapability.

In his present state of mind on the retreat he could therefore do no more than 'repeat Justus es, Domine, et rectum judicium tuum [Thou art just, Lord, and thy judgement right] and the like', and then 'being tired I nodded and woke with a start'. He had with him the copy of the Vulgate Bible which he had bought in 1866, on the day of his reception into the Roman Catholic church. He then wrote a horrifying summary of his stay in Ireland:

> What is my wretched life? Five wasted years almost have passed in Ireland. I am ashamed of the little I have done, of my waste of time, although my help-lessness and weakness is such that I could scarcely do otherwise. And yet the Wise Man warns us against excusing ourselves in that fashion. I cannot then

be excused; but what is life without aim, without spur, without help? All my undertakings miscarry: I am like a straining eunuch. (s. 262)

The conclusion Hopkins reaches after describing the aimless waste of his life in Ireland is that he is at one with his fatalistic contemporaries, his Oxford acquaintances who had killed themselves: 'I wish then for death'. But as a committed professional religious he cannot take the easy way out: 'Yet if I died now I should die imperfect, no master of myself, and that is the worst failure of all. O my God, look down on me'. That was his last note on the first evening of the New Year, 1889.

*   *   *

If these notes on the *Principium seu Fundamentum* are compared with those Hopkins made on the first day of other retreats (such as the August 1880 notes from Liverpool, *S.* 122–9), large differences are immediately obvious. The main one is that rather than meditating directly on the text – Man as God's creation with the purpose of serving God and saving his soul – Hopkins at Rahan focuses on his own moral situation, with its paradoxes, difficulties, and impossibilities. He pretends to be objective by starting with dividing moral good into passive and active states, but the application to himself is quick and direct. He is inescapably self-obsessed, and seeks radical self-assessment on terms which his own mind, not Ignatius's, dictates.

A similar, bitterly self-reflective, process happened the next morning, 2 January, when he started the exercise *De Tribus Peccatis*, on the Three Sins, those of the Angels, of Adam and Eve, and 'the particular sin of some one person who for one mortal sin has gone to hell'. Compared with his notes for December 1879 (s. 133), which discuss the words and concepts of the Latin text for this Exercise in a lively and objective manner, his Rahan note is short, and baldly personal:

Nothing to enter but loathing of my life and a barren submission to God's will. The body cannot rest when it is in pain nor the mind be at peace as long as something bitter distills in it and it aches. This may be at any time and is at many: how then can it be pretended there is for those who feel this anything worth calling happiness in this world?

This leads him to give a personal annotation of 'happiness', noticeably not a plea to God to grant it to him, as God is not imagined as a reality in these notes, but a sad description of its customary distance from him:

There is a happiness, hope, the anticipation of happiness herafter: it is better than happiness, but it is not happiness now. It is as if one were dazzled by a spark or star in the dark, seeing it but not seeing by it: we want a light shed on our way and a happiness spread over our life. (s . 262)

That afternoon, the same exercise brought 'more loathing', and the following day 'helpless loathing', and, ominously, almost no other comment, as though he were no longer capable of words. In fact there are no notes for the day after, 4 January.

On 5 January Hopkins attempted to free himself into more positive thinking, in meditation on Christ's Incarnation. As

my life is determined by the Incarnation down to most of the details of the day . . . why should I not make the cause that determines my life . . . determine it in greater detail still . . . and to my greater happiness in doing it? . . . But I say to myself that I am only too willing to do God's work and help on the knowledge of the Incarnation. But this is not really true: I am not willing enough for the piece of work assigned me, the only work I am given to do, though I could do others if they were given.

The job assigned to him was 'my work at Stephen's Green'. When his appointment to Dublin had been made, he had thought

that the Royal University was to me what Augustus's enrolment was to St Joseph . . . so resolution of the Senate of the R.U. came to me, inconvenient and painful, but the journey to Bethlehem was inconvenient and painful; and then I am bound in justice, and paid. I hope to bear this in mind. (s. 263)

Devlin comments that Hopkins was applying 'low but sturdy motives with which he begins to haul himself up', such motives being 'often the most useful to begin with in desolation' (s. 320), implying both that Hopkins's troubles were not extraordinary and that by following Ignatius's prescribed mental route Hopkins remained in control of himself and on the way to inevitable recovery. Like other Jesuit commentators Devlin prefers conformity with officially recommended patterns to description of the real situation.

Hopkins had not extricated himself from desolation, but on the next day, the Feast of the Epiphany, he had switched focus to the events, characters, and precise words of the Vulgate text. He enlarges on the Biblical text for the day and its contexts without deep engagement or insight. There is not the smallest personal reference in his notes: he seems afraid to return to his own situation, and to be taking refuge in official prescription. Again, Devlin's analysis seems poetically distant: Hopkins's notes, he says, 'end with the cliff-face scaled and his mind and heart at one, striding forward with great strides on a high plateau of light' (s. 221). Devlin ignores the discontinuity of Hopkins's writing – the unpredicted switch from self-preoccupation and self-loathing to undergraduate-ish dancing over prescribed texts, without subjective attachment.

*   *   *

In his despairing Rahan retreat, the summary of Hopkins's time in Ireland is shocking: no solution or alleviation seems possible: 'I could therefore do no more than repeat *Justus es, Domine, et rectum judicium tuum*' (s. 262). In response to feelings of weakness and worthlessness, this retreat had provided him with ineffective and fatalistic formulae.

But removed from the limitations of a retreat, Hopkins found himself able to draw on his personal, unofficial resource of poetic composition. Art could provide and succeed where religion had failed. Hopkins was, after all, a child of the nineteenth century. It was ten weeks after the retreat, on 17 March 1889. Nobody in Dublin on St Patrick's Day could be unaware of strong national feeling: tinkers selling dirty shamrock buttonholes, normal commerce and traffic interrupted, bunting and festive decoration, parades, bands, flags of favoured nations, idle sightseers and police abnormally evident, public houses and hotels bursting with visitors and new liveliness. Four years earlier, Hopkins's notes for the day had pictured St Patrick as a foreigner in Ireland, a suffering exile, gifted with patience (s. 260), and he had thus identified with him in feelings, though not in actions. He had asked for Patrick's help 'for Ireland in all its needs and for yourself in your position'.

On this St Patrick's Day, 1889, Hopkins wrote the poem '*Justus quidem tu es, Domine,* si disputem tecum; verumtamen justa loquar ad te: quare via impiorum prosperatur? etc (Jerem. xii 1.)' The retreat note's *Justus es, Domine* can now be qualified with *verumtamen justa loquar ad te,* 'but so what I plead is just'. There is now in this poem an argument, with two sides. Hopkins himself cannot be accused of unorthodoxy because he is quoting Jeremiah's words, but Biblical sanction enables him to question, explore and stand up for himself in ways which the retreat format had not allowed.

'Justus quidem . . .' opens in a completely different way from any other Hopkins poem. After the Vulgate text as title, the poem starts by translating that text, and then proceeds as though in Jeremiah's voice. This start partly resembles a sermon's, but its purpose, of self-justification and self-exploration, is quite unlike a sermon's. It does not preach, as many of Hopkins's earlier poems do, and it has dramatic characteristics beyond the dimension of written words. It is a declamation to a silent listener, called Lord, sir, or thou – a passive figure present at the beginning of the poem, fading away when the speaker becomes involved in the world of nature outside him, and who then reappears in the last line in a different guise.

The poem resembles the common practice of Elizabethan and Jacobean Protestants who versified Psalms as a penitential exercise if one were ill or in a low state. Psalm 136 had appealed to many poets (Campion, Bacon, Carew, Denham, and Crashaw) with its subject of creativity lost through the pressures of exile ('How shall we sing the Lord's song in a strange land?'). But Hopkins's poem has more in common with the late seventeeth- and eighteenth-century literary form, the Imitation, the freest kind of translation, which departs wilfully from the original text to create a new poem in its spirit, using the experience of a new age. This is Hopkins's method in 'Justus quidem . . .'. Part of the effect of an Imitation was that the reader was aware of the text from which the poet had departed, and recognised the variation upon the original, as one did in a parody. Yet while the Imitation could not be fully grasped without knowledge of the original, it could nevertheless stand on its own. In his poem Hopkins makes the reader aware of the text by incorporating it in the title, and by making its translation the start of the poem.

The poem's stilted start is caused by the conscious use of these biblical and literary precursors. But after the translation of the text in lines one to three the poem carries on in, apparently, the voice of Jeremiah for the fourteen lines, without telling us explicitly that Hopkins has taken over from the prophet. Hopkins has performed a kind of Ignatian exercise, a 'composition of person', by putting himself in the place of the speaker of the text.

Jeremiah was a poet of exile, just as Hopkins in Ireland was an exile, and a poet of exile; and they share exile characteristics. As foreigners they are both often called strangers (a common word in Jeremiah's text); their unearned punishment takes the form of being in a foreign land. There is the exile's constant emotional tension in their writings, the sense that they were never really at home, but longed for their native land, to which they would never return. Neither of them can relax on the assumption that peace and happiness are around. They convey a general sense that in this foreign land things are untrustworthy; people are not performing their proper roles. Hopkins had accused the two nationalist archbishops, Walsh and Croke, of immorality, while Jeremiah wrote: 'an appalling and horrible thing has happened in the land: the prophets prophesy falsely, and the priests rule at their direction' (5. 30–1). The sense of alienation would have been particularly strong in Hopkins on this 17 March in Dublin, with national feeling trumpeted around him, and no sympathetic fellow countryman to confide in, the other Oxford-educated Englishman at University College, Fr Joseph Darlington, being strongly republican. No wonder Hopkins returned to the unresolved problems of his January retreat, duty versus conscience, and clashing allegiances.

The Englishman Hopkins had come to Dublin amid an Irish row, in which his nationality was a key issue, and often, like Jeremiah, he mentions his consciousness of imminent battles and warfare. There was a common interpretation of Jeremiah 12.1 in Hopkins's time which related it to an earlier passage (11, 18–23), where Jeremiah tells how he had learned of a plot against his life by men of his native place, Anathoth. And in Chapter 12 he expostulates with Jehovah, according to this interpretation, on account of the impunity which the conspirators enjoyed. So it is not only that Jeremiah and Hopkins are asking the same question 'Why do the wicked prosper?', they also have a common background to their question. Jeremiah's enemies were opposed to God, and yet were all powerful, while Jeremiah was victimised by their evil plotting, though speaking the word of God. We can recall that Hopkins had written, ten weeks before this poem, of his church, Jesuit Province, and College being 'greatly given over to a partly unlawful cause', and that against his will 'my pains, laborious and distasteful, like prisoners made to serve the enemies' gunners, go to help on this cause'.

For Jeremiah, as for Hopkins in many poems and letters, there seems to be no audience or response. Jeremiah strives for recognition, but is not recognised by his countrymen as their spokesman in this land of corrupt values. Hopkins had written in 1885: 'England . . . would neither hear/ Me, were I pleading, plead nor do I', and the question of a poet's recognition occupies many letters to Patmore and Dixon. As a result both Jeremiah and Hopkins sometimes feel compelled to exaggerate their stance and force those around to take notice. But still people will not hear, and so their suffering is increased. It was said of Jeremiah, and it was probably as true of Hopkins, that as he was especially sensitive and affectionate his sufferings were all the more acute. They both had to wait for recognition until after death. Hopkins's feeling on 1 January of his pains being made 'to serve the enemies' gunners' is the same as Jeremiah's 'I will make you serve your enemies in a land which you do not know' (17. 4).

There are other common features. This is unique in Hopkins's poetry; he rarely invented speech or thoughts for other people, telling Bridges that he lacked sufficient experience of life to be a dramatist. His sympathy for St Alphonsus Rodriguez had been expressed in a restrained occasional poem, while the portrait of Caradoc in St Winefred's Well, which includes aspects of himself, is unfinished. Like Jeremiah he finds it difficult for his words to contain a message for other people which is not integrated with a dense autobiographical content; unhappily exiled they concentrated upon personal mental darkness. Old Testament thought before Jeremiah had concerned the relationship between God and Israel, but with Jeremiah religion became the relationship between God and the individual heart, his mental pain forcing him to speak.

Commentators argue about the logical difficulty with this Jeremiah text: 'If Jeremiah knows beforehand that God is just, what is the use of all the argument?' Hopkins makes the same point: 'Thou art just, but what I plead is just, and I (by implication) question your acts.' Jeremiah scholars are intrigued: how can a prophet chosen by God to speak for him, speak against him? This is where Hopkins is closest to Jeremiah. Jeremiah found a clever method of articulating his inner conflict between his God-disposed duty and commonsense.

Hopkins's poem is a dramatised exploration of his mental conflict; it is a mental conflict, though it takes the surface, literary form of a dispute between servant and master. His master is Hopkins's imposed sense of duty, while the servant is human nature which seeks reward. Thus far Hopkins is in a traditional mould – other servants of God have felt themselves unrewarded, including Old Testament prophets and St Teresa of Avila; there is a similar conflict in one of Michelangelo's last poems, 'Truth'.

The poem brims over with dramatic contrasts and conflicts, confrontations and oppositions: Thou/I; sinners/ I; prosper/disappointment; my enemy/my friend; sots and thralls/I; lust/thy cause; spare hours/life; birds/I; build/not build; eunuch/flourishing nature; and others. Another frequent opposition is the paradox, of which the most blatant, epitomising all paradoxes, is that the same person is called 'my enemy' and 'my friend' (in Lamentations 3. 2–3, Jeremiah complains that 'the Lord has become like an enemy'). Although this is modified by the conditional – '*Wert* thou my enemy, O thou my friend' – the reader's mind takes in the forceful opposition of enemy and friend, not the weak modification. Then 'Thou art just' but 'what I plead is just', which logically cannot be if I and thou are opposed. 'Sinners' ways prosper', which they should not do in a just world, which we have been told it is; and although by implication I am good, I only achieve disappointment, which again is unjust, although it happens in a just world.

Things are approved which should not be; things which go together should be opposite. Everything is topsy-turvy – except external nature, which is the opposite of the poet's inner nature. This wrongness is emphasised by pairs of the same word being forced into opposition. A word used once in conjunction with a concept is repeated in conjunction with that concept's opposite, creating a logical impossibility. A + B = A + not B. For example, 'Just' in line 1 is attached to 'Thou', whereas 'just' in line 2 is attached to the opposing 'I'. In line 5, 'thou my' is attached to 'enemy', and then, immediately afterwards, to 'friend'; 'why sinners' in line 3, 'why I' (who am good) in line 4; 'why prosper' and 'why disappointment'; and in line 12 'but build' and 'but strain'.

In the outside world the right things are conjoined, emphasised by the parallels and alliteration: 'banks and brakes'; 'leavèd' and 'lacèd'; 'fretty' and 'fresh'; 'fresh' and 'shakes'; 'birds' and 'build'. Then in lines 12 and 13 come blunt negatives, intensified by additional *b*'s: 'but not build'; 'no, but'; 'not breed', with their violent monosyllables, after the sweetness and smoothness of the natural scene. After these negatives comes a wishful begging for a return of rightness to the inner world, with the overdone alliterative harmony of the final line: 'Mine/ my; lord/life; roots/rain', representing creation and harmony; but the effect is muted into doubtfulness by the previous line's negative – 'not breed one work that wakes' – cancelling the positive force of 'work that wakes' before it can operate. It's not a 'work that wakes', it's '*Not* a work that wakes', it never wakes. This negative also affects the alliteration in the last line, so that its positive quality is weakened.

Another way in which the poet's inner world is contrasted with the world outside him is by the calm and simple statements describing nature ('See they are this: look at those there') being violently flung up against the restless fragments of the poet's inner nature. There are no simple statements when Hopkins is expressing the turmoil of his mind; it is all questions, conditionals – *if, but, why, indeed, must, wouldst, wert, more than, worse than*; there are interruptions in the middle of almost every statement – *Lord, indeed, but, sir, I wonder, sir* – what he is saying, and his attitude towards it are both uncertain. His attitude is neither simple nor constant: like Jeremiah, he is angry and yet insufficiently confident to show the full force of his emotion.

His use of the archaic 'thou' is unusual for Hopkins after 1884 ('[Carrion Comfort]' is the only other example). It helps to keep the poem at a respectful distance at times, but the temperature is soon raised again. Another device which lowers the temperature is the breaking-up of the pace and rhythm of arguments by a pacifying word or phrase – *Lord, sir, I wonder* (imagine the difference if Hopkins had written 'Thou art just if I contend with thee, but so what I plead is just'). The hectoring, interrogatory tone – question mark after question mark after question mark – is there, but is worked against by these modifying devices, suggesting two aspects of frustration working almost simultaneously – sharpened bitterness urging on the poet, while enervating hurt holds him back, half-scared. This is one of many ways in which the unresolved conflict is shown.

Effective devices swell out its plot, so that the poem becomes larger and more complex than its surface argument. There are breaks and bad logic in the arguments of several Hopkins poems, and in this one the plot noticeably changes. It starts with an ill-rewarded servant complaining about his bad treatment – a traditional pose of faithful but dissatisfied servants of God (such as Isaiah and St Teresa of Avila) – and then changes to the traditional situation of a dis-spirited poet observing the disparity between his own creative aridity and the fecundity of surrounding nature (Milton, Gray, Coleridge, and others wrote poems on this). In the main the poem's octave does not appear to cohere with the sestet. 'I' is at first a moral being opposed to sinners and immoral surroundings, and then becomes an uninspired poet contrasted with his productive natural surroundings. The octave is largely about morals, the sestet about artistic inspiration. (The movement between morals and aesthetics had been in the other direction in 'Spelt from Sibyl's Leaves'.)

With these two different groups of subject matter, does it mean that the stilted, derivative opening with Jeremiah provides a false start which has to be displaced when the true preoccupation of the poet's mind eventually enters the poem? Hopkins was writing a personal complaint, the first part against the injustice of his insoluble dilemma, of compulsorily serving two opposed sides simultaneously, and the second against his inspirational barrenness. In the first he is so close in feeling and situation to Jeremiah that he can use the prophet's exact words, but in the second, in spite of Jeremiah not sharing his creative barrenness, he can still use some of Jeremiah's imagery, though in a different cause. 'The sots and thralls of lust', in line 7, is less Hopkins than Jeremiah, who sees lust as the worst sin against God, and often uses the term to represent evil in general. In Jeremiah lust is punished by fruitlessness: 'You have polluted the land with your vile harlotry,/ Therefore . . . the spring rain has not come' (3. 2–3). In this way Jeremiah directly connects morality with creativity, although the connection is not apparent in Hopkins's poem.

Hopkins knew well the text and feelings of Jeremiah. Whereas (to contradict again Devlin's analysis) the rigid form of the religious retreat did not allow him to express and exorcise his most intimate feelings about his personal moral situation, but left him sinking ever deeper into the mire, the artistic form of a poem had enabled him, if not completely to exorcise his dissatisfaction and incompleteness, at least to express and explore them, which must have provided satisfactions of a different kind from those aimed for by Ignatius. In this poem, by expressing dissatisfaction at his moral paradoxes and artistic barrenness, he had achieved the satisfactory paradox of fine artistic creation.

Chapter Fifteen

SWAN SONG

→>-<←

Sweet fire the sire of muse, my soul needs this;
I want the one rapture of an inspiration.

Hopkins, 'To R.B.'

yet since
the sublimation of life whereto the Saints aspire
is a self-holocaust, their sheer asceticism
is justified in them.

Robert Bridges, 'The Testament of Beauty',
IV (Ethick), lines 441–4.

... now [the phoenix] sinks, and with spheral
swan-song immolates herself in flame.

Carlyle, 'Sartor Resartus', III, vii

At his unhappiest in Dublin, Hopkins was longer there than he had been in any other Jesuit posting. In other positions there had always been the likelihood of moving on, but in Ireland he was in a permanent academic post; his conscientiousness made him perform his professional duties adequately, so that while nobody estimated him a success, there were no reported complaints. Those people back in Britain who cared for him most, however, became increasingly worried. An influential English Catholic couple, the Paravicinis, who saw Hopkins in his last year, were so shocked by the change in him that they wrote to the English Jesuit Provincial, begging that he be posted away from Ireland; at the beginning of June 1889 they thought they had succeeded, but by then it was too late.

His external circumstances in Ireland almost look as though they were programmed to make Hopkins feel alien and unsuccessful. While people in Dublin fed on the obsessive self-righteousness and indignation of Irish politics, Hopkins also reacted strongly, in ways unsympathetic to and misunderstood by most Irish, and which he had no means of ventilating, except to correspondents away in England.

Always conscious of significant dates, in a letter to Patmore of 15 May 1888 Hopkins remembered that it was the anniversary of the Phoenix Park murders in 1882 of Lord Frederick Cavendish and T. N. Burke. On 18 April 1887 *The*

Times had printed in facsimile a short letter allegedly written by Charles Stewart Parnell on the day of the assassinations, saying that he had publicly condemned the deed merely from policy, and that though he regretted Cavendish's death, he could not 'refuse to admit that Burke got no more than his deserts'. This was the most prominent of a number of documents incriminating Parnell and some associates which had been sold to *The Times* by Richard Pigott, a former editor of the nationalist journal *The United Irishman*. Another political issue which obsessed Hopkins was the inquest held in late July 1888 to investigate the nationalist charge that John Mandeville had died from ill treatment received during his two months in Tullamore gaol the previous year. His fellow prisoner William O'Brien, in *United Ireland*, successor to *The United Irishman*, had charged the British government with having planned and executed Mandeville's death.

The Commission to inquire into *The Times*'s allegations over the Phoenix Park murders had first sat in September 1888, and the trial began in October. Mistrusting the easily available Irish newspaper accounts, Hopkins asked his mother to send him the weekly *Times* from England, now that his college had stopped taking the daily *Times*. Parnell having denied under oath that he had written the letter, *The Times* called Pigott as witness, and on 22 February 1889 Pigott broke down under cross-examination by Parnell's counsel, Sir Charles Russell, brother of Hopkins's colleague at St Stephen's Green, Fr Matthew Russell. The following day he confessed to the MP Henry Labouchere that he had forged all the documents.

The same day, 23 February, Hopkins wrote to Bridges who, having just returned from a month's tour of France and Italy, had complained that Italian opera singers sang out of tune and that some monks he had met abroad were inexcusably dirty. Hopkins retorted that spitting openly in the street was 'very, very common with the lower classes' in the North of England,

> And our whole [British] civilisation is dirty, yea filthy, and especially in the north; for is it not dirty, yea filthy, to pollute the air as Blackburn and Widnes and St. Helen's are polluted and the water as the Thames and the Clyde and the Irwell are polluted? The ancients with their immense public baths would have thought even our cleanest towns dirty. (LI. 299)

The news of Pigott's confession having just broken, he could not resist an inflamed finish to his letter. England was in 'a pretty mess – to speak jokingly of matter for tears', and Englishmen were 'boobies' over the Parnell Commission, 'giggling, yea guffawing at the wretched Pigot's mess'. For Hopkins the trial concerned the important issues of government and rebellion in Ireland, a fight between good and evil, showing up the blackness of the criminal Irish rebellion against the lawful British government. The British stupidly considered the trial as entertainment, disregarding the deep moral issues, 'making merry because a traitor to government [Pigott as nationalist] and then to rebellion [Pigott as betrayer of the rebel leader], both in a small way, has not succeeded in injuring an enemy of their own [Parnell] who is a traitor to government in a great way and a danger on an imperial scale [attacks legal government in Ireland, thus endangering the British empire]' (LI. 300).

Delving more deeply into his frustrations, Hopkins realised he did not wish to believe the letter was not genuine: 'And this I say as if Pigot were or employed the forger of those letters. For in my judgment, unless further evidence is forthcoming, those letters are genuine.' Even a week later, after the counsel for *The Times* in some disarray had withdrawn the letters from the case, he still wrote to his brother Lionel: 'I am not convinced . . . that the Facsimile letter, the one about the Phoenix Park, is not genuine after all' (L3. 194). And he reported the reaction of Irish nationalists around him, 'wild with triumph and joy'. Why, he asked Lionel (a genial and balanced man, who probably could not understood why his elder brother was so incensed) was there such a widespread interest in 'the charge against Mr. Parnell of, after the event, faintly approving or not disapproving of the murder', when O'Brien's accusation against the British of murdering Mandeville was a far weightier issue?

> I want Mr. Tom Burke [i.e., the spirit of the second Phoenix Park victim] to know when [Pigott's] successor O'Brien is going to confess to the falsehood of his charge against Mr. Balfour of planning in general and then carrying out in particular the murder of John Mandeville. [O'Brien's] charge is far more hideous.

He continued: 'I do not ask the Irish to see this [being blinded by nationalist fervour], but I should like the English dupes and dullards to see this.' His letter finished: 'If you knew the world I live in! Yet I continue to be a Home Ruler: I say it must be and let it be' (L3. 193–4).

In spite of the apparent crudity of his prejudices on the Irish struggle, Hopkins's *total* reactions were not as stupid as they at first appear. At least living in Ireland he could see what many British still could not appreciate over a hundred years later – that the tide of the nationalist cause was irreversible, and that allowing the inevitable to happen sooner rather than later would save continuing bloodshed and illegality. Clear-headed over that, he was nevertheless sufficiently inconsistent and prejudiced to grasp every chance of insulting the hated Gladstone, the one British politician with the foresight, imagination, and political skill to bring about Home Rule, and who, in spite of knowing that it would divide his party and lose himself vital support, had consistently advocated Home Rule. Hopkins can joke with his penfriends (all of whom are anti-Gladstone) about the Grand Old Man, calling him the Grand Old Traitor, or 'this fatal and baleful influence', seeing him with common contemporary Conservative prejudice as the disperser of the British Empire, 'without foresight, insight, or resolution himself, the bright form of the thoughts and wishes of the Liberal masses' (L3. 293), and agreeing with Baillie that he should be beheaded on Tower Hill.

Parnell was absolved of most of the charges and, the year following Hopkins's death, was paid by *The Times* agreed damages of £5000. Gladstone, who had firmly supported Parnell throughout the Commission's proceedings, put before Parliament a motion of reparation to Parnell. This was defeated, as also were Gladstone's many attempts at finding a Home Rule majority.

Most of Hopkins's letters are full of sane and thoughtfully worded epigrams and judgements; and there is always a lively individual style and humour, which make all his correspondents seem comparatively dull. But being so much on his own intellectually and culturally, without lively Oxford-type debates which might change opinions, kept intact many prejudices. A birthday message to his old mentor Newman, outlining the Irish situation as Hopkins saw it, was answered perceptively by the old cardinal, making one regret the infrequency during Hopkins's time in Ireland that he heard such shrewd commonsense from an Englishman whom he could respect:

> Your letter is an appalling one . . . . There is one consideration however which you omit. The Irish Patriots hold that they never have yielded themselves to the sway of England and therefore have never been under her laws, and have never been rebels. . . . Moreover, to clench [*sic*] the difficulty the Irish character and tastes [are] very different from the English. (L3. 413–14)

* * *

From 1884 to 1889 there had been a terrible trail of hopelessness and unfinished projects:

> [February 1886:] I am struggling to get together matter for a work on Homer's Art. I suppose like everything else of mine it will come to nothing in the end, but I cannot keep that likelihood always in view or I should do nothing at it at all. (L3. 257)

> [February 1887:] I do not want you to trouble about it; I am afraid it will be no good. I shd. like it [a list of transliterations from Egyptian into Greek that Baillie might do], but I shd. be sorry that you shd. have been throwing pains and time away. . . . I do something, what I can, but I cannot believe it will

come to anything. . . . I had some hope of bringing out somewhere . . . this year a preliminary paper not on the profounder matter of course but on the Dorian Measure itself; but I fear I shall not. . . Meantime my Homeric studies are postponed. (L3. 275–6)

[May 1888:] My paper on the *Angel* [Patmore's *The Angel in the House*] is really in hand and when finished will be printed without difficulty: there is more difficulty about getting it finished. (L3. 392.) [It was neither printed nor finished.]

[May 1888:] I see no sign of their [notes sent to the *Classical Review*] appearing; so I am afraid the whole will come to nought. However, to me, to finish a thing and that it shd. be out of hand and owe its failure to somebody else [i.e., the editor who rejected the notes] is nearly the same thing as success. (LI. 277)

No serious poem longer than a sonnet was completed in Dublin. His elegy, 'On the Portrait of Two Beautiful Young People', was unfinished because he could write it only on rare visits to County Kildare. Similarly, the inspiration for his drama, 'St Winefred's Well', was felt only occasionally:

There is a point with me in matters of any size when I must absolutely have encouragement as much as crops rain; afterwards I am independent. However I am in my ordinary circumstances unable, with whatever encouragement, to go on with *Winefred* or anything else. (LI. 218–19)

Ireland had seen the last six months of his life start with his writing at Tullabeg a deeply despairing summary of the uselessness and misery of his present position, and a wish for death. It continued with three poems about the death of his poetic inspiration.

If the Welsh poems of 1877 claim to be concerned with conjunction, but tell more about Hopkins's failure to unite aim with impulse, the 1889 Dublin poems not only purport to, but do, tell a tale of disruption and lack of integration. In Wales, the uncontrolled over-rich observation had sometimes distended the sonnet form into a swollen caricature of itself, whereas in these Irish poems the emotions are shown more poignantly by being skilfully displayed within the precisely limited conventional sonnet.

The three 1889 poems all start obliquely to their main subject. 'The shepherd's brow' and 'To R. B.' both keep away from the personal confession until the 'I' figure stands out on its own, in lines 11 ('And I that die') and 9 ('my soul needs') respectively. In 'Justus quidem' the 'I' is disguised at first by the confusion with Jeremiah, and engages in a jeremiad against the 'Lord' figure at the arbitrariness of the justice system, before the poet-figure 'I' makes its appearance in line 12, with ' . . . but not I build'. All three poems make out a larger, more general case, while the stripped 'I' is awaiting its opportunity to emerge. They all build *down* to the ending, explore larger layers of experience before the 'I' is left to make its final plea, alone and poignantly.

This is perhaps the most closely knit group of Hopkins's poems, composed within five weeks, after a gap in poetry writing of five months since October 1888. They are *small* works of art, signalling a drawing-in of the poet's resources. He has purposely turned his back on large-scale forms of the past: the two long shipwreck odes, the unfinished dramas, the longer poems abandoned incomplete, the extended sonnets. He has come down to the simple Italian sonnet, which he had mastered in the 1860s (at least ten Italian sonnets survive from 1865). But they are mature poems, Hopkins's last quartets. No longer the youthful delight in self-expression that you get in the St Beuno's poems; but no longer the accompanying over-pitched, bottled-up sudden release, nor the labouring to find a religious paradigm. He has also put behind him the pre-lapsarian sentiment of his epithalamion and 'On the Portrait of Two Beautiful Young People', which are moral and intellectual deep shelters. Now in Dublin there is a graver, detached labour, which produces more satisfactory poems. These 1889 sonnets are as highly personal as the comparable group of 1885 desolate sonnets, and yet more controlled and compact – compare the 1885 'Comforter, where, where is your comforting?' with the 1889 subtlety 'Wert thou my enemy, O thou my friend'.

In each of these 1889 poems a wry, not unattractive, self-deprecatory note sounds. The subject matter is primarily the relationship between the poet's emotions and the productions of his mind. Images of poetic creativity overlap: the creative urge likened to a flame in the second and third poems, and the process like that of birth in the first and third. Here Hopkins can retain a critical distance between his two personae: the protagonist who suffers the emotions and the poet who shapes the poem around them. In the 1885 sonnets the two functions were inseparable, the passionate act not modified by judgement, whereas in these sophisticated 1889 poems, Hopkins allows a retreat from dwelling on feeling into thinking about art.

* * *

Like 'Justus quidem tu es', the second of these last poems, 'The shepherd's brow', is more about the artist creating a poem than anything else. The first twelve lines express a cynical vision of Man, but beneath the surface is the major but muted theme of creativity, which eventually frees itself in the last two lines. Rather like the Jeremiah opening of 'Justus quidem', a traditional scene is taken over by the poet's cynical notion of his creative process. As early as lines 3–4 this final theme is predicted: 'a *story*/ Of just, majestical . . .', as also happens in line 8: 'What bass is *our* viol for tragic tones?', where the theory is advanced that artistic subject and creative means must both have adequate stature. And so the poet, at last revealing himself, accounts for the inferiority of this present work by describing his own creative act, and placing it within the already explored context of man's lowness. The poem Hopkins wrote nineteen days later, 'To R. B.', has a very similar conclusion.

A part of 'The shepherd's brow' is a cynically flavoured vision of life and death; but it is not a *single* vision. There are four in descending order: the divine, the fallen angels (or super-men), man, and sub-man (Hopkins); and these are followed in lines 13–14 by a new viewpoint which puts the poem in a different perspective.

The first vision is Moses': in Exodus, he seeks, receives, and acknowledges indications of divine glory. Then there is the magnificent fall of Satan's angels, probably taken from *Paradise Lost* (I. 44ff):

> Him the Almighty Power
> Hurled headlong flaming from the ethereal sky
> With hideous ruin and combustion down
> To bottomless perdition . . . .
> Who durst defy the omnipotent to arms.
> . . . .
> . . . . the sulphurous hail
> Shot after us in storm, o'erblown hath laid
> The fiery surge, that from the precipice
> Of heaven received us falling, and the thunder,
> Winged with red lightning and impetuous rage . . .

Satan was the embodiment of evil, but also of energy – and his condition of vitality must speak to Hopkins's loss of will and energy, connecting with the resentful comparison 'Why do sinners' ways prosper?' in the Jeremiah poem.

The majestical end of angels can inspire a great story, whereas man's progression to death is too petty for great art. Before 'lives and voids', there are two other life-death progressions: 'groundlong babyhood to hoary/ Age gasp' and 'breath . . . *mori*', 'voids' meaning the petty quitting (OED. 5) of man, which compares unfavourably with the magnificent angel-fall.

This poem's structure is similar to those of the 1885 sonnets 'No worst, there is none', 'To seem the stranger', and 'I wake and feel', where in the final two or three lines the poet removes himself from the immediacy of the described situation, and gives some kind of closure to the poem (not a solution to the problems), by making a third-person summary of his own troubles. The progression in this poem is from man to poet, followed by the first twelve lines being suddenly re-seen, and shown to be not reality, but a simulacrum caused by the poet's distorting vision (the anamorphic view in the reflective bowl of a spoon); he needs to distort his whole world-view, in order to control his passions.

The movement in the last three lines is a subtle, manifold one. On one level the switch is from 'Jack the man' and 'his mate', mankind in general out there, to 'And *I* that . . .', this individual here forming this poem. There is also the move from demonstration of emotions – indignation, disgust, cynicism – to their summary – 'deaths', 'tempests', 'fire and fever'. At the same time there is the third transference from a demonstration in subjective tones of man's objective state to an objective, even dispassionate, description of the poet's subjective state. And there is also a fourth change in movement: the turning away from emotions towards their expression in art; their present subjective reality transformed into an object, the reflection in a spoon. Many-dimensioned reality is collected together and flattened and compressed into art, as onto a small surface which only mirrors everything back as a tiny circumscribed, two-dimensional representation; even that, the poet modestly says, is distorted by his limited horizons and visions. Four different transferences.

But the point at which these changeovers occur is not necessarily the same for all four. The rhythmic and alliterative subtleties of lines 12 to 14 help to point to and artistically smooth over the changes. For instance, the poet sets up a rhythmical chant with 'That die these deaths, that feed this flame, that . . .', perhaps suggesting a rut of cynicism he has fallen into. Because of the easy sound parallelism the reader may not notice that a change in subject has occurred – the flame of creativity has suddenly taken over from emotions. The remarkable lengthening and slowing down of line 13, 'That . . . in smooth spoons spy life's masque mirrored: tame', effected by the elaborate alliteration shows the contrast between the poet's measured artistic poise and his staccato emotional jabs in the previous line.

In these three poems I think Hopkins says roughly this: I am in such a state of dissociation from the world outside me that I can only see it distortedly; my distorted world is a winter, barren one, although outside it is spring, where things are creative, lively, and fruitful, while I . . . I am a eunuch [not a virgin, one who has never created], deprived of his creative powers – for I did once have 'the roll, the rise, the carol, the creation', though now I do not breed one work that wakes.

Five weeks after he wrote 'Justus quidem tu es', nineteen days after 'The shepherd's brow', and just before his final illness, Hopkins created 'To R. B.'. It was unusual for Hopkins to send his poems to Bridges, to paste in his album, until they had lain about for some time, but he sent this only one week after he wrote it. This was because it is a letter, to be read by one individual, rather than an audience of poetry readers, and it functioned as the next communication in the close friendship of Hopkins and Bridges, employing arguments, imagery, and methods understood only by R. B.

Hopkins wrote to Bridges in a different style from that which he used for other correspondents. He was more at ease, more candid. Bridges was Hopkins's ideal audience, in a way that Dixon was not. Bridges was robust, Dixon delicate. He could speak his mind to Bridges, whereas he had to write to Dixon carefully. More useful to Hopkins than the strong faiths of Patmore and Dixon, a Catholic proselyte and an Anglican cleric, was Bridges's wavering between a liberal Anglicanism and agnosticism, a more English credo in the late nineteenth century (all Hopkins's surviving brothers were similarly vague in religious outlook). Bridges shared with Hopkins a wider range of interests and a greater time-span. Apart from the more sporadic contact with Mowbray Baillie, and to a lesser extent with others, Bridges was the last survivor of his vital Oxford days. Their affection had remained (except for one patch of misunderstanding) even when their opinions differed. Bridges represented the solid citizen, the average English reader whom he had to convert to his poetry, even if he had given up over religion. (Baillie was non-literary, and had always preferred Hopkins's undergraduate poems to the 'deliberate obscurity' of his later verse.) Hopkins chose Bridges as his poetic executor, entrusting him with the manuscripts and responsibility for eventual publication.

'To R. B.' borrows characteristics from Hopkins's letters to Bridges, such as mature calm and assured rhythm. It rationalises progressively, without self-assertiveness; Hopkins is authoritative, as in the letters, speaking out of mutual affection and knowledge, without shrillness.

This relationship enables Hopkins to express perhaps his finest sustained metaphor: the originating inspiration of his poetry as phallus and the mind as womb. So often in his poetry the reader senses Hopkins's uncertainty of communication; because he does not have experience of an audience, he sometimes *over*does explication to the point of patronage, and at other times *under*estimates, tending towards harmful obscurity and ambiguity. The balance in 'To R. B.' is remarkable (except for the obscure 'combs' [line 6], which R. B. understandably found unintelligible). Knowing this one-man audience well, Hopkins does not deviate from the metaphor by sideways looks or diversions. Unlike in the other two poems on artistic creativity, here, for Bridges's sake, he describes his poetic generative process in non-religious terms, although there are Christian models in the background: the (Holy) Spirit-like, non-human father, the sexless, sinless mother, carrying the child with the true father having disappeared after the conception, and the mother giving birth to an immortal, perfect child, who replaces her in a greater limelight.

In a letter eleven years before, Hopkins had replied to Dixon's recognition that his own literary works had been 'generally, almost universally, neglected': 'It is sad to think what disappointment must many times over have filled your heart for the darling children of your mind'. Then in 1885 he had written to Bridges:

> I can scarcely believe that . . . anything of mine will ever see the light . . . . For it is widely true, the fine pleasure is not to do a thing but to feel that you could and the mortification that goes to the heart is to feel it is the power that fails you . . . if I could but produce work I should not mind its being buried, silenced, and going no further; but it kills me to be time's eunuch and never to beget. (LI. 221–2)

And the year before this poem a letter to Bridges shows how he was further caring for and combing its imagery in his mind:

> It is now years that I have had no inspiration of longer jet than makes a sonnet. . . . it is what, far more than direct want of time, I find most against poetry and production in the life I lead. Unhappily I cannot produce anything at all. . . . All impulse fails me . . . . Nothing comes: I am a eunuch. (LI. 270)

In spite of this pessimism, in 'To R. B.' Hopkins finally gave birth to the now perfectly fashioned image of poetic creation he had conceived a wearily long time before, and had been nurturing in interim letters. R. B.'s response to this poem came thirty years later, in the moving, personal sonnet which prefaced the First Edition of Hopkins's *Poems*.

*   *   *

Soon after writing the poem 'To R. B.' Hopkins fell ill, with an undiagnosed complaint. He enclosed the poem in a letter to Bridges, which was cheerful in spite of his illness. But a few days later his mother, in the new family home, Court's Hill Lodge, Haslemere, in Surrey, received an uncharacteristically short letter from her son, stating that he had a rheumatic fever, which was inconvenient as he should have been setting examination papers. The following day he took to his bed and was visited by a doctor, 'who treated my complaint as a fleabite, a treatment which begets confidence but not gratitude' (L3. 196).

His illness was plainly getting worse; he was feverish, sleepless, in some pain, and had 'suspended digestion' (constipation) which had been painfully relieved; he was on a liquid diet and had nurses to look after him, but Dr Redmond had still not diagnosed his complaint. His only comfort was that he was relieved of all examination duties, which at that time of year were most arduous.

By 8 May too weak to write, he dictated a letter to his mother taken down by the minister in charge of the house, Fr Thomas Wheeler. His illness had at last been diagnosed as typhoid, and he had been moved from his upstairs room in 86 Stephen's Green, to a larger, lighter one on the ground floor of 85, where proper isolation could be observed, and the nurses from St Vincent's, on the corner of the Green, could come in by a different entrance from the students and staff at 86.

Hopkins had almost certainly caught the illness from the filthy sanitation at University College. Although it had been known that the plumbing badly needed an overhaul when the Jesuits first took over the Stephen's Green buildings in 1883, and jokes had been made about rats being found in a stew-pot, nothing had been done about it, both the bishops (the owners of the building) and the Jesuits (who leased it) being unwilling to spend funds on a complete overhaul (eventually done within a month of Hopkins's death).

The progress of Hopkins's illness was similar to the Prince Consort's earlier in the century, not just in the symptoms during incubation, of sleepless-ness and rheumatic pains, but in the two men having, before the onset of typhoid, expressed no desire to cling to life: Disraeli wrote of the Queen saying that Albert 'would die – he seemed not to care to live'.

Hopkins's relatives were told at one stage that he was mending, and had got over the worst of it. In fact he had 'a very virulent form of typhoid and his whole digestive system was paralysed'. Peritonitis set in about 4 or 5 June, and his parents were summoned. He received Holy Viaticum, with the final blessing and absolution on Saturday 8 June, and died at half-past one in the afternoon. The funeral took place at eleven the following Tuesday morning, at the Jesuit church on Upper Gardiner Street, on the opposite side of the River Liffey. A man who attended the funeral reported that the coffin was empty, and in disgust went out of the church to wait in his carriage. Although Hopkins was little known, a great show was made, and the funeral cortege, 'of very large dimensions', made its way on the long journey to the Prospect Cemetery, Glasnevin, where Irish Jesuits are buried.

Manley Hopkins was touched that so much trouble was taken over his son's death. Hopkins's brothers and sisters heard about his death on 10 June, and it took them all by surprise. His youngest brother, Everard, remembered Gerard's 'gifts his goodness & his sacrifice', while the third brother, Arthur, recalled their meeting on holiday at Whitby the previous summer, 'and the vision in my memory of the marvellously beautiful expression that was in his face as he bid us Goodbye when he left us. It brought tears into our eyes then, and in some distant way I felt that I should see his face no more' (Hopkins family letters). Inevitably many of Hopkins's friends, particularly his fellow undergraduates at Oxford, expressed regret at having seen him so infrequently during his years as a Jesuit. He was soon forgotten in Ireland.

*   *   *

Within two months of his death, Hopkins's best friend and the person to whom he had entrusted his poetic manuscripts, Robert Bridges, had approached Hopkins's parents and a printer, his friend C. H. O. Daniel, with a view to publishing some of the poems with a memoir. He wanted Canon Dixon to write his recollections of Hopkins, but Dixon apparently declined, and Bridges realised that he himself would have to provide the memoir.

But he had several difficulties. One was that the letters from which the memoir would be written were too personal, and he felt he would be betraying 'the understanding on which they were written'; a second reason was that the letters betrayed Gerard's nervous and depressed state of mind, which again would involve betrayal – releasing secrets to the public. Personal relationships were sacrosanct to Bridges, and the strength of his relationship with Hopkins can be judged by the dedicatory sonnet he wrote, printed on the back of the title-page to the edition of Hopkins's poems he published in December 1918.

Bridges was also afraid that the poems would be dismissed as freakish experiments unless he waited until there was a serious demand. (One has only to read the comments on the curious and impractical qualities of Hopkins's verse published by a former Oxford friend, George Saintsbury, to see what Bridges meant.) Bridges decided to try out some poems first in anthologies to see what the response would be. In 1891–2 he met with several refusals to publish Hopkins's verse in contemporary collections, but in 1893 he was invited to prepare a selection for Alfred Miles's *The Poets and The Poetry of the Century*, and chose eight complete poems and parts of three more. Bridges's short introduction gave a strong summary of Hopkins's poetry and life and temperament. Dixon thought there was too much fault-finding, but Mrs Hopkins 'did not think the note at all unkind in tone'. Bridges was always afraid that he would harm his friend's reputation if he appeared over fond and under critical, and he explained to Mrs Hopkins: 'I would much rather have it *said* that I was unkindly severe, than that I allowed my judgment to be led astray by my personal feelings, and I do not wish to leave anything but good for the critics to say.'

There was little reaction of any kind except for a hostile one from the *Manchester Guardian*, which said: 'Curiosities like the verses of the late Gerard Hopkins should be excluded', and that Bridges should employ his time on worthier objects. Nevertheless Bridges encouraged friends of his to read Hopkins's poetry in manuscript, and to put it into anthologies. Over a dozen anthologies, some religious, some not, printed one or more poems, and among the people who read the poems were Mary Coleridge, great-great niece of S. T. Coleridge, Francis Thompson, and Virginia Woolf.

Around 1910, two very different people expressed a wish to edit the poems. One was Edmund Gosse, the literary journalist, whom Bridges considered an unscrupulous opportunist, and the other was a Jesuit, Fr Keating, whom Bridges thought showed no evidence of literary or editorial competence, and would publish the poems only to boost the claims of the Roman Catholic church. Eventually, after Bridges had published in 1916 a justly famous anthology, *The Spirit of Man*, which contained six parts of or complete Hopkins poems, Bridges had the enthusiastic response he had been waiting for. In spite of a personally unhappy period when his house near Oxford burned down, his son was severely wounded in the trenches, and his wife was ill, he prepared the edition of Hopkins's poems, not just carefully editing them and writing the introduction and notes, but supervising the printing and make-up of the book (see HALB, 459–66, for the full story of how the first edition of *Poems* evolved). The 1918 first edition is still the most handsome and loving of all the many Hopkins poetry collections.

* * *

W. B. Yeats lived to see a Hopkins cult arise after the second edition of the *Poems* was published in 1930. Unlike Hopkins, Yeats had the opportunity to see and make a re-judgement of virtually all the other man's poems. But he refused or was unable to modify his prejudices, a caricature of a stereotype, the stereotype a common Irish view of a late Victorian English aesthetic Catholic convert, rather than a considered judgement of a real, highly individual and unique creative artist. One is reminded of Katharine Tynan's introduction to Christina Rossetti, whom she expected to find in trailing, beautifully coloured robes, and with long flowing hair. Tynan was shocked to see a lady wearing a suit, short-skirted, of iron-grey tweed and with stout boots (Tynan papers).

On each occasion Yeats was asked about Hopkins he found bad-tempered ways of denouncing both his personality and his poetry. (His opinions about other great contemporaries, such as Ibsen, also look odd today.) In March 1932 Yeats wrote to a young Irish poet, Monk Gibbon:

> Gerard Hopkins, whom I knew, was an excitable man – unfitted to active life and his speech is always sedentary. . . . [He] never understood the variety of pace that constitutes natural utterance. . . . Hopkins is the way out of life. . . .

Hopkins believed in nothing. Remember what Heine said about an Englishman saying his prayers [a Frenchman cursing was more pleasing in the sight of God].

In another letter to Gibbon Yeats wrote that Hopkins's 'whole life was a form of "poetic diction". He brought his faint theatrical Catholicism to Ireland where [it] is not relished by the sons of peasants and perhaps died of the shock' (Gibbon, 135–45). Hopkins could be understood in Dublin only as Yeats had seen him: his way of talking, his effeminate bearing and childish figure, his Newmanite Catholic Oxford conversion, his shyness and reclusiveness, his educated upper-class southern Englishness and Oxford mannerisms, scrupulous habits, interests in painting, music, architecture, and drawing, fondness for Nature, his poetic friendships, and his less well-known poetic compositions – all appeared to be facets of a typical English aesthete.

In 1935 Yeats was persuaded to edit *The Oxford Book of Modern Verse*. What should he do about Hopkins? The first generation of modernists had hardly known Hopkins: T. S. Eliot had disparaged him as 'a narrow technician, an unimportant devotional writer and a limited nature poet'; William Carlos Williams was fascinated by Hopkins's 'brutal chin', but misheard his speech rhythms, and was more influenced by Bridges; while Ezra Pound found Hopkins monotonous, did not own a copy of the poems, and preferred the metres of 'Rabbit Britches'. But by this time Hopkins was being regarded as a modern poet, having been championed by the influential new critics I. A. Richards, William Empson, Robert Graves, and F. R. Leavis. There was a considerable Hopkins cult after Richards had written that the best modern verse should compel slow reading: 'The effort, the heightened attention, may brace the reader, and that peculiar intellectual thrill which celebrates the step-by-step conquest of understanding may irradiate and awaken other mental activities more essential to poetry'. Hopkins best illustrated this thesis, as the most obscure, original, and audaciously experimental of poets.

Another factor influencing Yeats over the question of whether to include Hopkins in his anthology was that his editor at the Oxford University Press was Charles Williams, who had edited the second edition of Hopkins's *Poems*, whose preface praised Hopkins's 'passionate emotion' and 'passionate intellect'. Yeats sent a circular to Oliver St John Gogarty asking to include in 'a collection of modern verse from Gerard Hopkins to the present day' some poems of Gogarty's, whom he considered 'perhaps the greatest master of the pure lyric now writing in English'. Gogarty agreed to his poems being included, but asked not to be placed near Hopkins. Yeats replied that he need not be afraid of being put too near Hopkins: 'I do not even mention him in my introduction . . . and I do mention you with much praise' (McGarry, 72–87).

In spite of his personal dislike of Hopkins and his poetry, Yeats had felt obliged to include him, though he did so with bad grace. There was another strange episode involving Hopkins before the book was published. Yeats wrote to A. E. Housman asking permission to include some of Housman's *Last Poems*, and received the reply: 'I am unwilling to countenance an anthology which by its very conception allots so much importance to Hopkins'. Housman regarded Hopkins as 'a moth blundering round a candle'. This was in spite of the fact that it was Housman who had composed, at Bridges's request, the moving Latin dedication to Hopkins's mother at the start of the first edition of Hopkins's *Poems*. Yeats then wrote to Charles Williams, paraphrasing Housman's letter and saying that in order to placate Housman he had been obliged to deride Hopkins in his Preface, and, he added, 'I am not quite infidel where Hopkins is concerned'.

This seems to me a politic and dishonest answer, pretending an ambivalence he did not feel. *The Oxford Book of Modern Verse* came out in 1936 and was called by W. H. Auden 'the most deplorable volume ever issued' by its publishers. Ellmann described it as 'full of curious favouritisms' and pointed out that Yeats regarded the Introduction as a manifesto of his doubts about modern poetry. When he came to Hopkins, Yeats alluded to their meeting in Dublin but confessed to remembering nothing about it: 'A boy of seventeen, Walt Whitman in his pocket, had little interest in a querulous, sensitive scholar'. (Yeats was twenty-one when they met.)

In Section 17 of the Introduction Yeats describes his reactions to Hopkins's poetry in more detail than anywhere else:

> I read Gerard Hopkins with great difficulty, I cannot keep my attention fixed for more than a few minutes; I suspect a bias born when I began to think. He is typical of his generation where most opposed to mine. His meaning is like some faint sound that strains the ear, comes out of words, passes to and fro between them, goes back into words; his manner a last development of poetical diction. My generation began that search for hard positive subject-matter, still a predominant purpose. Yet the publication of his work in 1918 made 'sprung verse' the fashion, and now his influence has replaced that of Hardy and Bridges.

The selection of Hopkins's poems Yeats made is unrepresentative and suggests further insensitivity on Yeats's part – seven poems only, nothing from Hopkins's most experimental work, *The Wreck of the Deutschland*, and, even worse, there were none of the twenty-eight poems written in Ireland. Yeats's book of modern verse remains an oddity. A much more influential anthology, *The Faber Book of Modern Verse*, came out in the same year. Its editor, Michael Roberts, included thirteen representative poems of Hopkins's, which started the anthology, and Roberts's introduction sees no sharp discontinuity between Hopkins and his Victorian contemporaries, an opinion which stands up well, in view of the general present-day reallocation of Hopkins to the Victorian age to which he belongs.

Bibliography

✦✦✦

MANUSCRIPT MATERIAL

Library of Balliol College, Oxford; Bodleian Library, Oxford; Campion Hall, Oxford; Jesuit Archives, English Province, Farm Street, London; Jesuit Archives, Irish Province, Lr Leeson Street, Dublin; Stonyhurst College, Lancashire; Humanities Research Center, Austin, Texas; Library of University College Dublin.

BOOKS AND JOURNALS (unless otherwise stated, place of publication is London)

Apocryphal New Testament, The, trans. Montagu Rhodes James (Oxford, 1924).

Bible, The Holy, A Translation from the Latin Vulgate in the Light of the Hebrew and Greek Originals [by Mgr. Ronald Knox] (1961).

Bridges, Robert, *The Selected Letters of Robert Bridges*, ed. Donald E. Stanford (2 vols, Newark, Del., 1983/4).

Brown, Daniel, *Hopkins' Idealism* (Oxford, 1997).

Brown, Ford Madox:

    [Mary Bennett,] *Ford Madox Brown, 1821–1893* (exhibition catalogue, Liverpool, 1964).

    'Madox Brown's Diary Etc 1844–46', in *Praeraphaelite Diaries and Letters*, ed. William Michael Rossetti (1900).

Carlyle, Thomas, *Selected Writings*, ed. Alan Shelston (Harmondsworth, 1971).

Christ, Carol T., *Victorian and Modern Poetics* (1984).

Clayre, Alasdair (ed.), *Nature and Industrialization* (Oxford, 1977).

Crehan, Joseph, SJ, 'Some Hopkins Memories', *Hopkins Research Bulletin* 4 (1973), 29–30.

Curtis, L. Perry, Jr, *The Irishman in Victorian Caricature* (Newton Abbot, 1971).

Dacey, Philip, *Gerard Manley Hopkins Meets Walt Whitman in Heaven and Other Poems*, (Great Barrington, Mass., 1982).

Dessain, Stephen, *John Henry Newman* (1980).

Dixon, Richard Watson:

    Poems by the late Rev. Dr Richard Watson Dixon: A Selection . . . by Robert Bridges (1909).

    Songs and Odes (1896).

    Sambrook, J., *A Poet Hidden: The Life of Richard Watson Dixon* (1962).

Dowden, Edward, *New Studies in Literature* (1894).

Ellmann, Richard, *James Joyce* (New York, 1949).

English Dialect Dictionary, The, ed. Joseph Wright (1898–1904).

Evans, E. Estyn, *Irish Folk Ways* (1947).

Faber Book of Modern Verse, The, ed. Michael Roberts (1964).

Gardner, W. H., *Gerard Manley Hopkins, 1844–89: A Study of Poetic Idiosyncrasy in Relation to Poetic Tradition* (2 vols, 1966).

Gibbon, Monk, *The Masterpiece and the Man: Yeats as I Knew Him* (1949).

Giles, Richard F. (ed.), *Hopkins Among the Poets: Studies in Modern Responses to Gerard Manley Hopkins* (Hamilton, Ont., 1984).

Gladstone, Right Hon. W. E., MP, *Rome and the Newest Fashions in Religion* (1874).

Goffman, Irving, *Asylums: Essays on the Social Situation of Mental Patients and Other Inmates* (New York, 1961).

Goldie, Francis, SJ, *The Life of St Alonso Rodriguez* (1889).

Graves, Charles L., *Mr. Punch's History of Modern England* (4 vols, n.d.).

Harries-Jenkins, Gwynn, *The Army in Victorian Society* (1977).

Hepworth, Mike, and Turner, Bryan S., *Confession: Studies in Deviance and Religion* (1982).

Heraclitus:

    Kirk, G. S., *Heraclitus, The Cosmic Fragments* (1944).

    Walliser, Stephan, *That Nature is a Heraclitean Fire and of the Comfort of the Resurrection* (Bern, 1977).

    Wheelwright, Philip, *Heraclitus* (Oxford, 1949).

Hopkins, Gerard M., letters not in *L1*, *L2*, or *L3*:

    To Dr M. F. Cox, 26 Mar. 1887, *Hopkins Research Bulletin* 3 (1972), 6–7.

    To Dr M. F. Cox, 31 Mar. 1887, *Hopkins Research Bulletin* 3 (1972), 8–9.

Humphrey, William, SJ, *The Religious State. A Digest of the Doctrine of Suarez* (3 vols, 1888?).

Huxley, Aldous, *Mirage and Truth* (1934).

Ignatius, St:

    Curtis, John, SJ, *The Way of Religious Perfection in the Spiritual Exercises of St. Ignatius of Loyola* (Dublin, 1884).

    Downes, David A., *Gerard Manley Hopkins: A Study of his Ignatian Spirit* (1960).

    Hurter, Hugo, SJ, *Sketches for the Exercises of an Eight Days' Retreat* (1918).

    Rahner, Karl, *Spiritual Exercises*, trans. Kenneth Baker SJ (1967).

    Rickaby, Joseph, SJ, *The Spiritual Exercises of St. Ignatius Loyola* (1923).

Joyce, James:

    A Portrait of the Artist as a Young Man (1977 edn).

    Stephen Hero (1977 edn).

Judd, Denis, *The Victorian Empire* (1970).

Little, Sydney H., 'The Conversion of England: A Reply', *Dublin Review* (Oct. 1884), 348–87.

Lucy, Henry W., *A Diary of the Salisbury Parliament, 1886–1892* (1892).

Lyons, F. S. L., *Culture and Anarchy in Ireland, 1890–1939* (Oxford, 1939).

McGrath, Fergal, SJ, *Newman's University: Idea and Reality* (Dublin 1941).

MacKenzie, Norman H. (ed.):

    The Poetic Works of Gerard Manley Hopkins (Oxford, 1990).

    The Later Poetic Manuscripts of Gerard Manley Hopkins in Facsimile (New York, 1992).

Maher, Michael, SJ, *Psychology: Empirical and Rational* (1911).

Milroy, James, *The Language of Gerard Manley Hopkins* (1977).

Moore, George, *A Drama in Muslin* (1886).

Morris, John, SJ, *Journals Kept During Times of Retreat* (1894).

O'Connor, Frank, *My Father's Son* (this edn 1971).

O'Neill, George, 'Gerard Hopkins', *Essays on Poetry* (Dublin, 1919).

O'Shea, J.A., *Roundabout Reflections* (Dublin, 1901?).

Patmore, Coventry:

>Champneys, Basil, *Memoirs and Correspondence of Coventry Patmore* (2 vols., 1900).
>Patmore, Derek, *The Life and Times of Coventry Patmore* (1949).

Phillips, Catherine, *Robert Bridges* (Oxford, 1992).

Pickering, George, *Creative Malady* (1974).

Purcell, E.S., *Life of Cardinal Manning* (2 vols, 1894).

Raphael, Frederic, 'Aphrodite Ascendant', *New Statesman*, 24/31 Dec. 1976.

Rickaby, Joseph, SJ, *Moral Philosophy, Ethics, Deontology, and Natural Law* (1929).

Saint John of the Cross, *The Dark Night of the Soul* (edn of 1916).

Saintsbury, George, *A History of Nineteenth Century Literature* (1910).

Sargant, William, *Battle for the Mind* (1949).

Scotus:

>B. M. Bonansea, *Man and his Approach to God in John Duns Scotus* (1983).

Stewart, Robert P.:

>Vignoles, Olinthus J., *Memoir of Sir Robert P. Stewart Kt.* (1899?).

Thomas, Alfred, SJ, *Hopkins the Jesuit: The Years of Training* (1969).

Tynan, Katharine, *Twenty-five Years: Reminiscences* (1913).

Vaughan, J. S., 'Social Disturbances – their cause and cure', *Dublin Review* (Oct. 1886), 334–41.

Virgil, *Aeneid* and *Eclogues*, in *Virgil*, with an English translation by H. R. Fairclough, 1, rev. ed. [The Loeb Classical Library] (1963).

Ward, Mrs Humphry, *Helbeck of Bannisdale* (1898).

White, Norman:

>'Gerard Manley Hopkins: An Edition of the Last Poems (1884–89), with an Introduction and Notes' (MPhil thesis, University of London, 1968).
>'Gerard Manley Hopkins and the Irish Row', *Hopkins Quarterly* 9 (3) (1982), 91–107.
>*Gerard Manley Hopkins in Wales* (Bridgend, Wales, 1998).
>'G. M. Hopkins's Contributions to the *English Dialect Dictionary*', *English Studies* 68 (4) (1987), 324–34.
>'Hopkins and the Pre-Raphaelite Painters: The Community of Ideas' (PhD thesis, University of Liverpool, 1974).
>'Hopkins's Epithalamion', *Hopkins Quarterly* 4 (3–4) (1977–8), 141–49.
>'Hopkins' Sonnet 'No Worst, There is None', and the Storm Scenes in *King Lear*', *VP* 24 (1) (1986), 83–7.
>'Hopkins' Sonnet "Written in Blood"', *English Studies* 43 (2) (1972), 123–4.
>'Hopkins' 'Spelt from Sibyl's Leaves", *Victorian Newsletter* 36 (1969), 27–8.
>'Saint Gerard Manley Hopkins?', *Yale Review* (Spring 1980), 473–80.

Williams, Charles, Editorial Preface to *The Poems of Gerard Manley Hopkins* (2nd edn, Oxford, 1930).

Yeats, W.B., ed., *The Oxford Book of Modern Verse* (Oxford, 1936).

Index

✦━✦━✦